OF H

ad F

Az fuc sir

Vic tor Bla

thol- ic

1 nap sulp

Dioxy aline- phic A

tronath

MANUALS OF CHEMICAL TECHNOLOGY—1

EDITED BY GEOFFREY MARTIN, Ph.D., M.Sc., B.Sc.

DYESTUFFS

&

COAL-TAR PRODUCTS

THEIR CHEMISTRY, MANUFACTURE AND APPLICATION

INCLUDING

Chapters on Modern Inks, Photographic Chemicals, Synthetic Drugs, Sweetening Chemicals, and other Products derived from Coal Tar

BY

THOMAS BEACALL, B.A. (Cambridge); F. CHALLENGER, Ph.D., B.Sc.; GEOFFREY MARTIN, Ph.D., M.Sc., B.Sc., and HENRY J. S. SAND, D.Sc., Ph.D.

(*Reprinted with Additions from "Industrial and Manufacturing Chemistry," Vol. I.*)

NEW YORK

D. APPLETON AND COMPANY

MCMXV

Printed at
THE DARIEN PRESS
Edinburgh

PREFACE

A SERIES of short monographs on various branches of chemical technology, giving concise but sufficient information concerning the manufacture and utilisation of chemical products of great industrial importance at the present time, will undoubtedly supply a real want.

The present inaugural volume on Dyestuffs and Coal-Tar Products is based very largely on articles contributed to "Industrial and Manufacturing Chemistry," Vol. I., and concerns the manufacture and utilisation of certain chemical substances, whose exploitation has not been carried out in this country to anything like the extent that it should have been. It is intended for manufacturers, chemists, and students who desire to obtain in a separate form information on dyestuffs and coal-tar products, and who, consequently, do not wish to acquire the larger work, which treats of many branches of chemical technology unconnected with these subjects.

The lack of an English book on the subject, the sudden stoppage of the supply of German fine chemicals, and the preparations of the British Government for the establishment on a large scale of the synthetic dye industry in this country, all combine to provide opportunity and justification for the appearance of the present volume.

Although the book is entitled "Dyestuffs and Coal-Tar Products," yet it has been deemed advisable to include in it some products which are not derived from coal tar. The reason of this is that these substances find their main use when used in conjunction with coal-tar products, and a description of the one without the inclusion of the other would greatly diminish the value of the monograph for those classes of readers for whose use the volume is mainly intended. It must be recollected that mere

iii

academic distinctions in matters like this must be cast aside for practical considerations, as the work is primarily intended for practical men. At the same time it is hoped that there will be found here collected together a large amount of information which would otherwise be very difficult of access.

The section on dyes has been brought as thoroughly as possible up to date, and the remarkable new dyes derived from indigo, as well as the anthracene vat dyes and sulphide dyes, have received special attention.

Copious references to chemical literature will enable the reader, who seeks for fuller information than is possible to give in a work like this, to find it without much trouble. The Editor ventures to think that all the most recent practical advances in the subjects treated have been given in sufficient detail, but he would be very pleased to hear of omissions or suggestions for improving the present volume.

January 1915.

TABLE OF CONTENTS

CHAPTER I

INDUSTRY OF COAL TAR AND COAL-TAR PRODUCTS

CHAPTER II

INDUSTRY OF THE SYNTHETIC COLOURING MATTERS

v

CHAPTER III

THE INDUSTRY OF NATURAL DYESTUFFS

CHAPTER IV

THE DYEING AND COLOUR-PRINTING INDUSTRY

CHAPTER V

MODERN INKS

CHAPTER VI

SACCHARINE AND OTHER SWEETENING CHEMICALS

CHAPTER VII

THE INDUSTRY OF MODERN SYNTHETIC DRUGS

CHAPTER VIII

THE INDUSTRY OF PHOTOGRAPHIC CHEMICALS

CHAPTER I

Industry of Coal-Tar and Coal-Tar Products

CHAPTER I

INDUSTRY OF COAL-TAR AND COAL-TAR PRODUCTS

LITERATURE

LUNGE.—"Coal Tar and Ammonia." 1909.
SCHULTZ.—"Die Chemie des Steinkohlenteers." 2 vols. 1900-01.
SPILKER.—"Kokerei u. Teerprodukte." 1908.
DAMMER.—"Handbuch der Chemischen Technologie." Bd. iv. 1898.
SCHWALBE's "Benzoltabellen." 1903.
WINTHER's "Patente der Organische Chemie." 3 vols. 1877-1906.
See also under **Synthetic Dyes**.

COAL-TAR

COAL-TAR is the thick, black, evil-smelling liquid (sp. gr. 1.1 to 1.2) which accumulates in the hydraulic mains, condensers, and scrubbers of gasworks. Much, however, is now obtained from the coke ovens used for making hard coke for metallurgical purposes, and this source may eventually become the predominant one here, and has already become so in Germany, who derives two-thirds of her supply from this source.

In 1907 England produced 858,000 tons of tar ; Germany, 850,000 tons (1909); France, 170,000 tons (1904) ; United States, 200,000 tons (1904).

In 1913 England exported the following quantities of coal-tar and coal-tar products :—

		Value.
Crude coal-tar	88,000 cwt.	£16,000
Refined coal-tar and varnish	3,071,000 gals.	68,600
Pitch	9,731,000 cwt.	1,100,000
Tar oil, creosote	36,758,000 gals.	592,000
Coal-tar naphtha	515,000 ,,	24,600
Naphthalene	86,000 cwt.	37,700
Anthracene	564,000 lbs.	1,400
Benzol and toluol	6,655,000 gals.	303,000
Carbolic acid (phenol)	168,900 cwt.	190,000
Aniline and coal-tar oils	1,351,000 lbs.	28,900
Total value		£2,362,200

The United States in 1910 imported 37,000 barrels (280 lbs. per barrel) of tar and pitch, of value $92,000. The export was: 1906, 24,700 barrels ; 1908, 96,400 barrels ; 1910, 110,500 barrels (280 lbs. to the barrel). Value in 1910 was $138,800.

Coal-tar is the primary raw material of the colour industry. It has an extraordinary complex constitution, which varies not only with the nature of the coal or coke distilled, but also with the temperature of distillation.

The constituents employed in the colour industry are benzene, toluene, xylene, naphthalene, anthracene, phenol, and cresol. The composition is approximately given by the following table :—

The crude benzol is placed in the wrought-iron boiler A (Fig. 2, Heckmann's still) and heated to boiling by means of steam coils ; the vapours pass up the iron column B, which is divided into a series of compartments. The vapours pass into each compartment through the raised mouthpiece i, passing through the layer of liquid condensed in the compartment and maintaining it in continuous ebullition, while the excess of liquid overflows through a drop-pipe Z and discharges into the compartment below. Finally, the vapours reach the condenser C, where they are still further (but not completely) condensed to a liquid form by means of a water jacket ; the condensed liquids, pouring back through the U-tube, pass into the column B, maintain every compartment in B with its proper layer of boiling liquid. The more volatile parts pass on through n into the condenser D, where they are completely condensed by means of a water cooling jacket, and the separate fractions run off in succession through $s\,t\,u$.

The pure benzol and toluol thus obtained are used for making coal-tar dyestuffs.

The 90 per cent. benzol is used (mixed with petroleum ether) for motor cars, for carburetting illuminating gas, and as a cleansing solvent in laundry works. Solvent naphtha finds an extensive application in dissolving caoutchouc in the manufacture of waterproof stuffs.

2. **The Middle Oils,** B.P. 170°-230° C.; sp. gr. 1.01.—These contain much naphthalene and phenols.

The **naphthalene** is obtained by allowing the oil to stand, when large quantities crystallise out and are separated by centrifuging and pressing.

To obtain the naphthalene pure it is melted with 5 per cent. concentrated H_2SO_4, the acid drawn off, and the naphthalene distilled. Sometimes instead of being distilled the naphthalene is sublimed

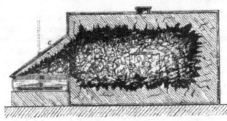

by placing in a shallow iron pan a, heated by the steam coil b, when the vapours sublime into the large chamber c.

For recrystallising naphthalene the ordinary solvent is petroleum spirit, and the operation is carried out in enamelled iron vessels provided with reflux condensers and heated by steam. The crystals are centrifuged and dried in air.

The naphthalene thus obtained is practically chemically pure, occurring in large crystalline plates, M.P. 79° C.

FIG. 3.—Apparatus for Subliming Naphthalene.

The mother liquors from which the naphthalene has been separated contain 30-40 per cent. of phenol. This is separated by fractionally extracting with a 10 per cent. caustic soda solution. The aqueous alkaline liquid is drawn off from the oil, and steam blown through in order to volatilise any traces of naphthalene or other hydrocarbons that it still contains.

The alkaline liquid is then neutralised by sulphuric or carbonic acid, the precipitated oily layer of phenol drawn off and fractionally distilled from stills with zinc or silver condensing coils ; the distillate is crystallised out in the cold, and separated from the still fluid cresols by a centrifugal machine.

The **phenol** is thus obtained almost chemically pure as a white solid. It is principally used for making picric and salicylic acid.

The **cresols,** separated from the phenol, occur as a fluid mixture of the three isomers. These bodies are much used for disinfecting purposes.

3. **The Heavy or Creosote Oils,** B.P. 230°-270° C., sp. gr. 1.04, form perhaps 10 per cent. of the tar. They consist of a complex mixture of neutral and acid oils, among which may be mentioned naphthalene, dinaphthylene, methyl-naphthalene, xylenol, naphthol, and paraffins. They are used for creosoting timber—especially telegraph poles and the sleepers of railways. See under **Timber Preserving** in Martin's "Industrial Chemistry," Vol. I. p. 190.

4. **Anthracene Oils,** B.P. 270°-400° C., sp. gr. 1.10, forming 12-17 per cent. of the tar, contain a certain amount of carbolic acid and a considerable amount

of **anthracene**, $C_{14}H_{10}$, M.P. 213° C. This latter is one of the most valuable constituents of coal-tar. To isolate the anthracene and free it from impurities the oil is cooled and the greenish crystals of impure anthracene which separate out are freed from the oily mother liquor by pressing or placing in a centrifugal machine. It then contains only 10-12 per cent. pure anthracene, being mixed with impurities such as phenanthrene, methylanthracene, diphenyl, naphthalene, pyrene, retene, carbazol, etc., which are exceedingly difficult to get rid of. To do this the whole is pressed to 200-300 atmospheres in a hydraulic press heated by steam. Most of the phenanthrene and naphthalene flows away in a liquid form, and the percentage of anthracene is increased to 28-40 per cent.

The anthracene is then washed with *solvent* naphtha. By washing with the pyridine *bases* mixed with solvent naphtha the carbazol is almost completely removed, and a product consisting of 90 per cent. anthracene is obtained, and made into alizarin.

Chemically pure anthracene is obtained by grinding up with caustic potash and lime, distilling, washing with solvents, and subliming.

The plant usually used for subliming anthracene is shown in Fig. 4. The anthracene is placed to the depth of 2-3 in. in a shallow iron pan C, heated from below. Superheated steam from the pipe B, which is perforated by many holes, carries away the vapours into the large chamber D, where they are suddenly chilled by a spray of cold water from the rose H, causing the anthracene to precipitate in the finest state of division—a necessary condition for its easy conversion into anthraquinone by the action of oxidising agents.

5. **Pitch.** — The residue which remains in the tar still is **Pitch** and forms 50-55 per cent. of the tar. Much of it probably consists of finely divided coal or coke, but undoubtedly 20-30 per cent. consists of solid unsaturated hydrocarbons, which give it its distinctive properties. Soft pitch has $C = 91.8$ per cent., $H = 4.6$ per cent.; hard pitch has $C = 93.2$ per cent., $H = 4.4$

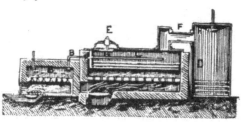

FIG. 4.—Anthracene Subliming Plant.

per cent. "**Hard Pitch**" is obtained by carrying the distillation as far as possible. It softens over 100°. **Soft Pitch** is obtained by a shorter distillation. The pitch is always run off while fluid from the still.

It is used for making briquettes from coal dust, for making varnishes and blacks (by mixing with certain oils), for making dolomites, stones, etc., in iron-works, and to a certain extent for paving streets, etc.—the natural asphalt being, however, both cheaper and better for the latter purpose.

Testing of Coal-tar and Pitch

(See Watson Smith, *Journ. Soc. Chem. Ind.*, 1883, p. 496.)

1. Free tar from water by placing a large glass beaker immersed in hot water and covered with a glass plate. After one and a half days decant off watery layer on surface.
2. Determine specific gravity by weighing accurately at 15° C. a given volume (say 1 l.) run into a standard flask.
3. Distil 2½ l. of tar freed from water as above from a large glass retort in usual way, placing apparatus on a large iron tray covered with ½ in. of sand (to diminish danger from fire), forcing in a slow current of air through a drawn out tube through the cork and reaching to the centre of the flask.

    (*a*) First heat slowly to 60°-70° C., heating at that temperature for a day or two to expel ammonia water.
    (*b*) Collect (1) Light oil, up to 170°; (2) Middle oil, up to 230° C.; (3) Creosote oil, up to 270° C.; (4) Anthracene oil.

The volumes of the different distillates are measured, and after treating the fractions much as they are treated on the large scale in the distillation of coal-tar, an estimate of the various proportions of the different substances likely to be obtained in the large scale distillation is arrived at and so the value of the coal-tar judged.

The **Free Carbon** in coal-tar is estimated (Kraemer) by extracting the coal-tar with forty times its weight of xylene, drying the residue at 100° C. and washing. The more free carbon, the thicker the tar and the greater the danger of frothing over during the distillation.

The **estimation of water** in tar is carried out by distilling 500 c.c. of carefully sampled and thoroughly agitated tar from a copper still, until finally a temperature of 200° C. is reached. Oil and water distil over into a graduated slanting glass tube 27 in. long, and separate out into two layers. The volume of water is then read off. To prevent boiling over add **toluene** to the crude tar.

Pitch is tested for its *softening* or melting point.

Soft pitch softens at 40° C., melts at 60° C.; medium pitch softens at 60° C., melts at 100° C.; hard pitch softens at 100° C., melts at 150°-200° C.

A rod of soft pitch, 4 × 4 × ¾ in., suitable for making patent fuel, will bend without breaking on heating in water at 60° C. for two minutes. Its **torsional value** is tested by special methods.

The amount of "**Free Carbon**" and "**Bitumen**" in pitch is estimated by boiling the pitch in a flask with a reflux condenser in succession twice each with benzene, carbon disulphide, and alcohol. The residue represents the "free carbon," the difference being the "bitumen."

To *distinguish* **coal-tar** pitch from *natural* asphalt, heat a sample in a crucible. **Coal-tar** pitch evolves *acrid* fumes, but natural asphalt (usually) a pleasant, bituminous smell.

Recovery of Pyridine Bases from the Distillation Products of Coal-tar

We have described how the various fractions of oil distilled from coal-tar are first washed with sulphuric acid, which abstracts the volatile bases contained in them.

Crude "pyridine-sulphuric acid," from washing the light oils with sulphuric acid, is a brownish liquid, sp. gr. 1.2-1.3, contains 15-20 per cent. of **bases** boiling between 100° and 200° C. Half of these bases is **pyridine**, the rest being the picolines, lutidines, etc.

Pyridine is separated from "pyridine-sulphuric acid" by passing in ammonia gas until a sample of the exit gas smells of pyridine. The liquid separates into two layers, the top one consisting of muddy impurities, the bottom being a solution of pyridine-ammonium sulphate. The bottom layer is run off and completely saturated with ammonia. Pyridine separates as an oil. It is drawn off and fractionated.

Pure pyridine is principally used for denaturing spirits in Germany.

Quinoline is separated in a similar manner from the sulphuric acid washings of the heavier coal-tar Oils. It is used for making the quinoline dyes.

Quinoline (on account of its high boiling point) does not occur largely in the acid washings from crude **benzol**, but is contained, together with acridine and other bases, in the crude sulphuric acid washings from the higher boiling tar oils.

Bone Tar or Bone Oil is the dark evil-smelling liquid formed during the dry distillation of bones in the preparation of bone black (animal charcoal). It contains considerable amounts of pyridine and quinoline, their homologues and other bases. These compounds may be extracted from it by the use of sulphuric acid, and separated as described above.

COAL-TAR PRODUCTS (see Table)

Distillation Products

Benzol (Benzene), C_6H_6.—Colourless, mobile liquid, B.P. 80.5°; M.P. 6° C; sp. gr. $\frac{18}{4} = 0.839$. Freezes to white crystals at 0° C. Distinguishable from light petroleum by (a) completely dissolving in fuming H_2SO_4 (petroleum does not); (b) easily dissolves picric acid and pitch (petroleum does not easily).

Valuation.—It should give no blue colour when shaken with concentrated H_2SO_4, and a fragment of isatin (thiophene); should not darken much when shaken with concentrated H_2SO_4 (unsaturated hydrocarbons or thiophene). No unnitrated hydrocarbon should be obtained on treatment with nitro-sulphuric acid and distillation with steam. " *Crude* benzol " is a mixture of benzene, toluene, xylene, etc., and is known as 30 per cent., 50 per cent., or 90 per cent. benzol, according as 30 per cent., 50 per cent., or 90 per cent. of the whole distils over before the thermometer reaches 100° C. Refined benzol should completely distil within half a degree Centigrade.

Toluol (Toluene), $C_6H_5.CH_3$.—Colourless liquid, freezes below – 20° C.; B.P. 111° C.; sp. gr. $\frac{13}{4} = 0.8708$.

Valuation.—Should only slightly darken on shaking with concentrated H_2SO_4.

Xylene, Xyol, $C_6H_4(CH_3)_2$.—Three isomers occur in coal-tar xylene, viz., 2·15 per cent. of **orthoxylene,** CH_3 $\diagup\!\!\diagdown$, B.P. 142°; 70-87 per cent. of **metaxylene,** CH_3

CH_3 $\diagup\!\!\diagdown$, B.P. 139°, sp. gr. (19° C.) = 0.8668; 3-10 per cent. **paraxylene,**

CH_3 $\diagup\!\!\diagdown$ CH_3, B.P. 138°, M.P. 15° C., sp. gr. 0.8621 (19° C.). **Metaxylene** is technically the most important.

Valuation.—Commercial xylol should distil between 135° and 140° C., and should only turn light brown when shaken with H_2SO_4.

Naphthalene, $C_{10}H_8$ (for preparation from coal-tar see preceding section, p. 418).—Colourless crystalline solid; M.P. 80.5°; B.P. 218° C.; sp. gr. (15° C.) = 1.1517. Sublimes when warmed.

Valuation.—No residue or colour change should be produced when sublimed in air; should melt and boil sharply; should produce no red colour with hot concentrated H_2SO_4, and when solution is diluted with water, filtered, and made alkaline, no smell of pyridine should be apparent. Boiling caustic soda should extract no phenol; should not melt below 79.5° C.

Uses.—Starting point for the production of synthetic indigo (see p. 46).

Anthracene, $C_{14}H_{10}$ (for preparation from **coal-tar** see p. 7).—Colourless crystalline plates with violet fluorescence (when pure); M.P. 213° C.; B.P. just over 360° C. Oxidised, produces **anthraquinone** (which gives with warm NaOH solution and zinc dust a red colour), and with picric acid in benzene gives red crystals M.P., 170° C., of the picrate, $C_{14}H_{10}.C_6H_2.(NO_2)_3.OH$.

To estimate the anthracene in the commercial product, oxidise into anthraquinone by boiling 1 g. for two hours with 45 g. glacial acetic acid to which are slowly added 15 g. of chromic acid dissolved in 10 c.c. of water, leave for twenty-four hours, add 400 c.c. water, stand two hours, filter off anthraquinone, wash with cold water, with boiling NaOH solution, with boiling water, dry in porcelain dish at 100°, heat ten minutes to 100° with 10 g. slightly fuming sulphuric acid, leave twelve hours in a damp place, pour into 200 c.c. cold water, filter off precipitate, wash with alkaline water and with hot water, transfer to dish, dry, *weigh.* Then heat dish until the anthraquinone has volatliised, and *weigh.* Loss of weight = anthraquinone. This multiplied by 85.6 gives percentage of anthracene in sample (see Luck, *Ber.*, 6, 1347). It may amount to anything between 30 and 90 per cent., the rest being phenanthrene, carbazol, chrysene, etc.

Uses.—Source of valuable dyes. See p. 39.

Phenol (Carbolic Acid), $C_6H_5.OH$.—White crystalline solid, M.P. 41°; B.P. 188° C.; sp. gr. (40° C.) = 1.05433. Commercial samples should melt about 39-40° C., boil about 183°-186° C., and dissolve completely in aqueous caustic soda.

Estimation by titration with standard bromine water. On account of the fact that phenol is extensively used for making picric acid and other explosives, the price in war time invariably rises enormously, and it then becomes profitable to make it from benzol by sulphonating and fusing with NaOH or KOH.

Cresol (Cresylic Acid), $C_6H_4(CH_3).OH$.—Three isomers occur in coal-tar, namely, ortho-, para-, and meta-cresol.

Halogen Derivatives

Benzyl Chloride, $C_6H_5.CH_2Cl$.—Prepared by leading chlorine over the surface of boiling toluene (placed in a sandstone vessel and heated by lead-coated steam pipes) until it has increased in weight by 38 per cent., washing with water, and fractionally distilling : $C_6H_5.CH_3 + Cl_2 = C_6H_5.CH_2Cl + HCl$. Colourless liquid, B.P. 178°; sp. gr. (14° C.) = 1.107. An estimate of the amount of benzotrichloride in it is obtained by observing the amount of green colouring matter produced on heating with dimethylaniline and zinc chloride.

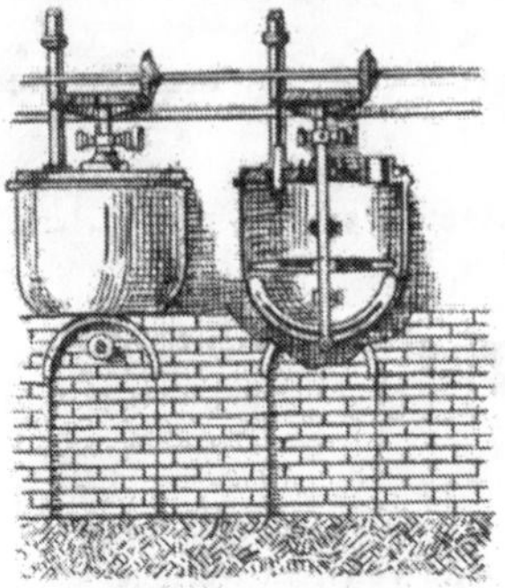

Benzal Chloride, $C_6H_5.CHCl_2$ (Benzylidene dichloride), and **Benzotrichloride**, $C_6H_5.CCl_3$, are simultaneously produced by the further chlorination of boiling toluene, and produce benzaldehyde and benzoic acid when heated with milk of lime. They are not usually separated.

FIG. 5.—Nitrating Apparatus for Nitro-Benzene.

Nitro Compounds

Nitro-benzene, $C_6H_5.NO_2$, is a light yellow liquid, smelling like bitter almonds, B.P. 207° C.; sp. gr. (15° C.) = 1.208. Is a very good solvent for other nitro compounds including guncotton, etc.

Preparation.—100 kg. benzol are placed in a cast-iron, round-bottomed vessel, fitted with a cover and stirring apparatus, and provided with a condensing tube and an opening for the addition of acid (both placed in the cover), while a tube at the bottom allows the contents to be emptied. A mixture of 115 kg. concentrated nitric acid, sp. gr. 1.38, and 180 kg. concentrated H_2SO_4 are now slowly run in, while the stirrers (lubricated with nitro-benzene) are kept in rapid movement, and the temperature of the whole kept below 25° C. by a stream of cold water flowing round the vessels ; when the greater part of the acid has been added, the temperature is allowed to increase to 50° C. The following action has taken place :—

$$C_6H_6 + HNO_3 = C_6H_5.NO_2 + H_2O$$
Benzene. Nitric acid. Nitro-benzene. Water.

The acid is run into the benzene (thereby keeping the latter in excess until the last), and the temperature is kept low in order to avoid the second reaction :—

$$C_6H_5NO_2 + HNO_3 = C_6H_4(NO_2)_2 + H_2O$$
Nitro-benzene. Nitric acid. Di-nitro-benzene. Water

The stirring and cooling apparatus must be efficient, as the nitrating mixture is otherwise liable to spontaneously inflame.

After all the acid has been slowly added the stirring is continued for some hours until no more action takes place. The whole is allowed to stand, and the **nitro-benzene** separates as an oil on the surface of the acid.

The acid is run off at the bottom. It contains about 1 per cent. of nitric acid, water, and organic compounds. It is "regenerated" for use by allowing it to slowly flow, cascade fashion, down a series of six porcelain vessels, heated in a stream of hot air.

During the heating the water and nitric acid vaporises (the nitrous fumes being condensed and used in the manufacture of nitric acid), and there finally flows out of the last vessel concentrated sulphuric acid, 66° Bé., which is used again for nitrating.

After the acid has been drawn off, the nitro-benzene is then run into large wooden vessels, and washed with water until all traces of acid are removed.

When required quite pure (for perfumery) it must be steam distilled. Usually any unused benzene present is first removed by blowing steam through the mixture, and the nitro-benzene coming over with the benzene is used again for nitrating.

For making dyes, etc., it is usually unnecessary to distil the benzol.

Yield.—100 parts of benzene give 150-152 parts nitro-benzene.

Metadinitrobenzene, $C_6H_4(NO_2)_2$.—Crystalline needles, M.P. 89.9° C. It is prepared in the apparatus used for making **nitro-benzene,** using stronger acids.

To 100 kg. benzene, 200 kg. nitric acid (40° Bé.) and 300 kg. concentrated sulphuric acid (66° Bé.), previously mixed together, are allowed to flow in, and after the action is over, the contents of the pot are withdrawn while still hot, the dinitrobenzene allowed to solidify, and purified by crystallisation. It is used for making diaminobenzene and explosives.

Trinitrobenzene, $C_6H_3(NO_2)_3$, is similarly made. It is used for making explosives.

Ortho- and Paranitrophenol, $C_6H_4.NO_2.OH$.—1 part of phenol is mixed with a little water, and then a mixture of 2 parts nitric acid (sp. gr. 1.38) and 4 parts of water is gradually added, cooling the liquid the whole time. After the reaction is completed the oil is washed with water and the *o*-nitrophenol steam distilled over, the paranitrophenol remaining behind.

Trinitrophenol, Picric Acid, $C_6H_2(NO_2)_3.OH$, is made by heating phenol sulphonic acid with nitric acid. For details see Martin's "Industrial Chemistry," Vol. I. p. 632. Used as an explosive.

Mono-Nitrotoluenes.—Three isomerides are known, viz. :—

	Melting Point.	Boiling Point.
Orthonitrotoluene - . . .	Liquid.	218°-219° C.
Metanitrotoluene - . . .	16° C.	230°-231° C.
Paranitrotoluene - . . .	54° C.	234° C.

Under ordinary conditions of nitrating, ortho and paranitrotoluene are principally produced, and may be separated (when necessary) by fractionally distilling under diminished pressure.

Mixtures of nitro-benzene and nitrotoluene and nitroxylene, $C_6H_3(CH_3)_2.NO_2$, are also prepared ; also nitro-benzylchloride, $C_6H_4(NO_2).CH_2Cl$; nitro-benzaldehyde chloride, $C_6H_4(NO_2).CHCl_2$, mono-nitronaphthalene, etc. etc.

Dinitrotoluene $C_6H_3(CH_3).(NO_2)_2$, is prepared in much the same way as dinitrobenzene (see p. 364).

The **Trinitrotoluenes** are used as explosives. See Martin's "Industrial Chemistry," Vol. I. pp. 633, 634.

α_1-α_3-**Dinitronaphthalene** is used for making explosives, alizarin black, and diaminonaphthalene. **Naphthalene** is allowed to stand twenty-four hours in contact with strong nitric acid, sulphuric acid is added, and the mixture heated twelve to twenty-four hours on the water bath, the product washed with water, and extracted in succession with carbon disulphide and acetone, in order to eliminate as much as possible the other isomerides formed at the same time. The pure product melts at 217° C.

α_1-α_3-Dinitro-naphthalene.

Bases

Aniline, $C_6H_5.NH_2$, is prepared on a very large scale by reducing nitro-benzene with **iron** and **hydrochloric acid.**

500 parts of nitro-benzene and 800 parts of water are placed in a large iron still provided with a mechanical agitator and condenser, and the whole is heated to boiling by blowing in steam. 16-20 parts of hydrochloric acid are now added, the steam is shut off, and 550 parts of finely ground cast-iron borings are gradually added during about eight hours. A vigorous action takes place, heat is evolved, and a mixture of water, aniline, and nitro-benzene distil over in a steady stream, and are continually returned to the still.

Great care must be taken in adding iron not to let the action become too violent, since violent explosions have been known to occur.

The following actions take place :—

$$C_6H_5.NO_2 + 3Fe + 6HCl = C_6H_5.NH_2 + 3FeCl_2 + 2H_2O.$$
Nitro-benzene. Iron. Hydrochloric acid. Aniline. Ferrous chloride. Water.

$$C_6H_5NO_2 + 2Fe + H_2O = C_6H_5NH_2 + Fe_2O_3.$$

$$Fe + 4Fe_2O_3 = 3Fe_3O_4.$$

According to the first equation 178 parts of HCl are required for the reduction of 100 parts of nitro-benzene.

In practice 9 parts of HCl are sufficient, in consequence of the reaction largely proceeding according to the second equation.

When all the iron has been added the heating is continued by steam, and the distillate returned so long as it is yellow (presence of nitro-benzene). When the distillate comes over colourless, it is collected in *h* (Fig. 6), and the distillation continued so long as aniline comes over. The aniline collects in a layer at the bottom and is drawn off from time to time. The

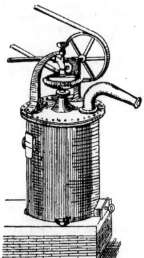

Full View.

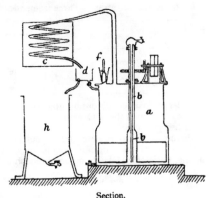

Section.

FIG. 6.—Reducing Apparatus for Nitro-Benzene
Steam is blown in through the hollow shaft of the stirrers.

water condensed from the steam distillation contains up to 3 per cent. dissolved aniline and toluidine, and is returned again to the boiler and used for another aniline distillation. The aniline thus obtained is purified by redistillation in special stills.

The residue in the still consists of metallic iron, and oxides and chlorides of iron, mixed with tarry impurities. Sometimes it is smelted for iron in iron-works, often it is worked up into green vitriol (iron sulphate). If allowed to accumulate the spontaneous oxidation of the finely divided iron may cause the mass to become incandescent.

Yield.—100 parts nitro-benzene give 70 aniline.

Properties.—Colourless oil, B.P. 182°; M.P. 8°; sp. gr. (15° C.) = 1.0275. Soluble in 32 parts of water at 15° C. Completely soluble in acids.

Tests.—Aniline water gives a violet colour with bleaching powder solution. It may be estimated by titrating with sodium nitrite solution. The presence of benzene or nitro-benzene, etc., in aniline is detected by their insolubility in acids.

Aniline for Red is a mixture of aniline with both toluidines, *e.g.*, 33.3 per cent. aniline, 28 per cent. paratoluidine, 42.7 per cent. *o*-toluidine, sp. gr. 1.008 at 15° C.; B.P. 190-198.

Aniline for Safranine consists of aniline (40 per cent.) and *o*-toluidine (60 per cent.).

"Aniline for Blue" or "light aniline" is aniline free from toluidine, 80 per cent. of which distils between 182°-182.5°. It is used for phenylating rosaniline. See under **Rosaniline Blue.**

Toluidine, $C_6H_4(CH_3)NH_2$ (ortho-, meta-, and para-), and

Xylidine, $C_6H_3(CH_3)_2NH_2$, and other similar bases are prepared in much the same way as aniline by reducing the corresponding nitro compounds.

Dimethylaniline, $C_6H_5.N(CH_3)_2$, is prepared by heating a mixture of aniline (75 parts), aniline hydrochloride (25 parts), and methyl alcohol (free from acetone) in a cast-iron autoclave (see Fig. 197) to 230°-270° C., and rectifying the product :—

$$C_6H_5.NH_2.HCl + 2CH_3OH = C_6H_5.N.(CH_3)_2 + HCl + 2H_2O$$
$$HCl + C_6H_5NH_2 = C_6H_5.NH_2.HCl.$$

Colourless oil; B.P. 192°; sp. gr. (15° C.) = 0.976. Used for making methylene blue, indophenol, malachite green, etc.

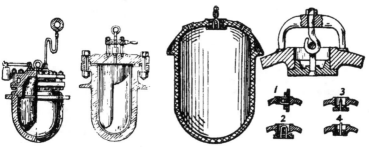

FIG. 7.—Autoclaves of Different Types.
1, 2, 3, 4 shows method of inserting stopper.

By treating the product (26 kg.) with HCl (100 kg. of 31 per cent. HCl), stirring, adding chopped ice (100 kg.) and then sodium nitrite (16 kg. in 351 kg. H_2O) we get *p*-nitroso-dimethyl-aniline as an oil :—

$$C_6H_5.N.(CH_3)_2 + HNO_2 = C_6H_4 \begin{array}{c} NO \\ \diagdown \\ N.(CH_3)_2 \end{array} + H_2O.$$

| Dimethylaniline. | Nitrous acid. | *p*-Nitroso-dimethylaniline. | Water. |

Used for making various dyes.

Diphenylamine, $(C_6H_5)_2.NH$, is prepared by heating molecular proportions of aniline and aniline hydrochloride together in an autoclave for some hours at 200° C., boiling with dilute HCl to remove aniline, and distilling the residual oil, which is diphenylamine. Forms monoclinic plates; M.P. 54° C.; B.P. 310°.

The **Phenylenediamines**, $C_6H_4(NH_2)_2$—All three varieties are in use :—

	M.P.	B.P.
Orthophenylenediamine -	- 102° C. -	- 252° C.
Metaphenylenediamine -	63° C. -	- 287° C.
Paraphenylenediamine -	- 147° C. -	- 267° C.

m-Phenylenediamine is prepared by reducing *m*-dinitro-benzene with iron and hydrochloric acid.

200 parts of *m*-dinitro-benzene and 200 parts of water are placed in a large iron vessel provided with a mechanical agitator and condenser (see under **Aniline**, Fig. 6). Steam is blown until the mixture boils, then 16 parts of hydrochloric acid are run in and 430 parts of finely ground cast-iron borings are slowly added ; when the action is complete the liquid is made alkaline with sodium carbonate, and boiled up with 800-1,000 parts of water, the liquid filtered from the iron sludge (which is again extracted with water) and the solution of the *m*-phenylenediamine either used directly for making substances like Bismarck brown, or it may be neutralised with hydrochloric acid, evaporated, and obtained as hydrochloride. On adding concentrated NaOH solution to the concentrated hydrochloride solution, the base is set free as an oil, which, rising to the surface, solidifies on cooling, and is purified by distillation.

Colourless solid ; M.P. 83° C. ; B.P. 287. Soluble in water.

p-**Phenylenediamine** is prepared by reducing *p*-nitraniline with iron and hydrochloric acid.

Benzidine, $\begin{array}{c} C_6H_4.NH_2 \ (1:4) \\ | \\ C_6H_4.NH_2 \ (1:4) \end{array}$, is prepared by reducing nitro-benzene with zinc dust and caustic soda in an iron vessel provided with a powerful stirrer. Any aniline formed is distilled off with steam, and the product run out and treated with cold dilute hydrochloric acid to dissolve out zinc hydrate. There is thus left hydrazobenzene, $C_6H_5.NH.NH.C_6H_5$:—$Zn + 2NaOH = Zn(ONa)_2 + 2H$

$$C_6H_5.NO_2 + C_6H_5.NO_2 + 10H = C_6H_5.NH - NH - C_6H_5 + 4H_2O.$$

This is converted into **benzidine** (by intramolecular change) thus :—

$$C_6H_5.NH.NH.C_6H_5 = NH_2.C_6H_4.C_6H_4.NH_2$$

by boiling with hydrochloric acid, filtering, and precipitating the base as sulphate by sulphuric acid or sodium sulphate. The base may be obtained by decomposing the sulphate by caustic soda and distilling. Crystalline plates ; M.P. 122° ; B.P. above 360° C. Nitrous acid converts it into tetrazodiphenyl $\begin{array}{c} C_6H_4 - N : N.OH \\ | \\ C_6H_4.N : N.OH \end{array}$ which combines with sulphonic acids of phenols and amines to form azo colours, such as Congo, Chrysamine, which dye cotton from an alkaline bath without a mordant. See **Synthetic Dyes**.

Nitraniline, $C_6H_4.NO_2NH_2$.—Of the three varieties the meta and para compounds are chiefly used in colour manufacture. **Metanitraniline** is prepared by the partial reduction of dinitro-benzene with iron and hydrochloric acid, or with ammonium sulphide; also from finely powdered aniline nitrate, by adding it, in a finely powdered condition, into concentrated sulphuric acid (cooled to $-5°$ C.), stirring, pouring into 400 l. water, and decomposing with caustic soda; yellow prisms, M.P. 114° C.

Paranitraniline is prepared from *p*-nitracetanilide (see Nölting and Collin, "Ber.," **17**, 262) by warming with dilute sulphuric acid; yellow prisms, M.P. 147° C.

Amidophenol, $C_6H_4.NH_2.OH$. — The ortho-amidophenol is obtained by mixing 50 parts of *o*-nitrophenol with 300 parts of ammonia and reducing by passing in H_2S. Meta-amidophenol is obtained by reducing *m*-nitrophenol, or by heating resorcinol with ammonia; para-amidophenol is obtained by reducing *p*-nitrophenol.

α-**Naphthylamines,** $C_{10}H_7.NH_2$, is manufactured by reducing α-nitro-naphthalene with iron and hydrochloric acid, as in the case of aniline.

800 kg. iron borings and 40 kg. hydrochloric acid are mixed, with the addition of some water, in a large vessel provided with a powerful stirring apparatus. The warmed mixture has then added to it in small portions about 600 kg. nitronaphthalene, and the reduction proceeds vigorously, continually stirring the whole time. The nitronaphthalene must be added at such a rate that the internal temperature is maintained about 50° C. Finally the mixture is, after the reaction has ceased, stirred vigorously for six to eight hours, while the temperature is maintained at about 50°-70° C. by blowing in steam. Samples are withdrawn from time to time, and the unchanged nitronaphthalene estimated (by distilling and dissolving the product in HCl). Finally milk of lime is added (about 50 kg.), the mixture vigorously stirred, and the vessel emptied. The following reaction takes place (Witt):—

$$24Fe_2Cl_2 + 4C_{10}H_7NO_2 + 4H_2O = 12Fe_2Cl_4O + 4C_{10}H_7NH_2;$$
$$12Fe_2Cl_4O + 9Fe = 3Fe_3O_4 + 24FeCl_2.$$

The crude naphthylamine is now distilled from box-shaped iron retorts, through which a stream of superheated steam is driven to facilitate distillation, the condensing worms being kept at 60° C. by immersion in hot water in order to prevent them from being choked by crystallising naphthylamine.

The α-naphthylamine is obtained pure by a single redistillation. *Flat* needles or plates with an unpleasant smell—M.P. 50° C.; B.P. 300° C.

β-**Naphthylamine,** $C_{10}H_7.NH_2$, is prepared by heating 10 kg. β-naphthol, 4 kg. NaOH, and 4 kg. NH_4Cl in an autoclave for sixty to seventy hours at 150°-160° C.—M.P. 112° C.; B.P. 294.

m-**Aminophenol,** $C_6H_4(OH).NH_2$, is manufactured by heating 20 kg. NaOH with 4 kg. water in an autoclave to 270° C., and then adding 10 kg. *m*-aminobenzol-sulphonic acid, $C_6H_4.SO_3H.NH_2$, and heating at 280°-290° C. for one hour, when the sodium salt of the base is produced thus :—

$$C_6H_4{<}^{SO_3Na}_{NH_2} + Na_2O = C_6H_4{<}^{ONa}_{NH_2} + Na_2SO_3.$$

The base, *m*-aminophenol, may be obtained by decomposing the sodium salt with acid or carbon dioxide.

m-**Oxydimethylaniline,** $C_6H_4{<}^{OH}_{N.(CH_3)_2}$, is prepared in a similar manner from the sulphonic acid of dimethylaniline.

Aminonaphthol, $C_{10}H_6\diagdown\begin{matrix}OH\\NH_2\end{matrix}$, is likewise prepared by fusing naphthylamine-

sulphonic acid, $C_{10}H_6\cdot\diagdown\begin{matrix}SO_3H\\NH_2\end{matrix}$, with caustic soda.

Pyridine, C_5H_5N, is obtained from the sulphuric acid washings of light benzol as described p. 420, also from **bone tar** or **bone oil** (obtained during the dry distillation of bones for animal charcoal). Colourless mobile oil, of unpleasant smell, B.P. 116.7° C.; sp. gr. (0° C.) = 0.9858.

Quinoline, C_9H_7N, is an oily liquid, B.P. 238° C.; sp. gr. (20° C.) = 1.094; occurs in the coal-tar and bone-oil bases. It is prepared by heating aniline (216 parts) and glycerol (600 parts) with concentrated sulphuric acid (600 parts) and nitro-benzene (144 parts) for one day at 125° C., then at 180°-200° C. until reaction is complete.

The glycerol decomposes thus :—

$$\underset{\text{Glycerol.}}{C_3H_8O_3} - \underset{\text{Water.}}{2H_2O} = \underset{\text{Acrolein.}}{CH_2 : CH.CHO,}$$

and the acrolein combines with the aniline thus :—

$$\underset{\text{Aniline.}}{C_6H_5.NH_2} + \underset{\text{Acrolein.}}{C_3H_4O} + \underset{\substack{\text{Oxygen}\\\text{from the}\\\text{nitro-benzene.}}}{O} = .C_9H_7N + 2H_2O.$$

The mixture is diluted wit h water, excess of nitro-benzene boiled off, the base set free by soda, the quinoline is distilled, purified from aniline by treating in acid solution with $K_2Cr_2O_7$ or $NaNO_2$. Yield, 70 per cent.

The quinoline of commerce, usually obtained from the basic portions of coal-tar oils, contains **quinaldine,** $C_{10}H_9N$, and isoquinoline, C_9H_7N. The former may be prepared in a similar manner by heating aniline and aldehyde, or paraldehyde with dehydrating agents, such as aluminium chloride and hydrochloric acid.

Acridin, $C_{13}H_9N$, a derivative of anthracene, is a crystalline body produced by treating diphenylamine, $C_6H_5.NH.C_6H_5$, and formic acid, $H.COOH$, with .zinc chloride. Also obtained, along with quinoline, from the sulphuric acid washings of the heavier coal-tar oils.

Phenylhydrazine, $C_6H_5.NH.NH_2$.— 10 parts aniline are dissolved in 200 parts concentrated HCl, the liquid cooled, and 7.5 parts of sodium nitrite, dissolved in 50 parts water, are gradually added. Diazobenzene chloride is formed. thus :—

$$C_6H_5.NH_2.HCl + NaNO_2 + HCl = C_6H_5 - N = N - Cl + NaCl + 2H_2O.$$

The solution is then neutralised and reduced by adding neutral potassium sulphite and acid metasulphite :—

$$C_6H_5.N_2.Cl + K_2SO_3 = C_6H_5.N_2.SO_3K + KCl.$$
$$C_6H_5.N_2.SO_3K + KHSO_3 + H_2O = C_6H_5.NH.NH.SO_3K + KHSO_4.$$

The phenylhydrazine-p-sulphonic acid, $C_6H_5.NH.NH.SO_3H$, thus obtained is used directly thus in the colour industry. If the base itself is required (for manufacturing antipyrene), the solution is boiled with concentrated HCl, when the chlorhydrate $C_6H_5.NH.NH_2.HCl$, is obtained, and from this the base may be set free by adding alkalki. When quite pure forms crystals, M.P. 23° C. As usually obtained it is an oil, B.P. 241°-242° C.

Sulphur Bases

When *p*-toluidine is heated with sulphur at 140° C. in the presence of lead oxide, **Thiotoluidine** is obtained (Merz and Werth, *Ber.*, **4**, 393), thus :—

$$2C_6H_4\!\!<\!\!{}^{CH_3}_{NH_2} + S_2 = H_2S + S\!\!<\!\!{}^{C_6H_3\!\!<\!\!{}^{CH_3}_{NH_2}}_{C_6H_3\!\!<\!\!{}^{CH_3}_{NH_2}}$$

p-Toluidine.   Sulphur.   Thio-*p*-toluidine.

The bases crystallise from alcohol in colourless, odourless plates, and unite with two molecules of HCl, thus :—$C_{14}H_{16}N_2S,2HCl$. If *p*-toluidine is heated with more sulphur to a higher temperature (eighteen hours at 180°-190° C. and six hours at 200°-220°), **Toluthiazol** is obtained :—

$$C_7H_9N + 2S_2 = 3H_2S + C_{14}H_{12}N_2S,$$

p-Toluidine.   Toluthiazol.

and has the constitution $CH_3.C_6H_3\!\!<\!\!{}^{S}_{N}\!\!>\!\!C.C_6H_4.NH_2$.

This is not a dyestuff, but if a higher temperature and more sulphur be employed in its preparation, a base is formed which on sulphonation yields **Primuline Yellow**.

A large and important class of sulphur colours are derived from these and similar bases, which are now rapidly increasing in value.

Aldehydes

Benzaldehyde (bitter almond oil), $C_6H_5.CHO$.

Preparation.—(1) By heating under 4 or 5 atmospheres pressure a mixture of benzylidene dichloride and benzotrichloride with the theoretical amount of caustic soda or lime, and distilling off the benzaldehyde with steam. Sodium or calcium benzoate remains behind :—

$$C_6H_5.CHCl_2 + 2NaOH = C_6H_5.CHO + 2NaCl + H_2O.$$

Benzal chloride.   Caustic soda.   Benzaldehyde.   Water.

Small quantities of chlorine compounds are contained in benzaldehyde prepared in this way. This does not matter for the colour industry, but if the benzaldehyde is to be used for perfuming purposes, it loses greatly in value, and now is successfully prepared for this purpose (2) by oxidising toluene with nickel or cobalt oxide (German Patent, 306,071, 1901 ; *Chemiker Zeitung*, 25, 439, 1901).

Colourless liquid with smell of bitter almonds, B.P. 180° C. ; sp. gr. (15° C.) = 1.0504.

Valuation.—90 per cent. of commercial product should distil between 177° C. and 181° C. ; should have sp. gr. at 15° C. = 1.0504 ; 1 volume should dissolve almost completely in 10 volumes warm aqueous sodium bisulphite, sp. gr. 1.11, and on extracting solution with ether, evaporating ether, no pungent-smelling residue should be left (benzyl chloride). Chlorine is detected by fusing with sodium hydrate and nitrate, and precipitating with silver nitrate. Adulteration with nitro-benzene is detected by a *green* colour on heating with strong potash solution, also by presence of N (heating with Na). On long keeping it oxidises to **benzoic** acid which crystallises out.

Carboxylic Acids

Benzoic Acid, $C_6H_5.COOH$, is prepared from the calcium or sodium benzoate left in the preparation of benzaldehyde (see above); after distilling off all the benzaldehyde the calcium benzoate is decomposed by hydrochloric acid, the precipitated benzoic acid is filtered off, dried, and sublimed. White needles, M.P. 121° C. ; B.P. 249° C. Soluble in boiling water.

Salicylic Acid, $C_6H_4(OH).CO_2H$, is prepared by submitting dry sodium phenate (from phenol and caustic soda) to the action of dry carbon dioxide gas at ordinary temperatures, when sodium phenyl carbonate is formed :—

$$C_6H_5.ONa + CO_2 = C_6H_5O.CO_2.Na.$$

This is then heated in a closed vessel at 120°·130° C. for several hours, when it is converted quantitatively into **sodium salicylate**—

$$\left(C_6H_5.O.CO_2.Na = C_6H_4\!\!<^{OH}_{COONa}\right),$$

which is dissolved in water and salicylic acid precipitated by adding hydrochloric acid. White needles, M.P. 156°. Steam-volatile. Sparingly soluble in cold water. Gives a violet coloration with ferric chloride.

Phthalic Acid (*o*-benzenedicarboxylic acid), $C_6H_4.(CO_2H)_2$ (1 : 2).

Preparation.—100 parts naphthalene, 1,500 parts concentrated sulphuric acid, 50 parts mercury are heated together until the naphthalene is dissolved ; then the mass is heated to 300° C. in a still, when sulphur dioxide, carbon dioxide, water, phthalic acid, and phthalic anhydride distil over. On cooling the crystals of phthalic acid are separated and dried by the centrifugal machine.

When heated with ammonia it yields **phthalimide,** $C_6H_4\!\!<^{CO}_{CO}\!\!>NH$.

Plates, M.P. 213° C. ; sparingly soluble in cold water, insoluble in chloroform.

The **anhydride,** $C_6H_4\!\!<^{CO}_{CO}\!\!>O$, forms long white needles, M.P. 128° C. ; B.P. 284° C. Largely used as a raw material for anthranilic acid, and so for synthetic indigo.

Anthranilic Acid (*o*-aminobenzoic acid), $C_6H_4(NH_2).CO_2H$, is prepared by dissolving 1 part phthalimide and 2 parts NaOH in 7 parts water, cooling, and gradually stirring in 10 parts of sodium hypochlorite solution (5 per cent. NaOCl) ; finally heating to 80° C. for some minutes, cooling, neutralising, and adding acetic acid in excess, when the greater part of the anthranilic acid separates out :—

$$C_6H_4\!\!<^{CO}_{CO}\!\!>NH + NaOCl + 3NaOH = C_6H_4\!\!<^{NH_2}_{COONa} + Na_2CO_3 + NaCl + H_2O.$$

The anthranilic acid still remaining in solution is precipitated in the form of a copper salt by adding copper acetate. Can also be easily prepared from *o*-chlorbenzoic acid, $C_6H_4.Cl.COOH$ (1 : 2), by heating with NH_3 in the presence of a trace of copper. (In the absence of copper no action takes place.) Colourless plates, M.P. 145° C. Used for manufacturing artificial indigo.

Diazo Compounds

LITERATURE

CAIN.—" Chemistry of the Diazo Compounds." London, 1908.
See also under **Synthetic Dyes.**

When a solution of sodium nitrite is added to a solution of a primary amine (containing the group NH_2), and the mixture is acidified, " Diazo Compounds," containing the group,—N=N—, are formed, which are usually unstable and sometimes explosive, but nevertheless give rise to a large number of valuable colouring matters.

Diazobenzene chloride, $C_6H_5—N=N—Cl$, one of the most frequently used diazo compounds, is only known in solution, and is obtained by "diazotising" aniline hydrochloride according to the following equation:—

$$C_6H_5.NH_2.HCl + NaNO_2 + HCl = C_6H_5-N\equiv N-Cl + NaCl + 2H_2O$$

Aniline hydrochloride.   Sodium   Hydrochloric   Diazobenzene   Sodium   Water.
       nitrite.   acid.   chloride.   chloride.

The solution of aniline hydrochloride is cooled by adding ice, and a 10 per cent. solution (accurately titrated) of sodium nitrite gradually run in, in the exact amount required to decompose the base, excess of nitrous acid being avoided (*test*: free nitrous acid turns KI + starch paper blue). The diazobenzene chloride is then immediately used while still in a liquid form.

Similarly **Diazobenzene nitrate**, $C_6H_5-N\equiv N-NO_3$, may be obtained by diazotising a solution of aniline in nitric acid (aniline nitrate), but although it can be obtained in a crystalline state, is always used in the liquid form, since the solid product is dangerously explosive.

All these diazo compounds are extremely reactive in the liquid form. For example, diazobenzene chloride, when added to aniline, immediately reacts as follows:—

$$C_6H_5-N_2-Cl + 2C_6H_5.NH_2 = C_6H_5-N\equiv N-NH.C_6H_5 + C_6H_5.NH_2.HCl$$

Diazobenzene chloride.   Aniline.   Diazoaminobenzene
                           (Gold yellow dye).

The product, in the presence of aniline salts, may undergo an intramolecular transformation, forming aminoazobenzol : $C_6H_5.N\equiv N-C_6H_5.NH_2$, which again can be diazotised. Besides monodiazo compounds di-, tri-, tetra-diazo compounds occur, containing two, three, four, and more "diazo groups," $-N\equiv N-$, and these bodies form an enormous number of colouring matters known as "azo dyes" (*q.v.*).

Sulphonic Acids

This important class of bodies contains the group SO_3H, and, accordingly as this occurs once, twice, or more, are known as mono-, di-, tri-, etc., sulphonic acids. They are, as a class, distinguished by their solubility in water, and thus arises the possibility of using many substances as "dyes" which, unless sulphonated, are insoluble and so useless. They are formed by acting on aromatic compounds with the following three agents:—

1. **Concentrated Sulphuric Acid**, 66° Bé. in the cold.

2. **Fuming Sulphuric Acid**, consisting of SO_3 dissolved in concentrated H_2SO_4.

3. **Chlorsulphonic Acid**, SO_3HCl, prepared by heating together fuming sulphuric acid and salt:—

$$H_2S_2O_7 + NaCl = SO_3HCl + NaHSO_4.$$

Fuming sulphuric acid.

In the last named agent, the sulphonation, although proceeding readily, has the disadvantage of being attended with the evolution of HCl gas, thus:—

$$SO_3HCl + C_6H_6 = C_6H_5.SO_3H + HCl$$

Chlorosulphonic   Benzene.   Benzene sulphonic   Hydro-
acid.   acid.   chloric
                                   acid.

Benzene-monosulphonic Acid, $C_6H_5.SO_3H + 1\frac{1}{2}H_2O$, is prepared by agitating together 2 parts of benzene and 3 parts fuming sulphuric acid, with gentle warming, until no more benzene is dissolved. Next chalk is added and the liquid filtered from the precipitated calcium sulphate, and concentrated. Needles, M.P. 40°-42° C.; deliquescent.

m- and *p*-**Benzene-disulphonic Acid**, $C_6H_4(SO_3H)_2$ (1:3) and (1:4).—A mixture of both these acids is used for preparing resorcin. 1 part benzene vapour is led into 4 parts concentrated sulphuric acid heated to 240° C. in retorts provided with reflux condensers. The acid is neutralised with chalk, and the calcium salts crystallised from water, when the meta compound crystallises first. Sometimes the calcium salts are transformed into potassium salts and the isomers separated by crystallisation, the potassium salt of the meta acid being less soluble than that of the para acid.

p-**Sulphanilic Acid,** $C_6H_4.NH_2.SO_3H$ (1 : 4), is prepared by mixing 100 parts of aniline with 105 parts of concentrated sulphuric acid, and heating on trays in an oven at 180°-220° C. m-**Sulphanilic Acid** is prepared by reducing m-nitrobenzene-sulphonic acid. Both varieties are colourless, crystalline solids, moderately soluble in water.

Xylidine Sulphonic Acid, $C_6H_2(CH_3)_2NH_2.SO_3H$, is prepared by heating commercial **xylidene** (120 parts) with 400 parts of fuming (20 per cent. SO_3) sulphuric acid, pouring the product into cold water, when the sparingly soluble sulphonic acid of metaxylidene, $C_6H_2.(CH_3)_2.NH_2.SO_3H$ (1 : 3 : 4 : 6), separates out. The mother liquor is converted into sodium salts and concentrated, when sodium p-xylidene sulphonate, $C_6H_2(CH_3)_2NH_2.SO_3H$ (1 : 4 : 2 : 5), separates out.

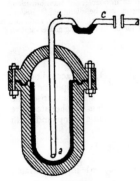

Nitrotoluene Sulphonic Acid, $C_6H_3.CH_3.SO_3H.NO_2$, is prepared by dissolving 1 part of p-nitrotoluol in 3 parts of fuming sulphuric acid and running the mixture into 15 parts of saturated brine, when the sodium salt of the acid crystallises out.

Naphthalene Sulphonic Acids, $C_{10}H_7.SO_3H$.—The a-acid is obtained by treating 1 part finely divided naphthalene with 2 parts concentrated H_2SO_4 or 10-15 per cent. fuming sulphuric acid, keeping the temperature between 20° C. and 40° C. By raising the temperature to 160°-180° C. the β-acid is obtained, and can be separated as a calcium salt.

FIG. 8.

Naphthalene - disulphonic Acid, $C_{10}H_6.(SO_3H)_2$, is obtained by heating 1 part naphthalene with 5 parts concentrated H_2SO_4 for four hours at 160°-180° C., and separating the a- and β-sulphonic acid, produced at the same time, as calcium salts.

Naphthylamine Sulphonic Acid $C_{10}H_6.SO_3H.NH_2$, is prepared by heating naphthalene sulphonic acid with a 20 per cent. ammonia solution in an autoclave under a pressure of 12 atmospheres :—

$$C_{10}H_7.SO_3H + NH_3 + H_2O = C_{10}H_6.(SO_3H).NH_2 + H_2 + H_2O.$$

Since hydrogen is formed and may not escape directly into the air (since it forms an explosive mixture with air) a special apparatus is used whereby contact of the hydrogen with air is avoided when the contents are discharged. A long tube $a b c$ passes through the cover down nearly but not quite to the bottom of the autoclave, the tube being bent at its upper end e, as in Fig. 8, and this part of the bend is filled with water, which prevents access of air to the hydrogen in the boiler. During the reaction the tube is firmly closed. But when the reaction is completed the tube is connected to another tube and the hydrogen pressure in the interior is used to force out the contents through the central tube—only a small residue of liquid finally remaining in the boiler, which is used again for another operation.

a_1a_4-**Dioxynaphthalene-**a_2**-sulphonic Acid,** [structure: HO OH ... SO_3H], is produced by melting $a_1a_2a_4$-naphthol disulphonic acid with solid NaOH at 250° C., or with NaOH solution under pressure. White crystals; produces valuable azo dyes.

$\beta_1\beta_8$-**Naphthylamine Sulphonic Acid,** [structure: HO_2S ... NH_2], is prepared by heating the ammonium salt of $\beta_1\beta_8$-naphthol sulphonic acid for two days at 180°-200° C. in an autoclave :—

$$C_{10}H_6 \!\!\begin{array}{c}\diagup OH \\ \diagdown SO_3.NH_4\end{array} = C_{10}H_6 \!\!\begin{array}{c}\diagup NH_2 \\ \diagdown SO_3H\end{array} + H_2O.$$

$\beta_1a_4\beta_8$-**Aminonaphthol Sulphonic Acid,** [structure: OH ... HO_3S ... NH_2], is produced by melting β-naphthylamine disulphonic acid with NaOH at 185° C. for six hours in an autoclave.

Phenylhydrazine-p**-sulphonic Acid,** $C_6H_4.(NH.NH_2).SO_3H$ (1 : 4), is obtained by reducing diazobenzene sulphonic acid (from p-sulphanilic acid) with sodium sulphite and boiling with concentrated HCl. Also by sulphonating phenylhydrazine (which see).

The Phenols (see Phenol, Cresol, p. 10)

Resorcinol, $C_6H_4.(OH)_2$. (1:3), is prepared by heating for eight to nine hours to a temperature of 270° C. 60 kg. of sodium benzene disulphonate with 150 kg. of caustic soda in a cast-iron vessel, provided with mechanical agitation. The product is dissolved in water, acidified, extracted with ether, the ether distilled, and the crude resorcinol so obtained purified by sublimation or crystallisation. Crystalline solid; M.P. 118° C.; B.P. 277° C.

Pyrogallol, $C_6H_3.(OH)_3$. (1 : 2 : 3), is prepared by heating gallic acid with three times its weight of water for half an hour at 200°-210° C. in an autoclave. A pad of pappè is inserted round the lid of the cover so that the CO_2 gradually escapes :—

$$\underset{\text{Gallic acid.}}{C_6H_2(OH)_3.COOH} = \underset{\text{Pyrogallol.}}{C_6H_3.(OH)_3} + \underset{\substack{\text{Carbon}\\\text{dioxide.}}}{CO_2}.$$

The solution is boiled with animal charcoal, filtered, and evaporated. White needles; M.P. 132° C.; B.P. 210° C.; easily soluble in water. Its solution in alkali rapidly absorbs oxygen from the air.

The Naphthols, $C_{10}H_7.OH$

Two varieties exist: a-naphthol, M.P. 94° C.; β-naphthol, M.P. 122° C. a-**Naphthol** is prepared by fusing sodium a-naphthalene sulphonate (1 part) with 2-3 parts caustic soda and a little water at 270°-300° C. in an iron vessel provided with an agitator. The sodium naphtholate rises to the surface, is separated from the lower layer of caustic soda and sodium sulphite, and decomposed with CO_2 gas. The precipitated naphthol is dried and distilled :— $C_{10}H_7.SO_3H + K_2O = C_{10}H_7.OK + K_2SO_3$. The β-**naphthol** is prepared in a similar way from the β-naphthalene sulphonic acid.

Usually the a-**naphthol** is contaminated with 5-10 per cent. β-naphthol. It may be prepared pure either by fractionally crystallising its salts, or, better, by decomposing a-naphthylamine with water in an autoclave :—$a.C_{10}H_7.NH_2 + H_2O = a.C_{10}H_7.OH + NH_3$.

Ketones

Anthraquinone, $C_6H_4\!\!<^{CO}_{CO}\!\!>C_6H_4$, is manufactured by oxidising anthracene.

Finely powdered commercial anthracene (containing 60-90 per cent. anthracene) is agitated with a boiling solution of sodium or potassium bichromate (1 molecule bichromate : 1 molecule of true anthracene), while dilute H_2SO_4 solution (4 molecules H_2SO_4 to every molecule of bichromate used) is slowly run in over nine to ten hours. The mixture is boiled, the crude anthraquinone filtered off, dried, and ground. It is then purified from any phenanthrene, acridine, carbazol, etc., present by heating with two to three times its weight of concentrated H_2SO_4 at 110° C. and pouring the mass into water. The impurities are changed into soluble sulphonic acids, while the anthraquinone is precipitated unchanged. It is washed with soda, filtered, and dried, and then contains 90-95 per cent. pure anthraquinone. It is then used immediately for making alizarin (*q.v.*). Yellow needles, M.P. 277° C. Fuming sulphuric acid converts it into monosulphonic acid, $C_{10}H_7O_2.SO_3H$, which, when fused with caustic soda, yields **alizarin.**

Benzophenone or **Diphenyl Ketone,** $C_6H_5.CO.C_6H_5$, and **Phenylmethylketone** or **Acetophenone,** $C_6H_5.CO.CH_3$, are obtained by the distillation of the calcium salts of the corresponding acids :—

$$(C_6H_5.CO_2)_2Ca = C_6H_5.CO.C_6H_5 + CaCO_3.$$
Calcium benzoate.　Benzophenone.

$$(C_6H_5.CO_2)_2Ca + (C_2H_3O_2)_2Ca = 2C_6H_5.CO.CH_3 + 2CaCO_3.$$
Calcium benzoate.　Calcium acetate.　Acetophenone.

Nitro-, amino-, and diamino-derivatives of these bodies are used, *e.g.*, **Diaminobenzophenone,** $NH_2.C_6H_4$—CO—$C_6H_4.NH_2$, prepared by nitrating benzophenone and then reducing.

Tetramethyldiaminobenzophenone, $CO\!\!<^{C_6H_4.N(CH_3)_2}_{C_6H_4.N(CH_3)_2}$, is manufactured by passing phosgene gas, $COCl_2$ (prepared by direct union of CO and Cl_2 in sunlight, and, since it easily liquefies at 8° C. under atmospheric pressure, condensed to a liquid by pressure and kept stored up in steel cylinders), is passed into **Dimethylaniline** at ordinary temperatures until the dimethylaniline has increased 50 per cent. by weight :—

$$2C_6H_5.N(CH_3)_2 + COCl_2 = CO[C_6H_4.N(CH_3)_2]_2 + 2HCl.$$
Dimethylaniline.　Phosgene gas.　Tetramethyldiaminobenzophenone.

The liquid is then heated for some time, the excess of dimethylaniline steam-distilled off, the residue dissolved in HCl and precipitated by alkali. Solid ; M.P. 179° C. It is converted on a large scale by reducing agents into **Tetramethyldiaminobenzhydrol,** $HO.CH.[C_6H_4N(CH_3)_2]_2$ (p. 54).

APPENDIX

Preparation of Organic Compounds by Electrical Processes

LITERATURE

WALTHER LÖB's "Die Elektrochemie der organische Verbindungen." **3rd Edition.** Halle, 1905.

ELBS' "Übungsbeispiele für die elektrolytische Darstellung Chemische Präparate." Halle, 1902.

FISCHER's *Jahresberichte der chem. Technologie.* 1884 onwards.

The electrolytic oxidation and reduction of organic compounds have been the subject of investigation for many years, and has been attended with important technical results.

Thus Elbs and Brunner (*Zeit. f. Elektrochemie*, **6**, 604, 1900) obtained a yield of 80 per cent. **formaldehyde** by electrolysing a sulphuric acid solution of **methyl alcohol**.

Iodoform may be prepared by electrolysing a mixture of 14 parts sodium carbonate (anhydrous), 10 parts KI, 100 parts water, 20 parts alcohol, at a temperature of 70° C. :—

$$CH_3.CH_2OH + 10I + H_2O = CHI_3 + CO_2 + 7HI.$$

A quantitative yield of **Bromoform**, $CHBr_3$, is obtained by electrolysing an aqueous solution of acetone and KBr (*Ztschr. für Elektrochemie*, **10**, 409, 1904).

Chloral is obtained (*Elektrochem. Ztschr.*, i. 70, 1894) by allowing alcohol to flow into the anode chamber of a cell in which a KCl solution is being electrolysed.

Crude sugar-rich liquids are now purified by electrolytic reduction (*Jahrbuch der Elektrochemie*, **3**, 322, 1896 ; **8**, 628, 1901).

Acetone is reduced by electrolysis in an acid or alkali solution tc Isopropylalcohol and Pinacone (D. R. Pat., Nr. 113,719, 1899).

Nitrobenzene, $C_6H_5.NO_2$, can be electrolytically reduced in stages, first to azo compounds, then to hydrazo compounds (*Jahresber. d. chem. Tech.* 1894, 1896, 1901). The same holds true of other nitro-aromatic bodies.

Thus, *m*-**Azo-toluol** is obtained by electrolytically reducing nitrotoluols (Rohde, *loc. cit.*, 1899). **Amino** compounds, however, are finally obtained by electrolysing certain nitro-bodies. Thus, *m*-**Nitro-dimethylaniline** gives on electrolytic reduction first **Tetramethyl-*m*-diaminoazobenzol**, and finally **Tetramethyl-*m*-diaminohydrazobenzol**. *m*-**Nitraniline** may be electrolytically reduced to *m*-**Diaminoazobenzol** (Wülfing, 1899).

Farbenfabr. *Bayer* (1901) made the important discovery that **nitro-bodies** are readily reduced to azo and hydrazo compounds without their necessarily being dissolved in a solvent (such as alcohol, nitrobenzene, etc.). The cathode consists of a metal such as zinc, tin, lead, etc., and surrounding it is placed an alkaline solution of the metal and the nitro-body to be reduced. The anode is separated from the cathode by a diaphragm, and consists of carbon, platinum, or some other inactive substance, immersed in a solution of soda, sodium sulphate, or sodium chloride. In the last case chlorine is evolved and may be employed to give rise to chlorine derivatives. The liquid about the cathode is vigorously stirred during the passage of the current. If the nitro-body is volatile, condensers must be attached to the cathodic chambers, since the heat evolved by the current may cause the nitro-body to volatilise. By such an apparatus they convert nitrobenzene completely into azobenzol in six to seven hours, the solid azobenzol separating when the cathodic fluid is cooled and is purified in the usual way. The production of hydrazobenzene requires a longer time.

Paranitrotoluene, $C_6H_4.NO_2.CH_3$, may be completely oxidised to **Paranitrobenzoic Acid**, $C_6H_4.NO_2.COOH$, by dissolving 7.5 parts paranitrotoluene in 40 parts glacial acetic acid, adding 20 parts concentrated H_2SO_4 and 20 parts water and 0.1 part $MnSO_4$, then placing the mixture in the *anodic* compartment of an electrolytic cell, and electrolysing at 80° C. with a current density of 175 amperes per square metre (Boehmiger, *Jahresberichte d. chem. Tech.* 1901).

Aniline may be somewhat similarly oxidised to **Quinone** at the *anode* of an electrolytic cell.

Benzidine may be prepared electrolytically from **nitrobenzene** (see Löb, *Jahresberichte d. chem. Tech.* 1900, 1901). 10 parts of nitrobenzene are dissolved in 50 parts of a 3 per cent. NaOH solution, placed in the cathodic compartment of an electrolytic cell, and vigorously stirred while a current of 10 amperes per 100 sq. cm. is passed at a temperature of 80°-100° C. until the whole is reduced to the azoxy state.

Then 20 parts H_2SO_4 in 50 parts water are added, and reduction carried further at ordinary temperatures, when the azoxybenzene passes completely into benzidine sulphate. *o*-**Nitrotoluene** may be in an exactly similar manner reduced to *o*-azoxytoluene, which is then acidified as above and reduced to tolidine sulphate.

The above brief account gives an idea of the technically important results which can follow the application of electrical processes to organic compounds.

CHAPTER II

Industry of the Synthetic Colouring Matters

INDUSTRY OF THE SYNTHETIC COLOURING MATTERS

LITERATURE

SCHULTZ.—"Chemie des Steinkohlenteers." Braunschweig, 1900-1901.

NIETZKI.—"Chemie der organische Farbstoffe." 1892.

SCHULTZ.—"Tabellarische Uebersicht der künstlichen organischen Farbstoffe." 1902. "Farbestofftabellen." 1911.

GREEN.—"Systematic Survey of the Organic Colouring Matters." 1904.

CAIN AND THORPE.—"Synthetic Dyestuffs." 1905.

GEORGEVICS.—"Chemistry of the Dye-Stuffs." 1903.

HEUMANN.—"Die Anilinfarben." 6 vols. 1888-1906.

LEHNE.—"Tabellen." 1906.

FRIEDLANDER.—"Fortschritte der Teerfarbenfabrikation." 1877-1910.

WINTHER.—"Patente der organischen Chemie." 3 vols. 1877-1905.

LEON LEFEVRE.—"Matieres Colorantes Artificielles." 2 vols. 1896.

BUCHERER.—"Die Teerfarbstoffe." Sammlung Göschen, 1904.

WICHELHAUS.—"Organische Farbstoffe." 1909.

ZERR.—"Tests for Coal-Tar Colours in Aniline Lakes." London, 1910.

Acknowledgments.—The authors desire to express their thanks to the following firms, who supplied them with much information regarding the more recent dyes:—

Read Holliday & Sons.	Kalle & Co.
Cassella & Co.	Levinstein & Co.
Farbwerke vorm. Meister Lucius & Brüning.	Farbenfabrik en vorm. F. Bayer & Co.
Badische Anilin- u. Soda-Fabrik.	

Introduction

THE origin and development of the coal-tar dye industry represents one of the greatest triumphs of modern chemistry.

In 1834 Runge discovered phenol and aniline in coal-tar. The researches of A. W. Hofmann (1842-63) revealed the chemical nature of several of the more important constituents of coal-tar. The industry practically dates from 1856, when Perkin obtained **Mauve** by oxidising aniline. In 1859 Verguin isolated **Fuchsine**. Soon afterwards **Aniline Blue** was discovered, which Hofmann in 1863 showed to be a derivative of Rosaniline. In 1868 and in 1869 Graebe and Liebermann synthesised **Alizarin** from anthracene by two methods, the second of these being almost simultaneously discovered by Perkin. In 1871 Baeyer discovered the **Phthaleins**. In 1876 E. and O. Fischer worked out the constitution of the **Rosaniline colours**. About the same time the manufacture of the **Azo colours** was begun. In 1884 the **Congo Red Cotton Dyes** were introduced. **Indigo** was synthesised by Baeyer in 1880, but its manufacture only became a commercial success after Heumann's synthesis in 1890, the product being placed on the market by the Badische Anilin- und Soda-Fabrik in 1897. The first sulphur dye, **Cachou de Laval**, was made by Croissant and Bretonnière in 1873, but the sulphide dye manufacture dates practically from **Vidal Black** (1893). In recent years the most noteworthy dates are 1901, the year of the discovery of the first **Anthracene Vat Dyes** by the Badische Anilin- und- Soda Fabrik, and 1905, when **Thioindigo** was produced by Friedländer.

Although the dye industry was founded in England by Perkin, who established a factory for the manufacture of Mauve, and later of Alizarin, the trade has gone largely into German hands. This has been attributed to a variety of causes which cannot be considered at length here. Suffice it to say that probably one of the most weighty of these causes was the unfortunate divorce of science from industry which largely prevailed in this country until recently, whereas the contrary was the case in Germany. It is noteworthy that the men who founded and built up the enormous German undertakings were not business men in the usual sense of the word, but were themselves chemists of note and realised to the full the importance of research. Then, too, every improvement was patented, and the industry was thus gradually surrounded by a ring of patents, which rendered the entry of new competitors into the market increasingly difficult. Among the German colour factories the following may be especially noted : The Badische Anilin- und Soda-Fabrik in Ludwigshafen am Rhein is the largest chemical factory in the world, employing 7,500 workmen, 197 university trained chemists, 95 engineers, and 709 clerks (1906). The Farbenfabriken vormals F. Bayer & Co. in Elberfeld and Leverkusen is almost as large. Other very large firms are Cassella & Co. in Frankfurt am Main, the Farbwerke vormals Meister Lucius & Brüning of Höchst, the Aktiengesellschaft für Anilin Fabrikation of Berlin, and Kalle & Co. of Biebrich. The most important English firms are Read Holliday & Sons of Huddersfield, and Levinstein & Co. of Manchester.

The worth of the coal-tar colours manufactured annually amounted in 1910 to £20,000,000 ; over three-quarters of this value are manufactured by the German firms.

Statistics.—The following numbers show the value of the import of synthetic dyes into the United Kingdom (almost entirely from Germany) :—

IMPORTS

	1906.	1913.	Value in 1913.
	Cwt.	Cwt.	
Alizarin and anthracene dye-stuffs · ·	57,300	60,800	£272,000
Aniline and naphthalene dye-stuffs - ·	188,600	283,000	1,543,000
Synthetic indigo - · · · ·	39,000	23,900	76,700
Other coal-tar dye-stuffs - · · ·	700	155	570,000
Total - · ·	285,600	367,855	£2,461,700

The export of coal-tar dyes from the United Kingdom amounted in 1910 to 56,000 cwt., value £196,000.

The United States *imported*, principally from Germany :—

	1906.	1910.	Value in 1910.
	Lbs.	Lbs.	
Alizarin colours - · · · ·	3,882,000	3,023,000	$648,000
Coal-tar colours and dyes · · ·	...	...	6,011,000
Indigo - · · · · ·	7,393,000	7,540,000	1,196,000

The United States exported of dyes and dye-stuffs—$491,000 in 1906, and $380,000 in 1910.
The German net export of coal-tar colours (including aniline oils and intermediate products) amounted in 1909 to 1,600,000 cwt. (more exactly, 83,250 metric tons), having a net value of £10,000,000.

For statistics regarding **Indigo** see p. 49.

Almost all the artificial colouring matters are derivatives of benzene, naphthalene, or anthracene, which are obtained from coal tar. 1,000 tons of coal-tar yield, when worked up, 2.5 tons of fuchsine, 0.75 ton of indigo, 0.2 ton of alizarin, and 0.2 ton of picric acid. Since the number of artificial dye-stuffs runs into several thousands, it is impossible within the limits of the present article to mention more than a few of the more important of each separate group, placing special emphasis on new classes of dye-stuffs, such as have been specially developed within the last few years. For particulars of special dyes the reader must consult the works cited at the beginning of this section.

Classification of Dyes.—Dyes may be classified either according to their chemical composition or according to their dyeing properties. In discussing the manufacture of dyes, the former method of procedure is the only suitable one, the second method being used when the technology of dyeing is under consideration.

The following scheme shows the arrangement followed in the present article, the three groups which are of the greatest importance at the present time being considered first :—

1. Azo dyes (including pyrazolone and stilbene dyes).
2. Dyes of the anthracene series.
3. Dyes of the indigo and thioindigo series.
4. Di- and tri-arylmethane dyes.
5. Pyrone dyes.
6. Azine dyes.
7. Oxazine dyes.
8. Dyes containing sulphur (thiazine, thiazole, and sulphide dyes).
9. Acridine dyes.
10. Minor groups of dyes—nitro and nitroso dyes, quinoline dyes, oxyketone dyes, indophenols, indamines, aniline black.

We will take them in this order in the following pages.

1. AZO DYES

The azo dyes form the largest group of dyes known ; they derive the name from their characteristic **azo** group, consisting of two nitrogen atoms and usually written $-N=N-$, or $-N_2-$. According as the azo group occurs one, two, three, four, etc., times in the molecule, the dyes are described as monoazo, disazo, trisazo, tetrakisazo, etc.

The azo dyes were discovered by Griess in 1858 and some were put on the market soon afterwards, but as a class the dyes did not come into existence until about 1876.

Method of Preparation.—When a primary amine is treated with nitrous acid at a low temperature, diazo compounds are formed according to the equation :—

$$R.NH_2 + HNO_2 = R.N=N.OH + H_2O.$$
Amine.   Nitrous   Diazo   acid.   hydroxide.

In practice aromatic amines only are used, and nitrous acid is replaced by sodium nitrite and an acid, usually hydrochloric acid. The reaction then becomes :—

$$R.NH_2 + NaNO_2 + 2HCl = R.N=N.Cl + NaCl + 2H_2O.$$
Amine.   Diazo chloride.

The diazo compounds can then react with other compounds, usually aromatic amines or phenols, producing azo compounds, which, if of suitable constitution, act as dyes. The reaction is :—

$$R.N=N.Cl + R^1H = R.N=N.R^1 + HCl.$$
Diazo   Second   Azo
compound.   component.   compound.

The amine which is diazotised is referred to as the diazo or first component, while the compound R^1H is called the second component.

The operation is carried out in practice as follows :—

A molecular proportion of the amine to be diazotised is dissolved in water with about $2\frac{1}{2}$ molecular parts of hydrochloric acid ; a solution of a molecular part of nitrite is then run in gradually while the reaction mixture is kept cool and stirred. After diazotisation is complete, the solution is added to a solution of a molecular proportion of the second component, and stirring is continued until the combination is finished ; the dye either precipitates or is salted out by means of salt or hydrochloric acid, and is filtered off, washed and dried.

The diazo reaction is capable of very wide application, but some amines cannot be diazotised except under special conditions, while others do not give the normal diazo salts—some of these will be noted later. The diazo compounds in general are not very stable, accordingly some amines (aniline, toluidines, etc.) must be diazotised at 0° C., while for others (nitranilines, naphthylamines, etc.) a temperature of about 10° C. is suitable. In some cases (*e.g.*, trinitraniline) the diazotisation is effected by nitrite in the presence of cold concentrated sulphuric acid, while the 1 : 2- and 2 : 1-aminonaphthols are diazotised in the presence of salts of copper, zinc, etc.

Besides nitrite, various other diazotising agents are occasionally employed, for instance, nitrosyl chloride, and nitrosulphonic acid.

It is unnecessary here to consider further the nature of the diazo compounds, or the various formulæ which have been proposed for them. A full discussion of these will be found in Cain's " Chemistry of the Diazo Compounds " (Arnold, 1908). Kekulé's formula, R.N=N.X, expresses the facts sufficiently for our present purpose.

In connection with the operation of coupling the diazo compounds with the second component, the following points should be noted : phenols are coupled in an alkaline solution (sodium carbonate), while if the second component is an amine it is coupled in a neutral or acid (usually hydrochloric or acetic) solution.

The azo group generally enters the molecule of the second component in the para-position to the amino or hydroxyl group of this body, or, if this combination be impossible, in the ortho-position. Thus aniline, phenol, α-naphthol, α-naphthylamine couple in the para-position, *p*-toluidine and *p*-cresol in the ortho-position, while β-naphthol couples in the α-ortho-position. In the case of the naphthylamine or naphthol sulphonic acids, the positions of the sulphonic groups often determine the position taken up by the azo group. In the case of some of the heteronuclear aminonaphthol sulphonic acids, *e.g.*, the 2 : 8 : 6, 2 : 5 : 7, 1 : 8 : 4, 1 : 8 : 5, 1 : 8 : 3 : 6 acids, different products are obtained according as the combination is effected in alkaline or in acid solution—in alkaline solution the azo group enters in ortho-position to the hydroxyl group, while in hydrochloric acid solution it enters in ortho-position to the amino group.

An important variation in the process of preparing azo dyes is the production of these dyes "**on the fibre.**" A typical instance is **Paranitraniline red** ; to produce this dye, the material to be dyed is impregnated with β-naphthol by passage through an alkaline bath of this compound, and is then passed into a second bath containing diazotised *p*-nitraniline, the dye thus being produced on the material. For use in this process the diazotised *p*-nitraniline is sometimes converted by the action of caustic alkali into a stable isomeric form, the so-called nitrosamine, which may be formulated $NO_2.C_6H_4.NNa.NO$, and is sold as such ; when required for use, the nitrosamine is reconverted into the active diazo compound by treatment with acid.

Monoazo Dyes, R.N=N.R[1]

The monoazo dyes are prepared according to the methods described above; their number is very great, and only a few typical ones are described here. Their dyeing properties vary according to their constitution ; a large number dye wool in acid baths; an important and growing group of these consists of the so-called ortho-oxyazo dyes, obtained from diazotised *o*-aminophenolic compounds—these dye wool with chrome mordants ; a large number of monoazo dyes are used as parent materials for the manufacture of pigments or lakes. Some typical monoazo dyes are tabulated below :—

Acid Wool Dyes

Acid yellow	Aminoazobenzene disulphonic acid.
Azococcine 2R	Xylidine + 1 : 4-naphthol sulphonic acid.
Crystal Ponceau } „ scarlet 6R }	α-Naphthylamine + 2 : 6 : 8-naphthol disulphonic acid.
Fast red A	Naphthionic acid + β-naphthol.
„ „ B	α-Naphthylamine + 2 : 3 : 6-naphthol disulphonic acid.
Lanacyl blue BB	1 : 8 : 3 : 6-aminonaphthol disulphonic acid + 1 : 5-aminonaphthol.
Metanil yellow	Metanilic acid + diphenylamine.
Orange II	Sulphanilic acid + β-naphthol.
Palatine red	α-Naphthylamine + 1 : 3 : 6-naphthol disulphonic acid.
Ponceau 2G	Aniline + 2 : 3 : 6-naphthol disulphonic acid.
„ 2R	*m*-Xylidine + 2 : 3 : 6-naphthol disulphonic acid.
„ 4R	ψ-Cumidine + 2 : 3 : 6-naphthol disulphonic acid.
„ 6R	Naphthionic acid + β-naphthol trisulphonic acid.
Tropaeoline O	Sulphanilic acid + resorcin.

Dyes for Chrome-Mordanted Wool

(a) **From Diazotised o-Aminophenols.**—Most of these dyes are of recent introduction, so it is difficult to ascertain the trade name of a dye of a particular constitution. Typical combinations are :—

4-acetylamino-2-aminophenol-5-sulphonic acid + β-naphthol, etc. (Cassella, English Patent, 3,182, 1903).

1-amino-2-naphthol sulphonic acids + naphthols, naphthol sulphonic acids, aminonaphthols, aminonaphthol sulphonic acids, dioxynaphthalenes, dioxynaphthalene sulphonic acids, resorcin, m-aminophenol, m-diamines, etc. (Geigy, English Patent, 15,025, 1904).

o-aminophenol and its methyl, chlor, nitro, etc., derivatives + chromotropic acid (M.L.B., English Patent, 26,383, 1905).

Nitro or chlor derivatives of o-aminophenol + 2-arylamino-5-naphthol-7-sulphonic acids (Bayer, English Patent, 14,921, 1906).

Nitro or chlor derivatives of o-aminophenol + alkyl or aryl derivatives of m-aminophenol (Bayer, English Patent, 25,177, 1908).

(b) Other Dyes for Chrome-Mordanted Wool.—

Alizarine yellow GG	.	.	.	m-Nitraniline + salicylic acid.
Azochromine	.	.	.	p-Aminophenol + pyrogallol.
Azofuchsine B	.	.	.	Toluidine + 1 : 8 : 4-dioxynaphthalene sulphonic acid.
Chromotrope 2B	.	.	.	p-Nitraniline + 1 : 8 : 3 : 6-dioxynaphthalene disulphonic acid.
Diamond yellow R	.	.	.	Anthranilic acid + salicylic acid.
Milling yellow	.	.	.	2-Naphthylamine sulphonic acid + salicylic acid.

Dyes used in the Manufacture of Lakes

Many of these dyes also are of recent introduction, so the trade names are difficult to obtain.

One of the best known is Lithol red (2-naphthylamine-1-sulphonic acid + β-naphthol) (B.A.S.F., English Patent, 25,511, 1899).

Other typical combinations are :—

o-Nitraniline-p-sulphonic acid or p-nitraniline-o-sulphonic acid + β-naphthol (M.L.B., English Patent, 16,409, 1901).

Aniline, etc. + 2 : 3-oxynaphthoic acid (Akt. Ges. für Anilin Fabrikation, English Patent, 1,235, 1903).

2-Naphthylamine disulphonic acids + naphthol sulphonic acids (Bayer, English Patent, 12,512, 1904).

Nitrochloranilines + β-naphthol (B.A.S.F., English Patents, 6,227. 1907. and 6,228, 1907).

Direct Cotton Dyes

The combination of diazotised dehydrothiotoluidine sulphonic acid or primuline (see p. 478) with various components give cotton dyes, *e.g.*—

Oriol yellow—primuline + salicylic acid.

Rosophenine 10B—dehydrothiotoluidine sulphonic acid + 1-naphthol-4-sulphonic acid.

Various derivatives of 2 : 5 : 7-aminonaphthol sulphonic acid when combined with diazo compounds (aniline, toluidine, xylidine, naphthylamines, etc.) give cotton dyes, *e.g.*—

2-acetylamino-5-naphthol-7-sulphonic acid, 2-benzoylamino-5-naphthol-7-sulphonic acid, aminobenzoyl-2-amino-5-naphthol-7-sulphonic acids, aminophenyl-1 : 2-naphthothiazole-5-oxy-7-sulphonic acids, aminophenyl-1-2-naphthiminazole-5-oxy-7-sulphonic acids, etc.

Disazo Dyes, R.N=N.R′.N=N.R″

There are three main types of disazo dyes : (a) primary, (b) secondary, (c) disazo dyes from tetrazotised diamines.

(a) **Primary Disazo Dyes.**—Certain azo dye components can be coupled with two diazo groups; such components are phenol, resorcin, α-naphthol, *m*-phenylenediamine, *m*-toluylendiamine, *m*-aminophenol, the aminonaphthol sulphonic acids referred to above, which can be coupled in acid or alkaline solution yielding different products, and the 1 : 8-dioxynaphthalene-4-sulphonic acid or -3 : 6-disulphonic acid. To prepare the primary disazo dyes, two molecular proportions of an amine, or one molecular proportion of each of two different amines, are diazotised and coupled with one molecular proportion of the second component. Thus **Resorcin Brown** is obtained by coupling *m*-xylidine (1 molecule) and sulphanilic acid (1 molecule) with resorcin (1 molecule).

$$C_6H_3(CH_3)_2.N\!\!=\!\!N\!\!-\!\!\underset{N\!\!=\!\!N.C_6H_4.SO_3Na}{\overset{OH}{\underset{OH}{\bigcirc}}} \quad or, \quad \genfrac{}{}{0pt}{}{m\text{-Xylidine}}{\text{Sulphanilic acid}}\!\!\Big\rangle Resorcin.$$

Naphthol Blue-Black is obtained by coupling 1 : 8-aminonaphthol 3 : 6-disulphonic acid (H acid) first with *p*-nitraniline in acid solution, and then with aniline in alkaline solution.

$$C_6H_5.N\!\!=\!\!N\!\!-\!\!\underset{NaO_3S\!\!-\!\!\!\!-\!\!SO_3Na}{\overset{OH\quad NH_2}{\bigcirc\bigcirc}}\!\!-\!\!N\!\!=\!\!N.C_6H_4NO_2 \quad or, \quad \genfrac{}{}{0pt}{}{p\text{-Nitraniline}}{\text{Aniline}}\!\!\Big\rangle H\text{-acid.}$$

It dyes wool in an alkaline bath.

Other primary disazo dyes are—

Terracotta F (dyes cotton).—Sodium salt of—
$$\genfrac{}{}{0pt}{}{\text{*Primuline}}{\text{Naphthionic acid}}\!\!\Big\rangle m\text{-phenylenediamine.}$$

Cotton Orange R (dyes cotton)—
$$\genfrac{}{}{0pt}{}{\text{Primuline}}{\text{Metanilic acid}}\!\!\Big\rangle m\text{-phenylenediaminedisulphonic acid.}$$

Fast Brown (acid wool dye)—
$$\genfrac{}{}{0pt}{}{\text{Naphthionic acid}}{\text{Naphthionic acid}}\!\!\Big\rangle resorcin.$$

(b) **Secondary Disazo Dyes** are obtained by coupling diazotised aminoazo compounds with amines, phenols, etc. In order, therefore, to prepare bodies of this type it is necessary to diazotise *twice*—first an amine is diazotised, then the diazo salt thus produced is coupled directly to another amine—the "middle" component —and the amino group in the aminoazo body thus produced is then diazotised, and finally the product thus obtained is coupled with an amine, phenol, etc.

The amines employed as "middle components" must be of such a nature that when combined with the first component they can be rediazotised to yield a diazo salt. Thus the amines generally employed are those which, on coupling with the first component, give either para-aminoazo compounds, or aminoazo compounds containing the amino and azo groups in different nuclei; examples of the first type are aniline, *o*- and *m*-toluidine, *p*-xylidine, *o*-anisidine, cresidine, α-naphthylamine and its 6- and 7-sulphonic acids (**Clève's acids**); examples of the second type are 2 : 5 : 7- and 2 : 8 : 6-aminonaphthol sulphonic acids, combined in alkaline solution, and the recently discovered derivatives of aminonaphthol sulphonic acids containing a heteronuclear amino group, such as the aminophenyl-1 : 2-naphthiminazoleoxy-sulphonic acids, and the aminobenzoylaminonaphthol sulphonic acids.

---

* See p. 66.

An example of such dyes is **Fast Violet R,** produced by (1) diazotising sulphanilic acid; (2) coupling the diazo compound with α-naphthylamine, giving

$$C_6H_4{\diagup}^{N=N-C_{10}H_6.NH_2}_{\diagdown SO_3H}$$; (3) diazotising once again; and (4) coupling with β-naphthol sulphonic acid S, thus obtaining the dye—

$$C_6H_4{\diagup}^{N=N-C_{10}H_6-N=N}_{\diagdown SO_3H}{\diagdown}C_{10}H_5{\diagup}^{SO_3Na}_{\diagdown OH}$$

Fast Violet R.

Biebrich Scarlet is prepared by coupling aminoazobenzene disulphonic acid with β-naphthol, and has, therefore, the constitution—

$$C_6H_4{\diagup}^{SO_3H}{-N=N-C_6H_3}{\diagup}^{N=N-C_{10}H_6.OH}_{\diagdown SO_3H}$$

Other secondary disazo dyes are—

Brilliant Croceine M (acid wool dye).—Aminoazobenzene + 2 : 6 : 8-naphtholdisulphonic acid.

Cloth Scarlet G (acid wool dye).—Aminoazobenzenesulphonic acid + β-naphthol.

Croceine Scarlet 7B ⎱ (acid wool dye).—Aminoazotoluene sulphonic acid + 2 : 8-naphtholsulphonic
      ,,   ,,   **8B** ⎰   acid.

Diaminogen (dyes unmordanted cotton blue).—Acetyl-1 : 4-naphthylenediamine-6- and -7-sulphonic acid + α-naphthylamine + 2 : 6-naphthol sulphonic acid (product saponified).

Janus Red (dyes cotton and wool).—*m*-Aminophenyltrimethylammonium chloride + *m*-toluidine + β-naphthol.

Naphthylamine Black D (acid wool dye).—Naphthylamine disulphonic acid + α-naphthylamine + α-naphthylamine.

Ponceau 4RB   ⎱ (dyes wool and cotton).—Aminoazobenzene sulphonic acid + 2 : 8-naphthol
Croceine Scarlet 3B ⎰   sulphonic acid.

Recently a number of secondary disazo dyes have been prepared having 2 : 5 : 7-aminonaphthol sulphonic acid and its alkyl, aryl, acidyl, etc., derivatives as end components. These dyes cotton blue to violet shades. (See English Patents, Nos. 14,248, 1907; 4,767, 1909; 4,768, 1909; 11,364, 1909.)

(c) Disazo Dyes from Tetrazotised Diamines.

This type of disazo dyes is prepared by tetrazotising, *i.e.*, diazotising both the amino groups of a primary diamine and combining the tetrazo compound so obtained either with two molecular proportions of one dye component or with one molecular proportion of one component and one molecular proportion of another component; in the first case the dyes are referred to as "symmetrical" and in the second case as "mixed" disazo dyes.

The most important diamines in this connection are the so-called para-diamines, of which benzidine, $H_2N-\langle\ \rangle-\langle\ \rangle-NH_2$, is typical; other well-known diamines of the benzidine type are *o*-tolidine, dianisidine, diethoxybenzidine, benzidine-*o*-disulphonic acid, benzidine sulphone. Similar diamines containing two benzene nuclei connected by another group and containing in each nucleus an amino group, usually in the para-position to the connecting group, are diaminostilbene disulphonic acid, *p*-diaminodiphenylurea, azoxyaniline, etc. The dyes derived from these diamines possess in general the highly important property of dyeing cotton directly (*i.e.*, without mordants), and hence are known as **direct or substantive cotton dyes.**

It should be noted, however, that the dyes derived from *m*-tolidine, *m*-dichlorbenzidine and benzidine-*m*-disulphonic acid do not dye cotton, but are acid wool dyes. It should be noted further that all diamines cannot be tetrazotised—thus ortho- and peri-diamines do not yield tetrazo salts but ring compounds, azimides. Some meta-diamines, *e.g.*, *m*-phenylenediamine, can be tetrazotised like the paradiamines. The case of *p*-phenylenediamine requires special mention ; this body cannot be readily tetrazotised ; accordingly disazo dyes are prepared from this body by first diazotising *p*-nitraniline or an acidyl- (*e.g.*, acetyl) -*p*-phenylenediamine, combining the diazo compound with a dye component, reducing the nitro group or saponifying the acidylamino group, of the dye so obtained, then diazotising the amino group so produced and combining with a second molecule of a dye component. A similar process is employed with the sulphonic acids of 1 : 4-naphthylenediamine.

The following are typical dyes of this class ; except where otherwise stated, they dye unmordanted cotton :—

a. Derived from Benzidine and its Derivatives

Benzopurpurine B	Tolidine	2-naphthylamine-6-sulphonic acid.
		2-naphthylamine-6-sulphonic acid.
,, 4B	Tolidine	naphthionic acid.
		naphthionic acid.
,, 6B	Tolidine	1-naphthylamine-5-sulphonic acid.
		1-naphthylamine-5-sulphonic acid.
,, 10B	Dianisidine	naphthionic acid.
		naphthionic acid.
Congo Blue 2B	Dianisidine	1-naphthol-4-sulphonic acid.
		2-naphthol-3 : 6-disulphonic acid.
Congo Corinth G	Benzidine	naphthionic acid.
		1-naphthol-4-sulphonic acid.
,, B	Tolidine	1-naphthol-4-sulphonic acid.
		1-naphthol-4-sulphonic acid.
Congo Red	Benzidine	naphthionic acid.
		naphthionic acid.
,, 4R	Tolidine	naphthionic acid.
		resorcin.
Diamine Black BH	Benzidine	2 : 8 : 6-aminonaphthol sulphonic acid (alkaline coupling).
		1 : 8 : 3 : 6-aminonaphthol sulphonic acid (alkaline coupling).
Diamine Blue BB	Benzidine	1 : 8 : 3 : 6-aminonaphthol sulphonic acid (alkaline coupling).
		1 : 8 : 3 : 6-aminonaphthol sulphonic acid (alkaline coupling).
Diamine Brown B	Benzidine	salicylic acid.
		2-phenylamino-8-naphthol-6-sulphonic acid (alkaline coupling).
Diamine Red 3B } Deltapurpurine 7B }	Tolidine	2-naphthylamine-7-sulphonic acid.
		2-naphthylamine-7-sulphonic acid.
Dianol Brilliant Red } Toluylene Red - }	Dichlorbenzidine	2 : 3 : 6-naphthylamine disulphonic acid.
		2 : 3 : 6-naphthylamine disulphonic acid.
Oxamine Red	Benzidine	salicylic acid.
		2 : 5 : 7-aminonaphthol sulphonic acid (alkaline coupling).

b. Derived from Phenylene and Naphthylene Diamines

Azoalizarine Bordeaux W (dyes wool with chrome mordants)—

p-phenylenediamine $\left\langle\begin{array}{l}\text{Salicylic acid.}\\\text{1-4-naphthol sulphonic acid.}\end{array}\right.$

Bismarck Brown, Manchester Brown (dyes wool, leather, and tannin mordanted cotton)—

m-phenylenediamine $\left\langle\begin{array}{l}\text{\textit{m}-phenylenediamine.}\\\text{\textit{m}-phenylenediamine.}\end{array}\right.$

Coomassie Black B (dyes wool)—

1 : 4-diaminonaphthalene-2-sulphonic acid $\left\langle\begin{array}{l}\text{2 : 3 : 6-naphthol disulphonic acid.}\\\text{2-naphthylamine.}\end{array}\right.$

Naphthylene Red—

1 : 5-diaminonaphthalene $\left\langle\begin{array}{l}\text{naphthionic acid.}\\\text{naphthionic acid.}\end{array}\right.$

Toluylene Orange RR—

Toluylenediamine sulphonic acid $\left\langle\begin{array}{l}\text{2-naphthylamine.}\\\text{2-naphthylamine.}\end{array}\right.$

c. Derived from other Diamines

Benzo Fast Pink 2BL—

p-diaminodiphenylurea disulphonic acid $\left\langle\begin{array}{l}\text{2 : 8 : 6-aminonaphthol sulphonic acid.}\\\text{2 : 8 : 6-aminonaphthol sulphonic acid.}\end{array}\right.$

Brilliant Yellow—

diaminostilbene disulphonic acid $\left\langle\begin{array}{l}\text{phenol.}\\\text{phenol.}\end{array}\right.$

Diphenyl Fast Black—

p-diaminoditolylamine $\left\langle\begin{array}{l}\text{2 : 8 : 6-aminonaphthol sulphonic acid}\\\text{(alkaline coupling).}\\\text{\textit{m}-toluylene diamine.}\end{array}\right.$

Hessian Yellow—

Diaminostilbene disulphonic acid $\left\langle\begin{array}{l}\text{salicylic acid.}\\\text{salicylic acid.}\end{array}\right.$

St Denis Red—

Diaminoazoxytoluene $\left\langle\begin{array}{l}\text{1 : 4-naphthol sulphonic acid.}\\\text{1 : 4-naphthol sulphonic acid.}\end{array}\right.$

Trisazo Dyes, R.N=N.R′.N=N.R″.N=N.R‴

Dyes containing three azo groups can be produced in a variety of ways :—

1. From Secondary Disazo Dyes—

(*a*) Where the end component of a secondary disazo dye is an amine capable of diazotisation, it may be diazotised and coupled with another component.

R.N=N.R′.N=N.R″.NH₂→R.N=N.R′.N=N.R″.N=N.Cl→R.N=N.R′.N=N.R″.N=N.R‴

EXAMPLE.—Acetyl-1 : 4-naphthylenediamine-7-sulphonic acid—→Clève's acid—→Clève's acid —→2 : 5 : 7-aminonaphthol sulphonic acid. (For Clève's acids, see p. 444.)
A similar dye is—
Clève's acid—→Clève's acid—→Clève's acid—→2 : 5 : 7-aminonaphthol sulphonic acid.

(*b*) When the end component of a secondary disazo dye is a component capable of combining with two azo groups, it may be combined with a further diazo compound. Similar products result on combining such a "double coupling" component with one molecular proportion of a diazoazo compound and one molecular proportion of a diazo compound.

EXAMPLE.—Chrome Patent Green A—
p-aminosalicylic acid—➤α-naphthylamine—➤1 : 8 : 4 : 6-aminonaphthol sulphonic acid◀—aniline.

2. From Tetrazotised Diamines—

(*a*) By combining a tetrazotised diamine, such as benzidine, etc., with 1 molecule of a diazotisable middle component, *e.g.*, α-naphthylamine, an intermediate compound is formed, which is then diazotised, thus giving a tetrazo body which is combined with two molecules of a component or one molecule of each of two components.

EXAMPLE.—Thus: dianisidine is tetrazotised and combined with 1 molecule of α-naphthylamine, giving the intermediate compound—

which is diazotised, and the tetrazo body—

is combined with 2 molecules of 1-naphthol-3 : 8-disulphonic acid to form the trisazo dye—

Congo Fast Blue B—

(*b*) If a tetrazotised diamine is combined with a molecule of a diazotisable amine and 1 molecule of another component to form a "mixed" disazo dye, the amino group of the middle component can then be diazotised and combined with an end component.

EXAMPLE.—Benzidine is combined with 1 molecule α-naphthylamine and 1 molecule salicylic acid, giving—

$$\text{HO}\diagdown_{\text{HOOC}}\diagup C_6H_3-N=N-C_6H_4-C_6H_4-N=N-C_{10}H_6.NH_2$$

The amino group is then diazotised and the diazo compound coupled with 1-naphthol-4-sulphonic acid, giving **Benzo Grey—**

$$\text{HO}\diagdown_{\text{HOOC}}\diagup C_6H_3.N=N-C_6H_4.C_6H_4.N=N.C_{10}H_6.N=N-C_{10}H_5\diagup^{\text{OH}}_{\text{SO}_3\text{Na}}$$

The following are typical dyes produced by the methods 2*a* and 2*b* (above):—

Crumpsall Direct ·} Benzidine⟨ salicylic acid.
Fast Brown O ·} aniline—➤2-phenylamino-8-naphthol-6-sulphonic acid.

Diamine Beta Black Benzidine⟨ 1 : 8 : 3 : 6-aminonaphtholdisulphonic acid.
p-xylidine—➤1 : 8 : 3 : 6-aminonaphtholdisulphonic acid.

Diamine Bronze G · Benzidine⟨ salicylic acid.
1 : 8 : 3 : 6-aminonaphtholsulphonic acid—➤*m*-phenylenediamine.

Oxamine Violet RR Benzidine⟨ 1 : 4-naphthol sulphonic acid.
m-phenylenediamine oxamic acid—➤1 : 4-naphthol sulphonic acid.

In each of the above processes, 2*a* and 2*b*, when *p*-phenylenediamine is employed, a procedure is adopted similar to that described under disazo dyes, *p*-nitraniline or acidyl-*p*-phenylenediamine being the starting point, and the nitro group being reduced, or the acidylamino group saponified at a suitable stage of the process. The process is similar in the case of $1:4$-naphthylenediamine sulphonic acids.

3. A further method may be illustrated by the dye **Diamine Green G**; p-nitraniline is diazotised and combined in acid solution with $1:8$-aminonaphthol-$3:6$-disulphonic acid, giving the monazo dye—

This is then combined in alkaline solution with the intermediate compound from 1 molecule of tetrazotised benzidine and 1 molecule of salicylic acid—

$$\begin{array}{c}\text{HO} \\ \text{HOOC}\end{array}\!\!\!>\!\!C_6H_3.N\!=\!N.C_6H_4.C_6H_4.N\!=\!NCl,$$

giving the trisazo dye—

$$\begin{array}{c}\text{HO} \\ \text{HOOC}\end{array}\!\!\!>\!\!C_6H_3.N\!=\!N\!-\!C_6H_4.C_6H_4.N\!=\!N\!-\!\!\langle\text{aminonaphthol ring}\rangle\!\!-\!N\!=\!N\!-\!C_6H_4NO_2$$

This dyes unmordanted cotton green shades.

Other dyes of this type are **Columbia Green, Diamine Green B, Diphenyl Green G** and **3G, Diamine Black HW, Diamine Black R.** All these are direct cotton dyes.

A similar method consists in taking a primary disazo dye in which, say, p-nitraniline or acet-p-phenylenediamine is one of the diazo components, reducing or saponifying, diazotising the free amino group so produced and combining with a component. Thus, a $1:8$-aminonaphthol, -dioxynaphthylene, or -naphthylene-diamine sulphonic acid is combined with 1 molecule diazo compound and 1 molecule p-nitraniline or acetyl-p-phenylenediamine, the product reduced or saponified, diazotised, and combined with amines or phenols.

Another type is afforded by $1:8:4$-aminonaphthol sulphonic acid which can combine with 3 molecules of a diazo compound.

Finally, we may note a case in which a triamine is diazotised and combined with 3 molecules of a component—

$$\textbf{Alizarine Yellow FS}\quad\cdot\quad\cdot\quad\cdot\quad\cdot\quad\cdot\quad\text{*Magenta}\!\!\begin{array}{l}\diagup\text{Salicylic acid.}\\ \!\!-\!\text{Salicylic acid.}\\ \diagdown\text{Salicylic acid.}\end{array}$$

Tetrakisazo Dyes, $R.N\!=\!N.R'.N\!=\!N.R''.N\!=\!N.R'''.N\!=\!N.R''''$

Here again various methods may be used. A few examples are :—

Benzo Brown G—

$$\begin{array}{l}\text{Sulphanilic acid}\\ m\text{-phenylenediamine}\!\!\begin{array}{l}\diagup\diagup m\text{-phenylenediamine.}\\ \diagdown m\text{-phenylenediamine.}\end{array}\\ \text{Sulphanilic acid}\end{array}$$

Mekong Yellow G—

$$\begin{array}{l}\text{Benzidine}\!\!\begin{array}{l}\diagup\text{Salicylic acid.}\\ \diagdown\text{Dioxydiphenylmethane.}\end{array}\\ \text{Benzidine}\diagdown\text{Salicylic acid.}\end{array}$$

Cuba Black, Diamond Black—

$$\text{Benzidine}\!\!\begin{array}{l}\diagup 2:8:6\text{-Aminonaphtholsulphonic acid}\!\longrightarrow\! m\text{-phenylenediamine.}\\ \diagdown 2:8:6\text{-aminonaphtholsulphonic acid}\!\longrightarrow\! m\text{-phenylenediamine.}\end{array}$$

* See p. 57.

Higher polyazo dyes are known, but need not be discussed here, as they are not made or used to any great extent.

Developing Dyes

Many azo dyes are capable of conversion into azo dyes of a higher order by "development" on the fibre; the process is analogous to the production of **paranitraniline red** previously referred to.

Two cases arise: (*a*) when the end component of an azo dye is a diazotisable amine, the dye is applied to cotton and is then diazotised in a bath of nitrite and acid, and then passed through a bath containing β-naphthol or other component; (*b*) when the end component is a compound capable of combining with two azo groups, the dyed material is passed through a bath containing a diazo compound, *e.g.*, diazotised *p*-nitraniline.

Pyrazolone Dyes

It will be convenient here to consider a group of dyes the constitution of which does not seem to be definitely established; from their method of preparation they may be regarded as containing either azo or hydrazone groups.

The prototype of these dyes is **Tartrazine**, a valuable yellow acid wool dye. Tartrazine was first prepared by condensing 1 molecule of dioxytartaric acid with 2 molecules of phenylhydrazine-*p*-sulphonic acid: thus—

$$\begin{array}{l} COOH \\ \ \ |\ \ OH \\ C \diagdown \\ \ \ |\ \ OH \\ \ \ \ \ OH \\ C \diagdown \\ \ \ |\ \ OH \\ COOH \end{array} \quad + \quad \begin{array}{l} H_2N.HN.C_6H_4.SO_3Na \\ \\ \\ H_2N.HN.C_6H_4.SO_3Na \end{array} \quad \longrightarrow \quad \begin{array}{l} N{-}C_6H_4.SO_3Na \\ \diagup \qquad \diagdown \\ CO \qquad N \\ \ \ \ \ \diagdown \qquad | \\ C{-}{-}{-}{-}C.COOH \\ NaO_3S.C_6H_4.NH.N \diagup \end{array}$$

i.e., the sodium salt of 1-*p*-sulphophenyl-3-carboxy-4-*p*-sulphophenylhydrazone-5-pyrazolone.

Tartrazine is also produced by condensing phenylhydrazine *p*-sulphonic acid (1 molecule) with oxalacetic ester (1 molecule), which yields the ester of 1-*p*-sulphophenyl-3-carboxy-5-pyrazolone, saponifying this ester, and acting upon it with diazotised sulphanilic acid (1 molecule)—

$$NaO_3S.C_6H_4.N = N.Cl + \begin{array}{l} N{-}C_6H_4SO_3Na \\ \diagup \qquad \diagdown \\ CO \qquad N \\ \ \ \ \ \| \qquad \| \\ H_2C{-}{-}{-}C.COOH \end{array} \xrightarrow{\hspace{1cm}} \begin{array}{l} N{-}C_6H_4SO_3Na \\ \diagup \qquad \diagdown \\ CO \qquad N \\ \ \ \ \ \| \qquad \| \\ NaO_3S.C_6H_4N = N.HC{-}{-}{-}C{-}COOH \end{array}$$

This latter reaction suggests that tartrazine is an azo, not a hydrazone, compound.

A large number of similar dyes have been prepared recently by combining various diazo compounds with pyrazolones, such as the 1-*p*-sulphophenyl-3-carboxy-5-pyrazolone formulated above, the 1-*p*-sulphophenyl-3-methyl-5-pyrazolone, and the two corresponding pyrazolones containing no sulphonic group. Generally these dyes give bright yellow, orange, or red shades; many are suitable for dyeing wool, others serve as the starting point for lakes, while some which contain a residue of benzidine, etc., dye unmordanted cotton.

Stilbene Dyes

Dyes containing a stilbene residue and obtained by tetrazotising diaminostilbene disulphonic acid and coupling with components, have already been considered. There remains a group of dyes also containing the stilbene residue and probably containing azo groups, although they are not formed by the reactions of diazotising and coupling. On heating *p*-nitrotoluene sulphonic acid with aqueous caustic alkalis a complicated reaction (or series of reactions) occurs, the chief products of which are yellow dyes, known as **Curcumine S** or **Sun Yellow, Direct Yellow, Mikado Orange, Stilbene Yellow**, etc., which dye unmordanted cotton.

Curcumine S was formerly considered to be azoxystilbene disulphonic acid, and **Direct Yellow** dinitrosostilbene disulphonic acid, but according to Green and Crosland (*Journ. Chem. Soc.*, 89, 1602), these dyes are more complex and contain two stilbene groups, Stilbene Yellow 4G and 8G being dinitroazodistilbenedisulphonic acid, Direct Yellow being mainly azoazoxydistilbenedisulphonic acid, and Mikado Orange chiefly disazodistilbenedisulphonic acid.

A number of other dyes of this class have been prepared, but little is known of their constitution; **Polychromine B** and **Diphenyl Orange RR** are obtained by heating *p*-nitrotoluene sulphonic acid and *p*-phenylenediamine with caustic soda; **Curcuphenine** is similarly obtained from *p*-nitrotoluene sulphonic acid and dehydrothiotoluidine sulphonic acid.

2. DYES DERIVED FROM ANTHRACENE

Under this heading are grouped a large number of dyes of varied structure and properties but possessing the common feature that the starting point in the preparation of each is anthracene, $C_{14}H_{10}$, , a residue or residues of this body or its oxidation product anthraquinone, $C_{14}H_8O_2$, , being always present in the molecule of these dyes.

The first group of these dyes to be considered is the oxyanthraquinones of which alizarin is the prototype.

Alizarin or 1:2-dioxyanthraquinone, , is one of the oldest dyes in use and, after indigo, is perhaps the most important. It occurs in nature in madder in the form of a glucoside and was first obtained from this source. The natural alizarin is now almost entirely superseded by the synthetic product. Alizarin was first synthesised in 1868 by Graebe and Liebermann. In 1869 another and better synthesis was effected by them, and almost simultaneously by Perkin. This process consisted in sulphonating anthraquinone to produce the β-sulphonic acid, -SO₃H. By fusing this body with caustic alkali the sulphonic group is replaced by a hydroxyl group and at the same time another hydroxyl group enters in the α-position. This process has since been improved by the addition of oxidising agents, such as $KClO_3$, to the alkali, and this is now the usual process for preparing this dye. Alizarin is a mordant dye giving different shades with various mordants. Its chief application is for dyeing bright yellowish red shades on cotton mordanted by Turkey red oil (see Martin's "Industrial Chemistry," Vol. I. p. 43) and alumina.

Closely related to alizarin are two trioxyanthraquinones :—

Anthrapurpurin, 1:2:7-trioxyanthraquinone, and **Flavopurpurin**, 1:2:6-trioxyanthraquinone :—

Anthrapurpurin.

Flavopurpurin.

These bodies are obtained by fusing with caustic alkalis the disulphonic acids which are obtained by sulphonation of anthraquinone.

Commercial alizarin often contains one or both of these bodies, since the anthraquinone sulphonic acid used for the manufacture of alizarin often contains a certain amount of the disulphonic acids. Both these trioxyanthraquinones dye alumina-mordanted cotton red shades.

A third trioxyanthraquinone, **Purpurin**, $1:2:4$-trioxyanthraquinone, which occurs with alizarin in madder, is obtained by oxidising alizarine by manganese dioxide and sulphuric acid, and also dyes red shades with alumina mordants.

A fourth trioxyanthraquinone, **Anthragallol**, $1:2:3$-trioxyanthraquinone, is obtained by an entirely different process, viz., condensation of gallic acid with benzoic or phthalic acid, *e.g.* :—

It dyes brown with chrome mordants.

Alizarin Bordeaux, $1:2:5:8$-tetraoxyanthraquinone, is obtained by treating alizarin with fuming sulphuric acid, whereby a sulphuric ester of the tetraoxy body is first formed, and is then saponified ; it dyes wool bordeaux with alumina mordants, and violet-blue with chrome mordants.

Alizarin Cyanine R, $1:2:4:5:8$-pentaoxyanthraquinone, is formed by oxidising **Alizarin Bordeaux** by various oxidising agents, *e.g.,* manganese dioxide in sulphuric acid, arsenic acid, lead peroxide, persulphates, nitric acid, or by electrolytic oxidation ; it dyes blue to violet shades with mordants.

Similar oxidation of this pentaoxy body gives a hexaoxyanthraquinone :—

Anthracene Blue, $1:2:4:5:6:8$-hexaoxyanthraquinone, is obtained by treating with sulphuric acid and sulphur sesquioxide, $1:5$ or $1:8$-dinitroanthraquinone, or the mixture of these two bodies formed by nitrating anthraquinone ; apparently the nitro groups are reduced to amino groups, which are then replaced by hydroxyl groups, while the other hydroxyl groups enter the molecule ; the dyeing properties of this dye are similar to those of Alizarin Cyanine R.

Rufigallol, $1:2:3:5:6:7$-hexoxyanthraquinone, is obtained by condensation of 2 molecules of gallic acid (*cf.* **Anthragallol** above) ; it dyes brown with chrome mordants.

It will be noticed that all the above-described oxyanthraquinones are mordant dyes, and all contain at least two hydroxy groups in ortho-position to one another ; probably the property of forming lakes with mordants is dependent upon this structure. The dioxyanthraquinones isomeric with alizarin, *e.g.,* **quinizarin** ($1:4$), **anthrarufine** ($1:5$), **chrysazine** ($1:8$), **anthraflavic acid** ($2:6$), do not possess dyeing properties.

We have now to consider a number of dyes which are derivatives of the oxyanthraquinones.

Alizarin Brown, α-nitroalizarin (OH : OH : $NO_2 = 1:2:4$), is produced by nitrating alizarin in fuming sulphuric acid or in sulphuric acid containing arsenic acid, or by nitrating mono- or di-benzoylalizarin in sulphuric acid ; nitration of alizarin in sulphuric acid containing boric acid gives **Alizarin Orange,** β-nitroalizarin (OH : OH : $NO_2 = 1:2:3$) ; nitration of flavopurpurin gives **Alizarin Orange G** (OH : OH : OH : $NO_2 = 1:2:6:3$). Reduction of α-nitroalizarin gives α-aminoalizarin, **Alizarin Garnet R ; Alizarin Maroon** is a mixture of aminoalizarin and aminopurpurins, and is produced by nitrating commercial alizarin and then reducing.

Sulphonation of alizarin gives alizarin monosulphonic acid, **Alizarin Red S** (OH : OH : $SO_3H = 1:2:3$). Sulphonation of flavopurpurin gives **Alizarin Red 3WS** (OH : OH : OH : $SO_3H = 1:2:6:3$).

The above simple nitro-, amino-, and sulphonic derivatives are also mordant dyes.

The bodies next to be discussed are acid wool dyes dyeing without mordants, though some can be subsequently chromed.

Alizarin Saphirol B, diaminoanthrarufin disulphonic acid, is produced by sulphonating anthrarufin, nitrating, and finally reducing.

Sulphonation and nitration of anthrachrysone (1 : 3 : 5 : 7-tetraoxyanthraquinone) gives **dinitroanthrachrysone disulphonic acid** dyeing brown shades ; reduction gives the corresponding diamino bodies which dye violet ; boiling the last named with alkali gives a hexaoxyanthraquinone disulphonic acid, Acid **Alizarin Blue BB** and **GR.**

An important property of the anthraquinone derivatives is the readiness with which negative substituents (Br, Cl, NO_2, OH, SO_3H) and also amino groups can be replaced by substituted amino groups NHR, where R is an alkyl or aryl radical. This reaction is applied in the production of a number of wool dyes; for example, quinizarin when condensed with aniline, p-toluidine, etc., gives—

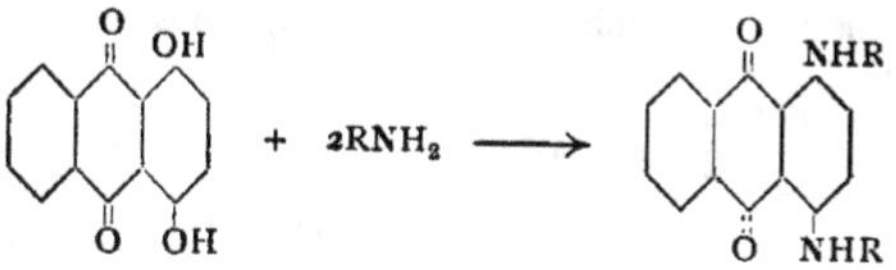

Sulphonation of these compounds gives **Quinizarin Greens—**

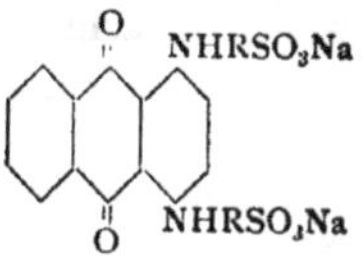

Leuco Quinizarin, 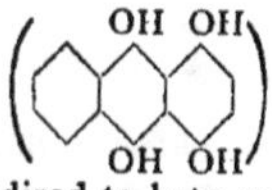 , gives the same products, the two meso-hydroxy groups being reoxidised to keto groups.

Other dyes of this type are—

Anthraquinone Violet—

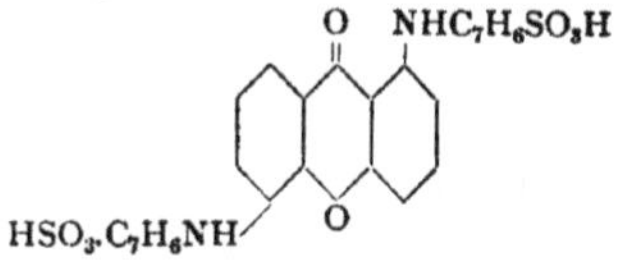

Alizarin Pure Blue—

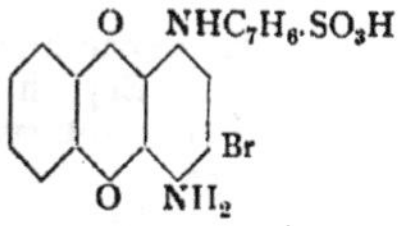

Alizarin Cyanine Green—

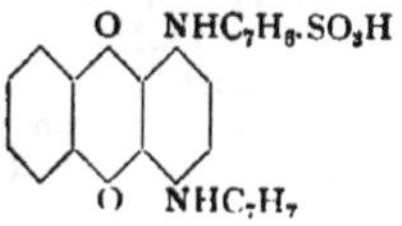

Alizarin Irisol—

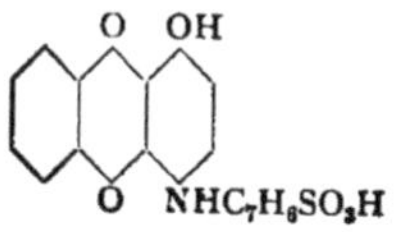

Alizarin Astrol—

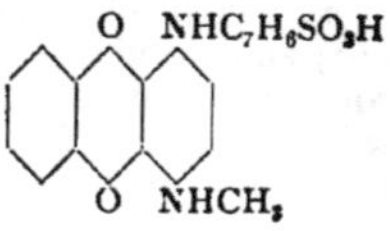

Another type of anthraquinone derivative is that in which a nitrogen-containing ring is added to the anthracene nucleus—the **anthraquinolines**; these are obtained from nitro- or amino-oxyanthraquinones by Skraup's quinoline synthesis, viz., by treating these bodies with glycerol and sulphuric acid; in this manner β-nitro- or β-aminoalizarin gives **Alizarin Blue**, while a-aminoalizarin gives **Alizarin Green**—

Alizarin Blue.   Alizarin Green.

Both these compounds give soluble bisulphite compounds, **Alizarin Blue S** and **Alizarin Green S**, on treatment with sodium bisulphite, which are used in printing with chrome mordants.

A similar quinoline compound, **Alizarin Black P**, and its bisulphite combination, **Alizarin Black S**, are obtained from β-nitro- or β-amino-flavopurpurin.

Treatment of Alizarin Green with strong sulphuric acid at high temperatures produces a 1 : 2 : 5 : 7 : 8-pentaoxyanthraquinoline, **Alizarin Indigo Blue**, which also gives a soluble bisulphite compound, **Alizarin Indigo Blue S**; concentrated or fuming sulphuric acid with Alizarin Blue gives 1 : 2 : 5 : 8-tetraoxyanthraquinoline, **Alizarin Green**, bisulphite compound **Alizarin Green S**.

Recent Developments in Anthracene Dyes—Anthracene Vat Dyes

In recent years there has been a great development in the anthracene dyes, chiefly in the production of the so-called "vat" dyes, i.e., dyes which, like indigo, are insoluble, or practically so, in water, but yield on reduction colourless or slightly coloured "leuco" compounds which are soluble in alkali. The fabric to be dyed is impregnated with a solution of the leuco compound, and the dye is developed by oxidation in air or otherwise.

Vat Dyes derived from Anthracene.—The oldest anthracene vat dye is **Indanthrene**, **Indanthrene Blue R**, which is prepared by melting 2-amino-anthraquinone with caustic alkali (B.A.S.F., English Patents, 3,239, 1901; 22,762, 1901).

Indanthrene is N-dihydro-1 : 2 : 1' : 2'-anthraquinoneazine—

and dyes blue shades.

Indanthrene can also be prepared by condensing 1-amino-2-halogenanthraquinone (or 2-amino-1-halogenanthraquinone) with itself (F. v. Bayer, English Patent, 7,692, 1904); by condensing 1 : 2-diaminoanthraquinone with 1 : 2-anthraquinone and oxidising the product (F. v. Bayer, English Patent, 12,756, 1905); by condensing 1 : 2-diaminoanthraquinone with alizarin (F. v. Bayer, English Patent, 9,102, 1906); and together with Flavanthrene (v. infra) by treating 1-aminoanthraquinone with acid condensing agents (B.A.S.F., English Patent, 19,322, 1906). Halogenised indanthrenes (**Indanthrene Blue GC, GCD, and CE, etc.**) are prepared by chlorinating or brominating indanthrene (B.A.S.F., English Patents, 4,035 1902; 23,179, 1903; 17,242, 1905). **Algol Blue K** (N dimethylindanthrene) is made from 1-methylamino-2-bromanthraquinone by the second method mentioned above.

Indanthrene disulphonic acid (B.A.S.F., English Patent, 12,185, 1901) and monosulphonic acid (B.A.S.F., English Patent, 339, 1909) are also known, as well as other derivatives.

Another azine dye is **Flavanthrene** (Indanthrene Yellow) prepared by heating 2-aminoanthraquinone with alkali at a higher temperature than that required for Indanthrene; oxidising agents, *e.g.*, potassium nitrate, may be added to the melt; it is also obtained by heating 2-aminoanthraquinone with condensing agents, for instance, antimony pentachloride in nitrobenzene, or aluminium chloride alone, or by the action of acid oxidising agents, such as bichromate and sulphuric acid, manganese dioxide and sulphuric or nitric acid or lead peroxide (B.A.S.F., English Patent, 24,354, 1901). Flavanthrene dyes cotton blue shades which on standing become a bright yellow.

The following synthesis by Scholl (*Ber.*, 40, p. 1691) shows its constitution :—

1-amino-2-methylanthraquinone.

2:2'-dimethyl-1:1'-dianthraquinonyl.

Flavanthrene.

Analogous to Indanthrene and Flavanthrene, but containing methine groups in place of nitrogen, are **Anthraflavone** and **Pyranthrone**.

Anthraflavone— or the stilbenze derivative $C_{14}H_7O_2.CH=CH.C_{14}H_7O_2$
(Ullmann, *Ber.*, **46**, 712).

is prepared by treating 2-methylanthraquinone or its ω-halogen derivatives with
condensing agents (B.A.S.F., English Patent, 10,677, 1905; D.R.P., 199,756); it
dyes citron-yellow shades.

Pyranthrone (Indanthrene Gold Orange)—

is prepared by treating 2:2'-dimethyl-1:1'-dianthraquinonyl with alkali or zinc
chloride, with or without oxidation (B.A.S.F., English Patent, 14,578, 1905; Scholl,
Ber., **43**, p. 346); it dyes orange tints. Treatment with halogens (English
Patents, 10,505, 1906; 12,568, 1909) gives redder dyes.

The next group of dyes to be considered are the **benzanthrone** dyes. The
benzanthrones are compounds containing the group—

and are prepared by heating anthraquinone or its reduction products (anthranol,
oxanthranol, or anthracene) or its amino, sulphonic, etc., derivatives with glycerin,
preferably in presence of condensing agents, such as sulphuric acid. The benzanthrones undergo further condensation on being melted with alkalis, and yield blue
to violet dyes (B.A.S.F., English Patent, 16,538, 1904; D.R.P., 176,018; Bally,
Ber., **38**, p. 194).

The dye prepared from anthranol is known as **Violanthrene,** and that obtained
from 2-aminoanthraquinone as **Cyananthrene.** Violanthrene has the formula of
a dibenzanthrone (see English Patent, 16,271, 1910)—

Among the derivatives of benzanthrone we may note: **benznaphthanthrone** from naphthanthraquinone (English Patent, 853, 1905) gives a reddish blue dye; **benzanthronequinolines** from α-aminoanthraquinones (English Patent, 3,819, 1905) give violet-blue dyes; green dyes (**Indanthrene Green, etc.**) by nitrating benzanthrone dyes, with or without subsequent reduction (English Patent, 1,818, 1905); halogen derivatives from halogenanthraquinones (English Patent, 7,022, 1905), or by halogenising the dyes (English Patent, 22,519, 1905); the latter dye violet-blue to red-violet shades. Halogenised benzanthrones, on treatment with alkali, give dyes which usually contain no halogen, and are known as **isoviolanthrenes** (English Patent, 20,837, 1905). Other derivatives are obtained by heating aminobenzanthrones with metallic salts or oxides (English Patents, 10,770, 1907; 3,156, 1908). Brombenzanthrone condensed with 1-aminoanthraquinone gives benzanthronyl-1-aminoanthraquinone, which, by treatment with condensing agents, gives a **green dye** (English Patent, 24,604, 1908; D.R.P., 212,471).

Another group of dyes is that containing two or three anthraquinone nuclei united by NH groups, the **dianthraquinonylamines** and **trianthraquinonylamines**, α-β-**Dianthraquinonylamine** (Algol Orange R)—

is prepared by condensing 2-aminoanthraquinone with 1-chloranthraquinone, or 1-aminoanthraquinone with 2-chloranthraquinone (D.R.P., 162,824; B.A.S.F., English Patent, 19,199, 1905); it dyes orange shades (F. v. Bayer, English Patent, 24,810, 1908).

Trianthraquinonylamines, dyeing red shades, are produced by condensing two molecular proportions of 2-chloranthraquinone with 1 : 5-diaminoanthraquinone (**Indanthrene Bordeaux B**, B.A.S.F., English Patent, 10,324, 1906), or by condensing two molecular proportions of 1-aminoanthraquinone with β-β-dihalogenanthraquinones (**Indanthrene Red G**, B.A.S.F., English Patent, 4,235, 1907). A number of derivatives of di- and tri-anthraquinonylamines giving a variety of shades are known (English Patents, 10,860, 1906; 13,057, 1906; 7,418, 1908; 12,167, 1908; 5,382, 1909; 9,219, 1909).

A further group of dyes is the **acidylaminoanthraquinones**, obtained by introducing the formyl, acetyl, benzoyl, succinyl, salicylyl, thiosalicylyl, anisyl, cinnamyl, etc., radicals into the amino groups of aminoanthraquinones (F. v. Bayer, English Patents, 2,709, 1909; 3,055, 1909); these dye yellow, red, orange, blue, violet, etc., shades (**Algol Yellows, Algol Reds**, etc.). **Helindon Yellow 3GN** (English Patent, 24,920, 1909), is a symmetrical urea derived from 2-aminoanthraquinone.

A number of anthracene vat dyes containing sulphur are also known, *e.g.*, **mercaptans** (English Patent, 10,387, 1908), **thiazoles** (English Patent, 12,828, 1911), **thiazines** (English Patents, 18,240, 1911; 28,479, 1911), **thioureas** (English Patent, 11,473, 1910).

Two groups of dyes which are at present attracting attention are the **anthraquinone acridones** and **thioxanthones.**

Anthraquinone 1 : 2-acridone,

is prepared by condensing anthranilic acid with *a*-chlor- or *a*-nitro-anthraquinone and heating the resulting carboxyanilido-anthraquinone,

with condensing agents (Ullmann, English Patent, 12,653, 1909).

Anthraquinone- 1 : 2-thioxanthrone,

is similarly prepared from thiosalicylic acid (Ullmann, English Patent, 30,480, 1909).

A number of derivatives of these dyes have been prepared (B.A.S.F., English Patent, 13,907, 1909, etc.).

3. DYES OF THE INDIGO, THIOINDIGO, AND INDIGOID SERIES

Indigo (Indigo Blue, Indigotin)

Is the most important dye of commerce. It was originally obtained from natural sources, but the natural indigo has been very largely replaced by synthetic indigo, the manufacture of which is perhaps the greatest triumph of dyestuff chemistry.

Indigo has the formula, $C_{16}H_{10}N_2O_2$, or . It occurs in

nature as a glucoside, **indican**, in various plants—*Indigofera tinctoria, Indigo anil, Polygonium tinctorium, Isatis tinctoria.* Hydrolysis of the indican gives indigo and a sugar, indiglucin; this hydrolysis is effected in practice by fermenting the leaves and stems of the indigo-bearing plants.

Indigo has been synthesised by a number of processes, only the more important of which can be dealt with here.

Baeyer in 1880 synthesised it from o-nitrocinnamic acid, $C_6H_4\begin{smallmatrix}CH=CH.COOH\\NO_2\end{smallmatrix}$. Treatment of this compound with bromine gives o-nitrodibromhydrocinnamic acid, $C_6H_4\begin{smallmatrix}CHBr—CHBr.COOH\\NO_2\end{smallmatrix}$, from which alkalis remove hydrobromic acid, giving o-nitrophenylpropiolic acid, $C_6H_4\begin{smallmatrix}C\equiv C.COOH\\NO_2\end{smallmatrix}$; this compound, on treatment with alkaline reducing agents, splits off carbon dioxide and condenses to indigo. An alternative method consists in treating o-nitrocinnamic acid with chlorine, which gives phenylchlorlactic acid, $C_6H_4\begin{smallmatrix}CHOH—CHCl.COOH\\NO_2\end{smallmatrix}$; alkalis convert this compound into o-nitrophenyloxyacrylic acid, $C_6H_4—CH—CH.COOH$, which condenses on heating in solution into indigo.

In 1882 Baeyer synthesised indigo from o-nitrobenzaldehyde; treatment of this body with acetone gives o-nitrophenyllactomethylketone, $C_6H_4\begin{smallmatrix}CHOH.CH_2COCH_3\\NO_2\end{smallmatrix}$, which is converted into indigo by treatment with alkalis. These syntheses of Baeyer's were not, however, a commercial success, although o-nitrophenyllactomethylketone has been employed under the name of Indigo salt for producing indigo on the fibre (the bisulphite compound of the ketone being printed on the fibre which is then passed through an alkaline bath).

Heumann's synthesis of indigo in 1890 from phenylglycine, and soon afterwards from phenylglycine-o-carboxylic acid, led to the commercially successful placing of synthetic indigo upon the world's markets.

Two main processes are now worked on a very large scale:—

1. **The Phenylglycine Process,** worked by the Höchst Farbwerke, consists in heating aniline with chloracetic acid, when phenylglycine is formed, thus:—

$$\underset{\text{Aniline.}}{C_6H_5.NH_2} + \underset{\text{Chloracetic acid.}}{Cl.CH_2.COOH} = \underset{\text{Phenylglycine.}}{C_6H_5.NH.CH_2.COOH} + HCl.$$

(Phenylglycine has also been made by heating aniline with HCN and formaldehyde.) The phenylglycine is next melted with caustic soda to form indoxyl, $C_6H_5\begin{smallmatrix}NH\\CO\end{smallmatrix}CH_2$ or $C_6H_5\begin{smallmatrix}NH\\C(OH)\end{smallmatrix}CH$, thus :—

$$\underset{\text{Sodium salt of phenylglycine.}}{C_6H_5.NH.CH_2.COONa} + NaOH = \underset{\text{Indoxyl.}}{C_6H_4\begin{smallmatrix}NH\\CO\end{smallmatrix}CH_2} + 2NaOH.$$

But since at the high temperature necessary for proper fusion a large portion of the parent materials are destroyed by the alkali, with a resulting poor yield of indoxyl, it is preferable to add materials to the caustic soda to lower the temperature of melting. A great improvement was effected by the Frankfurter Scheideanstalt by adding sodamide, $NaNH_2$ (M.P. 120° C.; prepared by heating metallic sodium in a stream of dry NH_3), when the following change takes place:—

$$\underset{\text{Phenylglycine.}}{C_6H_5.NH.CH_2.COOH} + \underset{\text{Sodamide.}}{Na.NH_2} = \underset{\text{Indoxyl.}}{C_6H_4\begin{smallmatrix}NH\\CO\end{smallmatrix}CH_2} + NaOH + NH_3.$$

The escaping ammonia is collected and used again. Carbides and nitrides have also been used instead of sodamide. To obtain indigo the melt is dissolved in water, and air blown through to oxidise and condense the indoxyl (probably present in the alkaline solution as the sodium salt, $C_6H_4\begin{smallmatrix}NH\\C(ONa)\end{smallmatrix}CH$) to indigo;

or the solution is acidified so as to give free indoxyl, which is then oxidised and condensed to indigo :—

$$2C_6H_4\!\!<^{NH}_{CO}\!\!>CH_2 + 2O = C_6H_4\!\!<^{NH}_{CO}\!\!>C = C\!\!<^{NH}_{CO}\!\!>C_6H_4 + 2H_2O$$

Indoxyl.   Indigo blue.

In this process the starting point is benzene (from which aniline is obtained by nitrating and reducing as described on p. 424), while intermediately chloracetic acid, caustic soda, and sodamide are used. The success of the synthesis depends entirely upon the price at which these materials are obtainable.

2. The Phenylglycine-*o*-Carboxylic Acid Process, worked by the Badische Anilin- und Soda-Fabrik, depends upon the fact that when phenylglycine-*o*-carboxylic acid is melted with caustic alkalies, it condenses, thus :—

$$C_6H_4\!\!<^{COOH}_{NH.CH_2.COOH}\longrightarrow C_6H_4\!\!<^{CO}_{NH}\!\!>CH.COOH\longrightarrow C_6H_4\!\!<^{CO}_{NH}\!\!>CH_2 + CO_2 + H_2O.$$

Phenylglycine-*o*-carboxylic   Indoxylic acid.   Indoxyl.
acid.

The starting point in this process is **Anthranilic Acid**, $C_6H_4\!\!<^{NH_2 \, (1)}_{COOH \, (2)}$, which the B.A.S.F. obtain from the cheap and abundant naphthalene by the following series of operations : (1) The naphthalene is oxidised to phthalic acid, $C_6H_4(COOH)_2$, by heating with concentrated sulphuric acid and mercury (see **Phthalic Acid**, p. 430), when the anhydride of the acid distils over ;

(2) the phthalic anhydride, $C_6H_4\!\!<^{CO}_{CO}\!\!>O$, thus obtained is converted into phthalimide, $C_6H_4\!\!<^{CO}_{CO}\!\!>NH$, by heating with ammonia ; which (3) on treating with bleaching powder or NaOCl gives anthranilic acid, $C_6H_4(COOH).(NH_2)$ (see p. 430) ; (the anthranilic acid may also be obtained by heating *o*-chlorbenzoic acid, $C_6H_4.Cl.COOH$ (1 : 2) with NH_3 in the presence of Cu) ; (4) next, the anthranilic acid is treated with chloracetic acid to obtain phenylglycine-*o*-carboxylic acid—

$$C_6H_4\!\!<^{COOH}_{NH_2} + Cl.CH_2.COOH = C_6H_4\!\!<^{COOH}_{NH.CH_2.COOH} + HCl ;$$

Anthranilic acid.   Chloracetic acid.   Phenylglycine-*o*-carboxylic acid.

and (5) the phenylglycine-*o*-carboxylic acid is finally converted into indoxyl and then into indigo as above described.

It has also been shown that for phenylglycine-*o*-carboxylic acid one may substitute methyl-anthranilic acid, $C_6H_4\!\!<^{COOH}_{NH.CH_3}$, when melting with sodamide for indoxyl. According to this latter process the use of chloracetic acid is abolished, since methylanthranilic acid may be produced directly from anthranilic acid by treating with methyl chloride, or from phthalic anhydride by treating with methylamine.

On comparing the two main processes for manufacturing synthetic indigo, it will be seen that the one starts from benzene, and the other from naphthalene. Both processes at present work with monochloracetic acid, thereby creating a huge demand for glacial acetic acid (about 3,000 tons are used annually, being obtained from the distillation of about 150,000 cub. yds. of wood). The chlorine for chlorinating the acetic acid is obtained by electrolysing alkali chlorides, which, also produces caustic alkali. Finally the demand for a concentrated sulphuric acid for oxidising naphthalene to phthalic acid, coupled with the escape of large amounts of SO_2 and SO_3 during the heating process, contributed very essentially to the industrial development of the contact process for the manufacture of sulphuric acid. The manufacture of synthetic indigo thus furnishes a very interesting series of examples of the interaction of one branch of chemical industry on others.

The following statistics show that although **synthetic indigo** has largely diminished the culture of **natural indigo** in India and other tropical countries, yet the demand for indigo is also not increasing, probably owing to the competitive action of several very fast blue dyes, derived from anthracene, which are now on the market.

Imported into Great Britain :—

	1896.	1906.	1907.	1908.	1909.	1913.	Value. (1913).
		Cwt.	Cwt.	Cwt.	Cwt.	Cwt.	
Synthetic indigo - -	o	39,042	41,379	37,761	33,494	23,889	£76,695
Natural indigo - -	...	7,641	11,116	8,644	10,051	4,174	54,739

Practically all the synthetic indigo imported into Great Britain comes from Germany : (1910) **Germany**, 28,182 cwt. (value, £101,183) ; **Netherlands**, 4 cwt. (value, £16) ; **Belgium**, 10 cwt. (value, £50) ; **other countries**, *nil*. The total amount of synthetic indigo exported from Germany in 19.9 amounted to 161,100 dz. = 16,110 metric tons, or roughly, 320,000 cwt. representing a value of 40.3 million marks (say £2,000,000).

The United States imported of Indigo : 1906, 7,393,000 lbs. ; 1910, 7,539,000 lbs. ; value in 1910, $1,196,000. Of this quantity Germany imports 7,000,000 lbs., value $1,000,000.

Indigo is a typical vat dye, *i.e.*, before dyeing it is reduced to its leuco compound, indigo white, $C_6H_4\begin{matrix}NH\\ C(OH)\end{matrix}C—C\begin{matrix}NH\\ C(OH)\end{matrix}C_6H_4$, which is soluble in alkalies ; the fibre (cotton, wool, or silk) is immersed in an alkaline solution of this body, and is then withdrawn and oxidised to indigo by exposure to air. The old method of obtaining the vat was by fermentation by means of dung ; other methods consisted in the use of glucose and alkali, lime and ferrous sulphate, or zinc and alkali ; the vat is now usually prepared by means of sodium hydrosulphite and alkali.

Indirubin or Indigo Red is an isomer of indigo and has the constitution It occurs as an impurity in natural indigo, and may be prepared by the condensation of indoxyl with isatin, $C_6H_4\begin{matrix}NH\\ CO\end{matrix}CO$; it is of no value as a dye.

Sulphonation of indigo yields a disulphonic acid, **Indigo Carmine**, which is an acid wool dye.

Halogenised Indigo Dyes

Halogenised indigo dyes, *i.e.*, indigo derivatives in which one or more of the hydrogen atoms of the benzene nuclei has or have been replaced by bromine or chlorine, may be prepared by two general methods :—

1. Treatment of indigo or a derivative thereof, either alone or suspended or dissolved in various media, with halogen or with halogenising agents.

2. Obtaining a halogenised parent material, *e.g.*, brom- or chlor-phenylglycine-*o*-carboxylic acid, which is then subjected to suitable treatment, say condensation and oxidation, to yield a halogenised dye.

These two methods have been known for some years, but until 1907 had only been applied to the production of mono- and di-halogen derivatives, except as regards a tetrachlorindigo prepared in 1901 from dichlorinated phenylglycine-*o*-carboxylic acid (B.A.S.F., English Patent, 20,552, 1901).

From 1907 onwards both methods have been largely extended, and halogen-indigos containing from 3 to 6 atoms of halogen in the molecule are now known.

By treating indigo, suspended in an inert medium such as nitrobenzene, with the theoretical amount of bromine (two atomic proportions of bromine for each bromine atom to be introduced into the indigo molecule), at a raised temperature, **tri-** and **tetra-bromindigos** are obtained (S.C.I.B., English Patent, 5,122, 1907 ; D.R.P., 193,438). By applying this method to mono- and di-chlorindigos, mixed tri- and tetra-halogenindigos are produced, and from the para-dihalogenindigos (*i.e.*, containing halogen in para position to the carbonyl group) penta- and hexa-halogenindigos result (S.C.I.B., English Patent, 10,326, 1907).

4

Chlorination of indigo in similar media in presence of chlorine carriers yields **tri-** and **tetra-chlorindigos** (S.C.I.B., English Patent, 19,793, 1908).

The above-described products dye reddish-blue shades.

The constitution of these bodies has been established by Grandmougin (*Ber.*, 42, p. 4408) in the following way :—

Tetrabromindigo obtained by bromination in nitrobenzene is oxidised by means of nitric acid to a dibromisatin of M.P. 249°-250° C., which is identical with the known 5 : 7-dibromisatin,

Distillation of the dibromisatin with potash gives 2 : 4-dibromaniline. The tetra-bromindigo is, therefore, 5 : 7 : 5′ : 7′-tetrabromindigo,

The nomenclature here employed is that of Friedländer (*Ber.*, 42, p. 765). The di- and tri-bromindigos obtained similarly are the 5 : 5′ and 5 : 7 : 5′ bodies. The tetrabromindigo is known in commerce as **Ciba Blue.***

Another method of bromination consists in treating indigo suspended in concentrated sulphuric acid with bromine in the cold (F. v. Bayer, English Patent, 4,423, 1908). In this process the hydrobromic acid formed is partly oxidised by the sulphuric acid, so that less than the theoretical amount of bromine can be used; for the same reason bromides may be used instead of bromine in this process (F. v. Bayer, English Patent, 5,582, 1908). The tri- and tetra-bromindigos so obtained dye greenish-blue shades. Grandmougin asserts that they are identical with the products obtained by bromination in nitrobenzene (*Ber.*, 43, p. 937). A closely allied process is that of Kalle & Co. (English Patent, 15,088, 1909), in which chlorsulphonic acid is used as the suspension medium during the bromination.

Another process (F. v. M.L.B., English Patent, 25,513, 1907) consists in treating dihalogenindigos with excess of bromine alone; greenish black products are thus obtained which appear to be perbromides of bromindigos; treatment of these bodies with sodium bisulphite removes the loosely combined bromine, giving the brominated dyes. Similar perbromides are obtained by using excess of bromine in presence of concentrated sulphuric acid (English Patent, 25,514, 1907).

The above-described processes—bromination in sulphuric or chlorsulphonic acid, or with bromine alone—can also be applied to produce **penta-** and **hexa-bromindigos** (English Patents, 13,789, 1908; 2,609, 1909; 3,019, 1909), which also dye greenish blue shades.

According to Grandmougin (*Ber.*, 43, p. 937) the penta- and hexabromindigos obtained by bromination in sulphuric acid are the 4 : 5 : 7 : 5′ : 7′ and 4 : 5 : 7 : 4′ : 5′ : 7′ bodies respectively.

An interesting process is that of Kalb in which dehydroindigo forms the starting point (*Ber.*, 42, p. 3642 *et seq.*, p. 3653 *et seq.*; B.A.S.F., English Patents, 16,377, 1909; 22,714, 1909).

Dehydroindigo, is obtained by careful oxidation of indigo, for instance by means of silver oxide, lead dioxide, manganese dioxide, or

---

* The trade names are here given on the authority of Bohn, *Ber.*, 43, p. 987.

permanganates, in absence of water, and in presence of indifferent diluents, *e.g.*, chloroform, benzene, or nitrobenzene. If anhydrous acids are also present the corresponding dehydroindigo salts are formed. Dehydroindigo is also formed by treating indigo with halogen or halogenising agents under suitable conditions. With sodium sulphite or bisulphite, dehydroindigo forms soluble compounds, which can be readily halogenised by treatment with chlorine or bromine, even in presence of water; the tetrahalogen bodies thus produced are the $5:7:5':7'$ bodies. The other salts of dehydroindigo can be halogenised similarly; on reduction they yield the halogenindigos.

The unsymmetrical condensation product from isatin and indoxyl, indirubin, has been brominated by various processes; mono- to hexa-brom derivatives, dyeing reddish blue shades, have thus been obtained (S.C.I.B., English Patents, 6,106, 1907; 8,530, 1908; 6,351, 1910). The **tetra-bromindirubin** is known as **Ciba Heliotrope**.

Under the second method we may note two processes of the B.A.S.F. (English Patents, 6,991, 1909, and 6,992, 1909). According to the first of these a halogenised anthranilic acid is treated with formaldehyde, giving a compound of the formula $\text{Hal}\underset{\text{CO—O}}{\overset{\text{NH—CH}_2}{\bigcirc}}$; this on treatment with a cyanide gives the corresponding ω-cyanmethylanthranilic acid, $\text{Hal}\underset{\text{COOH}}{\overset{\text{NHCH}_2\text{CN}}{\bigcirc}}$, which is saponified to halogenphenylglycine-*o*-carboxylic acid, for instance $3:4$-, $4:5$-, and $4:6$-dihalogenphenylglycine-*o*-carboxylic acid. The $4:6$-dichlorphenylglycine-*o* carboxylic acid thus prepared is identical with that prepared by chlorinating phenylglycine-*o*-carboxylic acid (English Patent, 20,552, 1901), and the tetrachlorindigo of this last-mentioned Patent is, therefore, the $5:7:5':7'$ body. According to the second Patent, No. 6,992, 1909, dihalogenphenylglycine-*o*-carboxylic esters are used as parent materials; by this process the $5:7:5':7'$-, $4:5:4':5'$-, $4:4':6:6'$-, and $5:5':6:6'$-tetrachlorindigos and the $4:4'$-dichlor-$5:5'$-dibrom- and $5:5'$-dichlor-$7:7'$-dibromindigos have been prepared.

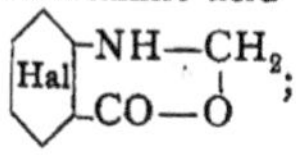

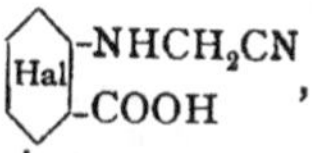

In connection with the halogenindigos it is noteworthy that the ancient **Tyrian purple** obtained from *Murex Brandaris* has been shown by Friedländer (*Ber.*, 42, p. 765) to consist essentially of $6:6'$-dibromindigo.

Thioindigo Dyes

Thioindigo is an analogue of indigo containing sulphur in place of the NH groups—

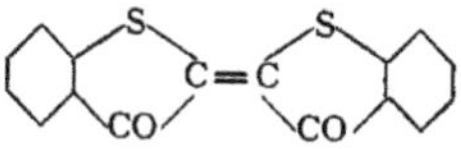

It was discovered by Friedländer (*Ber.*, 39, p. 1060) and first put on the market as Thioindigo Red B by Kalle & Co. (English Patents, 22,736, 1905; 23,316, 1905; 14,261, 1906; 16,100, 1906; 16,101, 1906).

The process for its production is shown by the following scheme :—

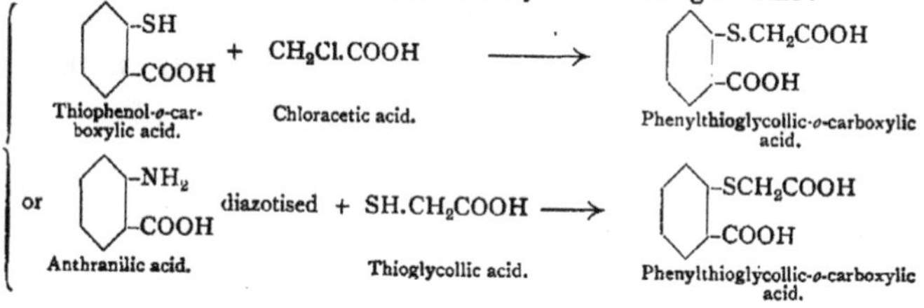

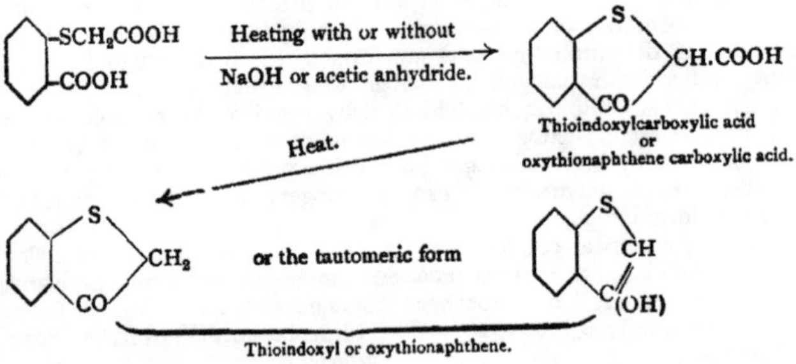

Heating with or without
NaOH or acetic anhydride. →

Thioindoxylcarboxylic acid
or
oxythionaphthene carboxylic acid.

← **Heat.**

or the tautomeric form

Thioindoxyl or oxythionaphthene.

Condensation and oxidation of this latter body gives thioindigo.

It will be seen that this process corresponds with the Heumann synthesis of indigo from phenylglycine-*o*-carboxylic acid.

This synthesis has been followed by the production of a large number of derivatives of thioindigo and allied dyes. The following general methods may be noted :—

2. Treatment of arylthioglycollic acids or their salts or esters, $RSCH_2COOR_1$, with acid condensing agents, such as sulphuric acid, phosphorus pentoxide, acetic anhydride, zinc chloride, potassium bisulphate, or oxalic acid, and oxidation of the resulting thioindoxyl derivatives (B.A.S.F., English Patent, 28,578, 1906).

3. Conversion of arylthioglycollic acids into the acid chlorides, $RSCH_2COCl$, by means of phosphorus tri- or pentachloride or oxychloride; the acid chlorides on treatment with aluminium chloride give thioindoxyl derivatives (B.A.S.F., English Patent, 14,191, 1906).

4.

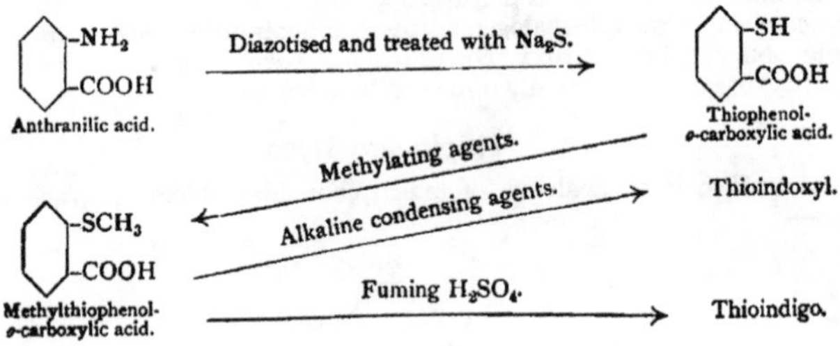

Diazotised and treated with Na₂S. - - →

Anthranilic acid.

Thiophenol-
o-carboxylic acid.

← **Methylating agents.**
← **Alkaline condensing agents.** →

Methylthiophenol-
o-carboxylic acid.

Thioindoxyl.

Fuming H₂SO₄. →

Thioindigo.

(F. v. M.L.B., English Patent, 593, 1907.)

5.

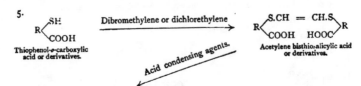

Thiophenol-*o*-carboxylic
acid or derivatives.

Dibromethylene or dichlorethylene →

Acetylene bisthiosalicylic acid
or derivatives.

Acid condensing agents. ←

Thioindigo or derivatives.

(B.A.S.F., English Patent, 26,053, 1907.)

6.

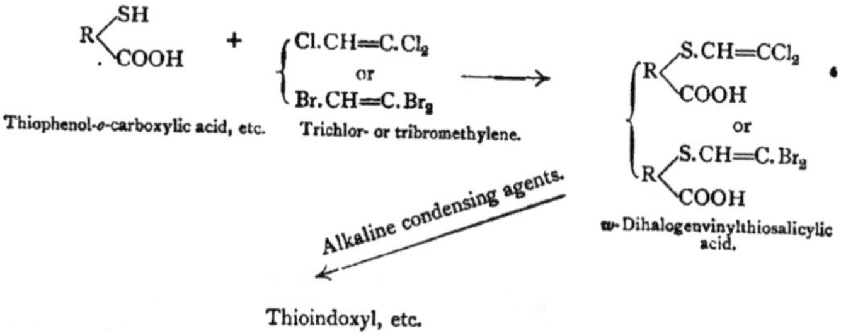

$$R\begin{cases}SH\\COOH\end{cases} + \begin{cases}Cl.CH{=}C.Cl_2\\ \text{or}\\ Br.CH{=}C.Br_2\end{cases} \longrightarrow \begin{cases}R{<}^{S.CH=CCl_2}_{COOH}\\ \text{or}\\ R{<}^{S.CH=C.Br_2}_{COOH}\end{cases}$$

Thiophenol-*o*-carboxylic acid, etc.   Trichlor- or tribromethylene.   *ω*-Dihalogenvinylthiosalicylic acid.

Alkaline condensing agents. ←

Thioindoxyl, etc.

(B.A.S.F., English Patent, 90, 1908.)

7.

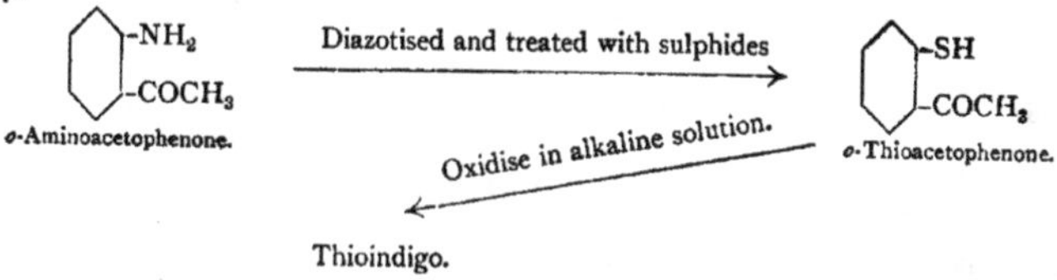

o-Aminoacetophenone $\begin{cases}-NH_2\\-COCH_3\end{cases}$ → Diazotised and treated with sulphides → $\begin{cases}-SH\\-COCH_3\end{cases}$ *o*-Thioacetophenone.

Oxidise in alkaline solution. ←

Thioindigo.

(F. v. M.L.B., English Patent, 4,541, 1908.)

Among the **derivatives of thioindigo** we may note the following: Halogen derivatives obtained from halogenised parent materials or by halogenising the dyes, as in the case of indigo (S.C.I.B., English Patent, 6,490, 1907); alkyloxy and alkylthio derivatives (F. v. M.L.B, English Patent, 1,472, 1907); amino derivatives (F. v. M.L.B., English Patent, 16,584, 1907). The *m*-amino compound (H_2N- [thioindigo structure] $-NH_2$) dyes brown shades, and the

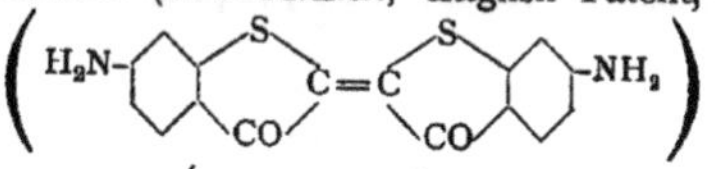

p-amino compound (H_2N- [thioindigo structure] $-NH_2$) black shades; their

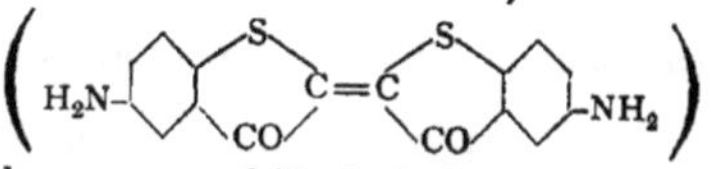

halogen derivatives dye orange and black shades respectively.

Unsymmetrical dyes containing only one thionaphthene residue have also been prepared. The condensation of thioindoxyl with isatin gives **Thioindigo Scarlet R,** the analogue of indirubin—

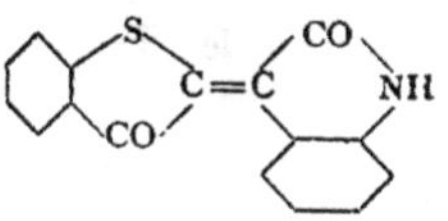

[structure: thioindoxyl condensed with isatin, C=C linking, CO, NH groups]

(Kalle, English Patent, 17,162, 1906.)

Condensation of thioindoxyl with α-isatinanilide gives **Ciba Violet A—**

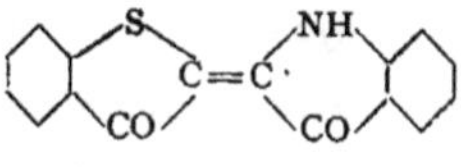

[structure: C=C linking, S, NH, CO groups]

(S.C.I.B., English Patent, 11,760, 1906.)

The same product is obtained from α-isatin chloride and thioindoxyl (Kalle, English Patent, 11,609, 1907.)

Condensation of thioindoxyl with acenaphthenequinone gives **Ciba Scarlet G**—

(S.C.I.B., English Patent, 344, 1908.)

Other Indigoid Dyes

Friedländer (*Ber.*, 41, p. 772) has described dyes which contain half the indigo molecule, and may be termed indigoid dyes. They are obtained by condensing α-isatin derivatives with phenolic compounds such as 1-naphthol, 1-anthrol, or their derivatives. The reactions between α-isatin chloride and 1-naphthol may be given thus—

See also for these dyes, English Patents, 7,819, 1909 (Bayer); 3,206, 1910 (Kalle).

4. DI- AND TRIARYLMETHANE DYES

Under this heading are grouped a number of dyes, which may be regarded as derivatives of diphenylmethane and triphenylmethane—

Diphenylmethane.   Triphenylmethane.

One or more of the phenyl groups may be replaced by naphthyl groups to give, *e.g.*, diphenylnaphthylmethane dyes.

(a) Diphenylmethane Dyes

The only important dyes of this class are the **Auramines**.

Auramine is obtained by treating tetramethyldiaminobenzophenone with ammonia; the reaction may be expressed :—

$$CO{<}^{C_6H_4N(CH_3)_2}_{C_6H_4N(CH_3)_2} + NH_3 = HN{=}C{<}^{C_6H_4N(CH_3)_2}_{C_6H_4N(CH_3)_2} + H_2O.$$

This represents the dye base as an imide; the dye is employed in the form of its hydrochloride, which may be formulated either as the hydrochloride of the imide base, or as—

$$H_2N{-}C{<}^{C_6H_4N(CH_3)_2}_{\underset{\underset{Cl}{|}}{C_6H_4{=}N(CH_3)_2}}$$

Auramine may also be obtained by treating tetramethyldiaminodiphenylmethane, $CH_2{<}^{C_6H_4N(CH_3)_2}_{C_6H_4N(CH_3)_2}$, with sulphuric acid and then with ammonia.

The parent materials, tetramethyldiaminobenzophenone and tetramethyldiaminodiphenylmethane, are prepared by the action of phosgene and formaldehyde, respectively, on dimethylaniline.

Auramine dyes wool, silk, or tannin-mordanted cotton bright yellow shades.

Auramine G is prepared similarly from dimethyldiaminoditolylmethane.

(b) Triphenylmethane Dyes

These may be divided broadly into two types: (1) those containing amino groups; (2) those containing hydroxy groups, with or without carboxylic groups. The first of these, which is the more important, may again be subdivided into dyes containing two amino groups (Malachite Green type) and dyes containing three amino groups (Rosaniline type).

Before discussing the individual dyes of these groups, it will be well to consider generally their constitution. There are three stages to be considered in the formation of the amino dyes—the leuco base, the carbinol base, and the dye itself. The leuco bases are the triphenylmethane derivatives—thus Paraleucaniline, the leuco base of Pararosaniline, is triaminotriphenylmethane; oxidation of this body gives the carbinol base—

$$HC \Big\langle \begin{matrix} C_6H_4NH_2 \\ C_6H_4NH_2 \\ C_6H_4NH_2 \end{matrix} \qquad\qquad HO.C \Big\langle \begin{matrix} C_6H_4NH_2 \\ C_6H_4.NH_2 \\ C_6H_4NH_2 \end{matrix}$$

Triaminotriphenylmethane.   Carbinol base of triaminotriphenylmethane.

The dye **Pararosaniline** is the hydrochloride of this body, less the elements of water. Several formulæ are possible for such a body, and there has been considerable controversy as to the correct one. The balance of evidence appears to favour Nietzki's formula representing this body as quinonoid—*

$$C \Big\langle \begin{matrix} C_6H_4NH_2 \\ C_6H_4NH_2 \\ C_6H_4\!=\!NH_2 \\ \quad | \\ \quad Cl \end{matrix}$$

It should be noted that both the leuco base and the carbinol base are colourless—it is only when the carbinol base is converted into a salt that the dye results.

General Methods of Production

Triphenylmethane derivatives may be produced by a variety of processes. In each of these some compound must be present which will supply the methane carbon. Thus, for instance, benzaldehyde condenses with two molecules of dimethylaniline giving tetramethyldiaminodiphenylmethane, the leuco base of **Malachite Green**—

$$C_6H_5CHO \; + \; \begin{matrix} C_6H_5N(CH_3)_2 \\ C_6H_5N(CH_3)_2 \end{matrix} \longrightarrow C_6H_5.CH \Big\langle \begin{matrix} C_6H_4N(CH_3)_2 \\ C_6H_4N(CH_3)_2 \end{matrix}$$

Benzaldehyde.   Dimethylaniline.   Leuco base of Malachite Green.

Or a methyl group attached to an aromatic nucleus may supply the methane carbon as in the production of Paraleucaniline (v. supra) by oxidising a mixture of p-toluidine and aniline:—

$$NH_2.C_6H_4.CH_3 \; + \; \begin{matrix} C_6H_5NH_2 \\ C_6H_5NH_2 \end{matrix} \longrightarrow NH_2.C_6H_4.CH \Big\langle \begin{matrix} C_6H_4NH_2 \\ C_6H_4NH_2 \end{matrix}$$

p-Toluidine.   Aniline.   Paraleucaniline.

In the "New Fuchsine" process formaldehyde is employed. This condenses with two molecules of aniline to form diaminodiphenylmethane, which is then oxidised together with aniline and aniline hydrochloride to give Pararosaniline—

$$CH_2O \; + \; 2C_6H_5NH_2 \longrightarrow CH_2(C_6H_4NH_2)_2;$$

Formalde-   Aniline.   Diaminodiphenylmethane.
hyde.

---

* For a summary of the evidence see Sidgwick's "Organic Chemistry of Nitrogen," Oxford, 1910, p. 61.

$$CH_2 \underset{C_6H_4NH_2}{\overset{C_6H_4NH_2}{\diagup}} + C_6H_5NH_2HCl \longrightarrow ClH_2N = C_6H_4 = C \underset{C_6H_4NH_2}{\overset{C_6H_4NH_2}{\diagup}}$$

Diamino-   Aniline hydro-   Pararosaniline.
diphenylmethane.   chloride.

Phosgene, again, reacts with dimethylaniline to give tetramethyldiaminobenzophenone—

$$CO \underset{Cl}{\overset{Cl}{\diagup}} + \underset{C_6H_5N(CH_3)_2}{\overset{C_6H_5N(CH_3)_2}{}} \longrightarrow CO \underset{C_6H_4N(CH_3)_2}{\overset{C_6H_4N(CH_3)_2}{\diagup}} + 2HCl.$$

Phosgene.   Dimethylaniline.   Tetramethyldiaminobenzophenone.

This may be converted into the chloride and condensed with a further molecule of dimethylaniline, or reduced to the benzhydrol, which is condensed with dimethylaniline and the leuco compound oxidised, giving **Crystal Violet**, hexamethyl pararosaniline hydrochloride—

$$C \diagup \begin{array}{l} C_6H_4.N(CH_3)_2 \\ C_6H_4N(CH_3)_2 \\ C_6H_4 = N(CH_3)_2Cl \end{array}$$

Crystal Violet.

Oxalic acid has also been employed, as in the manufacture of **Aurine** (trioxytriphenylcarbinol anhydride) from phenol, oxalic acid, and sulphuric acid. We may suppose that formic acid is first produced, which then reacts with the phenol, giving **Aurine**—

$$C \diagup \begin{array}{l} C_6H_4OH \\ C_6H_4OH \\ C_6H_4 = O \end{array}$$

The preparation and properties of some typical triphenylmethane dyes are given below :—

Diamino Compounds (Malachite Green Series).

Malachite Green is essentially a salt of tetramethyldiaminotriphenyl carbinol. It usually appears in commerce as the zinc or iron double chloride, or the oxalate. Its method of preparation has already been indicated. It dyes wool, silk, and tannin-mordanted cotton green.

Brilliant Green is prepared similarly from benzaldehyde and diethylaniline ; its dyeing properties are similar to those of Malachite Green.

Setoglaucine is prepared from *o*-chlorbenzaldehyde and dimethylaniline.

Setocyanine, Victoria Green 3B, and **Glacier Blue** are other dyes of this type.

The above-described dyes are basic dyes ; the sulphonic acids of this series are acid wool dyes. Examples are **Erioglaucine A**, from benzaldehyde-*o*-sulphonic acid and ethylbenzylaniline sulphonic acid, **Night Blue B**, from *o*-chlor-*m*-nitrobenzaldehyde and ethylbenzylaniline sulphonic acid ;

$$C \diagup \begin{array}{l} C_6H_4N(C_2H_5)_2 \\ C_6H_2 \diagleft \begin{array}{l} OH \\ SO_3Na \\ SO_3 \end{array} \\ C_6H_4 = N(C_2H_5)_2 \end{array}$$

Patent Blue V is obtained by condensing *m*-oxybenzaldehyde with diethylaniline and sulphonating the product, or from *m*-nitrobenzaldehyde and diethylaniline, reducing and diazotising to form the hydroxy group, and sulphonating.

Patent Blue A is the corresponding product from ethylbenzylaniline.

The mordant dyes, **Chrome Green**, **Chrome Violet**, and **Chrome Blue**,

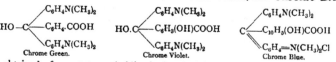

Chrome Green.   Chrome Violet.   Chrome Blue.

are obtained from tetramethyldiaminobenzhydrol and benzoic, salicylic, or α-oxynaphthoic acid respectively, and may also be included in this class.

Triamino Compounds—Rosaniline Series.

Pararosaniline (Parafuchsine, Paramagenta) has already been referred to (pp. 55, 56).

Rosaniline (Fuchsine, Magenta) is the hydrochloride of triaminodiphenyl-tolylcarbinol—

$$C \underset{\diagdown C_6H_4=NH_2Cl}{\overset{\diagup C_6H_3(CH_3)NH_2}{-C_6H_4NH_2}}$$

and is prepared similarly either by oxidising a mixture of aniline and *o-* and *p-*toluidine by various oxidising agents, or by the New Fuchsine process from formaldehyde, aniline, and *o*-toluidine. **New Fuchsine** (hydrochloride of triamino-tritolylcarbinol) is prepared from formaldehyde and *o*-toluidine.

These three dyes are basic dyes, dyeing wool, silk, and tannin-mordanted cotton red shades.

Rosaniline is one of the oldest synthetic dyes, having been put on the market in 1859 by Verguin. The constitution of this and Pararosaniline was not, however, ascertained until 1878 by E. and O. Fischer (see for example Georgevics, "Chemistry of Dyestuffs," p. 137). The alkylated, benzylated, and arylated rosaniline dyes are also basic dyes; they are obtained either by alkylating, etc., the rosanilines or by treating the corresponding tertiary amines according to the general processes indicated above. Examples are :—

Hofmann Violet, a mixture of mono-, di-, and tri-methyl or -ethyl rosaniline and pararosaniline hydrochloride, from methyl or ethyl halides and rosaniline and pararosaniline.

Aniline Blue, spirit soluble, triphenylrosaniline and triphenyl-pararosaniline hydrochloride, by the action of aniline on impure rosaniline.

Methyl Violet, penta- and hexa-methyl-pararosaniline, by the oxidation of dimethylaniline.

Crystal Violet, from dimethylaniline (*v.* above).

Ethyl Violet, the corresponding dye from diethylaniline.

$$C \underset{\diagdown C_6H_4=N(CH_3)_2Cl}{\overset{\diagup C_6H_4N(CH_3)_2}{-C_6H_4N(CH_3)_2Cl}}$$

Methyl Green, heptamethylpararosaniline chloride, by acting on Methyl Violet with methyl chloride.

Ethyl Green, ethylhexamethyl pararosanilinechlorbromide, by treating Methyl Violet with ethyl bromide.

Benzyl Violet, obtained by acting on Methyl Violet with benzyl chloride.

The sulphonic acids of the rosaniline series are obtained either by sulphonating the basic dyes, or from the amine sulphonic acids. Typical examples are :—

Acid Magenta, a mixture of trisulphonic acids of rosaniline and pararosaniline obtained by sulphonation of the bases, dyes wool in acid baths.

Alkali Blue, monosulphonic acid of triphenylrosaniline and triphenylpararosaniline, obtained by sulphonation, dyes wool in an alkaline bath.

Soluble Blue is the corresponding trisulphonic acid, and dyes silk and mordanted cotton.

Höchst New Blue, a trisulphonic acid obtained by sulphonation of trimethyltriphenylpararosaniline (obtained from phosgene and methyldiphenylamine), dyes wool from acid baths.

Acid Violet 6B, disulphonic acid of dimethyldiethyldibenzyltriaminotriphenylcarbinol, obtained from dimethyl-*p*-aminobenzaldehyde and ethylbenzylaniline sulphonic acid, dyes wool from acid baths.

Eriocyanine A, tetramethyldibenzylrosanilinedisulphonic acid, from tetramethyldiaminobenzhydrol sulphonic acid and dibenzylaniline sulphonic acid, dyes wool reddish blue in acid baths.

We may include here the triaminodiphenylnaphthylmethane dyes :—

$$C \Big\langle \begin{array}{l} C_6H_4N(CH_3)_2 \\ C_6H_4N(CH_3)_2 \\ C_{10}H_6{=}NC_6H_5.HCl \end{array}$$

Victoria Blue B is obtained from phenyl-*a*-naphthylamine and tetramethyldiaminobenzophenone chloride or tetramethyldiaminobenzhydrol. It dyes wool, silk, or cotton from acid baths, or mordanted cotton.

$$C \Big\langle \begin{array}{l} C_6H_4N(C_2H_5)_2 \\ C_6H_4N(C_2H_5)_2 \\ C_{10}H_6{=}NC_7H_7.HCl \end{array}$$

Night Blue is similarly obtained from *p*-tolyl-*a*-naphthylamine, and has similar dyeing properties.

Hydroxy Compounds—Aurine Series

Aurine, rosolic acid, has already been referred to; it is used for colouring varnishes.

$$HO{-}C \Big\langle \begin{array}{l} C_6H_3(OH)COOH \\ C_6H_3(OH)COOH \\ C_6H_3(OH)COOH \end{array}$$

Chrome Violet, aurine tricarboxylic acid, is obtained from formaldehyde and salicylic acid; used for printing chrome mordanted cotton.

A number of mordant dyes of this series have been prepared recently; see English Patents, 15,204, 1907 (Geigy); 14,311, 1909; 14,312, 1909; 368, 1910; 1,411, 1910; 6,364, 1910 (Bayer); 12,130, 1910; 17,087, 1910 (M.L.B.).

We may finally note the azotriphenylmethane dyes, one of which, **Alizarin Yellow F.S.,** has already been referred to under azo dyes. They are obtained from triphenylmethane dyes containing free amino groups by diazotising and coupling with components and oxidising. For example—

$$HO{-}C \Big\langle \begin{array}{l} C_6H_4N(CH_3)_2 \\ C_6H_4.N{=}NC_6H_3(OH).COOH \\ C_6H_4N(CH_3)_2 \end{array}$$

Azo Green is obtained from diazotised *m*-aminotetramethyldiaminotriphenylmethane and salicylic acid; dyes chromed wool.

Phenolphthalein, the lactone of dioxytriphenylcarbinolcarboxylic acid, obtained from phenol and phthalic anhydride, may be classed in the aurine series, though its production is analogous to that of the phthaleins (*q.v.*); it is employed as an indicator in volumetric analysis.

5. PYRONE DYES

The dyes of this class are closely allied to the di- and tri-phenylmethane dyes, and are sometimes classed with them. It is more convenient, however, to treat them as a separate group and to regard them as pyrone or xanthene derivatives. They all contain the pyrone ring—

and may be regarded as derivatives of Xanthene, $C_6H_4 \underset{CH_2}{\overset{O}{\diagup\diagdown}} C_6H_4$, or of **Meso-**

Phenylxanthene, $C_6H_4 \underset{H\diagup C \diagdown C_6H_5}{\overset{O}{\diagup\diagdown}} C_6H_4$.

The **Pyronines** are obtained by condensing formaldehyde with dialkyl-*m*-aminophenols, thus—

$$(CH_3)_2N \diagdown_{C_6H_4} \diagup^{OH} \qquad HO \diagdown_{C_6H_4} \diagup^{N(CH_3)_2}$$

$$CH_2O$$

$$\downarrow$$

$$(CH_3)_2N \diagdown_{C_6H_3} \diagup^{OH} \quad HO \diagdown_{C_6H_3} \diagup^{N(CH_3)_2}$$

$$CH_2$$

$$\downarrow$$

$$(CH_3)_2N.C_6H_3 \underset{CH_2}{\overset{O}{\diagup\diagdown}} C_6H_3N(CH_3)_2$$

which on oxidation gives **Pyronine G**, $(CH_3)_2N—C_6H_3 \underset{CH}{\overset{O}{\diagup\diagdown}} C_6H_3=N(CH_3)_2Cl.$

Pyronine B is the corresponding product from diethyl-*m*-aminophenol. These dye cotton, wool, and silk red, but are not very fast.

The next group to be considered are **Fluorescein** and its derivatives, the **Eosines,** etc.

Fluorescein is obtained by the reaction of phthalic anhydride on resorcin thus—

$$HO \diagdown_{C_6H_4} \diagup^{OH} \; HO \diagdown_{C_6H_4} \diagup^{OH} \qquad \longrightarrow \qquad HO \diagdown_{C_6H_3} \diagup^{O} \diagdown_{C_6H_3} \diagup^{OH}$$

$$\underset{C_6H_4 \overline{\quad} CO}{\overset{CO}{\underset{\diagdown O}{|}}} \qquad \qquad \underset{C_6H_4—CO}{\overset{C}{\underset{\diagdown O}{\diagup\diagdown}}}$$

It may also be formulated $HO—C_6H_3 \underset{C}{\overset{O}{\diagup\diagdown}} C_6H_3=O.$ Its alkali salts are soluble

$$C_6H_4COOH$$

in water with a beautiful green fluorescence, whence the name. They dye silk and wool yellow. **Eosine**, tetrabromfluorescein, is obtained by brominating fluorescein. **Erythrosine**, tetraiodofluorescein, is obtained by iodising. **Erythrene** and **Spirit Eosine** are methyl and ethyl ethers of eosine. **Phloxine**, tetrabrom-tetrachlorfluorescein, is obtained by brominating the tetrachlorfluorescein from tetrachlorphthalic acid and resorcin. **Phloxine P** is the tetrabromdichlorfluorescein obtained by brominating the dichlorfluorescein from dichlorphthalic acid and resorcin. **Rose Bengal** and **Rose Bengal 3B** are the corresponding tetraiododichlor- and tetraiodotetrachlorfluorescein. These dye animal fibres yellowish red to bluish red shades ; not very fast.

Fluorescein, as formulated above, is a dioxy-mesophenylxanthenecarboxylic acid or its lactone ; the next group to be considered, the **Rhodamines,** are amino derivatives of mesophenylxanthene carboxylic acid.

Rhodamine B, $Cl(C_2H_5)_2N=C_6H_3 \underset{C—C_6H_4.COOH}{\overset{O}{\diagup\diagdown}} C_6H_3—N(C_2H_5)_2$, can be obtained either by condensing two molecular proportions of diethyl-*m*-aminophenol with phthalic anhydride, or by condensing equimolecular proportions of diethyl-m-aminophenol and phthalic anhydride to form diethyl-p-amino-o-oxybenzoylbenzoic acid, which is then condensed with a further molecular proportion of diethyl-m-aminophenol.

$$(C_2H_5)_2N\diagdown_{C_6H_4}\diagup^{OH} \ + \ \begin{matrix}CO-O\\ |\quad\ |\\ C_6H_4-CO\end{matrix} \longrightarrow (C_2H_5)_2N\diagdown_{C_6H_3}\diagup^{OH}_{CO}$$
$$\qquad\qquad\qquad\qquad\qquad\qquad\qquad\qquad\overset{|}{C_6H_4-CO.OH}$$

$$(C_2H_5)_2N\diagdown_{C_6H_3}\diagup^{OH}_{CO} \ + \ HO\diagdown_{C_6H_4}\diagup N(C_2H_5)_2 \longrightarrow (C_2H_5)_2N-C_6H_3\diagdown\overset{O}{\diagup}\diagdown C_6H_3-N(C_2H_5)_2$$
$$\qquad\qquad\overset{|}{C_6H_4.COOH}\qquad\qquad\qquad\qquad\qquad\qquad\qquad\qquad\overset{|}{C_6H_4COOH}$$

By this second method unsymmetrical rhodamines can be obtained, for example :—

Rhodine 2G from dimethylaminooxybenzoylbenzoic acid and ethyl-m-aminophenol, the carboxylic group of the dye being finally converted into its ethyl ester.

Rhodamine 12GM, from dimethylaminooxybenzoylbenzoic acid and resorcinmethyl ester, and esterification of the product.

Irisamine G, from dimethylaminooxybenzoylbenzoic acid and m-amino-p-cresol, the product being esterified.

Rhodamine B can also be obtained by converting fluorescein into its chloride by PCl_5, and treating the chloride with diethylamine :—

$$HO-C_6H_3\diagdown\overset{O}{\diagup}\diagdown C_6H_3-OH \longrightarrow Cl-C_6H_3\diagdown\overset{O}{\diagup}\diagdown C_6H_3-Cl \longrightarrow$$
$$\qquad\overset{|}{C_6H_4COOH}\qquad\qquad\qquad\qquad\overset{|}{C_6H_4COOH}$$

$$(C_2H_5)_2N-C_6H_3\diagdown\overset{O}{\diagup}\diagdown C_6H_3-N(C_2H_5)_2$$
$$\overset{|}{C_6H_4COOH.}$$

By applying this method the corresponding arylaminoxanthene derivatives can be produced, the sulphonic acids of which are acid wool dyes (whereas the Rhodamines described above are basic dyes, dyeing tannined cotton, wool, or silk various shades of red).

Examples of such acid dyes are :—

Fast Acid Violet B (Violamine B), $C_6H_5N=C_6H_3\diagdown\overset{O}{\diagup}\diagdown C_6H_3-NH.C_6H_4SO_3Na$, obtained
$$\qquad\qquad\qquad\qquad\qquad\qquad\qquad\overset{|}{C_6H_4COONa}$$

by sulphonating the product of reaction of aniline on fluorescein chloride.

Fast Acid Violet A2R (Violamine R), and **Violamine G,** are the corresponding sulphonic acids obtained by sulphonation of the products from o-toluidine and p-phenetidine respectively.

The above derivatives of phthalic acid are known as **Phthaleins**; succinic anhydride gives similar products known as **Succineins.** For example :—

Rhodamine S, $Cl(CH_3)_2N=C_6H_3\diagdown\overset{O}{\diagup}\diagdown C_6H_3N(CH_3)_2.$
$$\qquad\qquad\qquad\qquad\overset{|}{C_2H_4COOH}$$

Finally, mention should be made of two phthaleins of somewhat different properties, viz. :—

Galleine from gallic acid or pyrogallol and phthalic anhydride, a violet mordant dye, and **Caeruleine,** an anthracene derivative, obtained by treating galleine with concentrated sulphuric acid ; a green mordant dye :—

Galleine.

Coeruleine.

6. AZINE DYES

The azines are characterised by containing the azine (pyrazine, paradiazine) ring :—

The azine dyes of the anthracene series (indanthrene, etc.) have already been described. We shall consider here those azines which contain other aromatic nuclei. The simple azines, like diphenazine, , or naphthophenazine,

, like the simple azo compounds, are not dyes. But when the nuclei contain suitable substituents ("auxochromes"), such as NH_2 or OH, the products are in general dyes. It is now usual to formulate the azine dyes as possessing an ortho-quinonoid structure, and this practice will be followed in the succeeding pages.

In some cases, *e.g.*, the safranines, alkyl or aryl groups are attached to one of the two nitrogen atoms, which is then regarded as quinquevalent, the dyes being then referred to as azonium compounds,—*e.g.*, **Safranine T**—

i.e., meso-phenyldiaminoditolylazonium chloride, mixed with the corresponding meso-tolyl body.

The principal group of azines to be considered are the **Eurhodines,** the **Rosindulines** and **Isorosindulines,** the **Safranines,** and the **Indulines.**

The **Eurhodines** are aminodiphenazines, the **Rosindulines** and **Isorosindulines** are naphthophenazine compounds, the **Safranines** are, as previously stated, meso-alkyl- or -aryl-diaminoazines, while the **Indulines** are meso-alkyl- or -aryl- tri- and -tetraaminoazines.

The following general methods for the production of azines should be noted :—

1. Condensation and Oxidation of a *p*-nitroso derivative of an amine with a second amine. For example :—

p-Nitrosodimethyl aniline.   *m*-Toluylene diamine.   Neutral Red (an eurhodine).

Instead of a *p*-nitroso compound, a *p*-diamine or a *p*-aminoazo compound may be used; for example :—

$$(CH_3)_2N-C_6H_4 \underset{NH_2}{\overset{NH_2}{\big<}} + C_6H_4.NH_2 + 3O + HCl \rightarrow (CH_3)_2N-C_6H_3 \underset{N}{\overset{N}{\big<}}\rangle C_6H_3-NH_2.HCl$$

p-Aminodimethylaniline.   *m*-Phenylenediamine.   Neutral Violet (an eurhodine).

$$(CH_3)_2N-C_6H_4 \underset{+}{\overset{N=N-C_6H_5}{\big<}} \quad \underset{C_6H_5}{\overset{C_6H_5}{\underset{NH}{|}}} C_6H_3 \underset{NH_2}{\overset{CH_3}{\big<}} + O + HCl \longrightarrow$$

p-Phenylazodimethyl   Phenyl-*m*-toluylene
aniline.   diamine.

$$C_6H_5NH_2 + (CH_3)_2N.C_6H_3 \underset{N}{\overset{N}{\big<}} C_6H_3 \underset{NH_2}{\overset{CH_3}{\big<}}$$
Aniline.

$$\underset{C_6H_5 \quad Cl}{}$$

Rhoduline (a safranine).

In the latter reaction it will be noted that the azo compound splits up and an amine forms as a bye-product.

2. Both the azine nitrogen atoms may be obtained from an *o*-diamine or *o*-aminoazo compound, *e.g.* :—

$$CH_3\underset{}{\overset{}{\diagdown}}C_6H_3 \underset{NH}{\overset{NH_2}{\big<}} + C_{10}H_7NH_2 + 3O + HCl \longrightarrow CH_3-C_6H_3 \underset{N}{\overset{N}{\big<}} C_{10}H_5.NH_2$$
$$\underset{C_2H_5}{|}$$

Ethyl-*o*-toluylene   α-Naphthylamine. $$\underset{C_2H_5 \quad Cl}{}$$
diamine.   Induline Scarlet (a rosinduline).

or

$$CH_3-C_6H_3 \underset{NH-C_6H_5}{\overset{N=NR}{\big<}} + C_{10}H_7NH_2 + O + HCl \longrightarrow CH_3-C_6H_3 \underset{N}{\overset{N}{\big<}} C_{10}H_5NH_2 \quad + R.NH_2$$
$$\underset{C_2H_5 \quad Cl}{}$$

Azo derivative of ethyl-*p*-   α-Naphthylamine.   Induline Scarlet.
toluidine.

3. The most important method is that in which three components are used; this method is largely employed for obtaining Safranines.

Obviously this method is capable of yielding a great variety of products. The process may be carried out either in one step or two. If, for example, a *p*-nitroso compound of an amine is condensed with another amine, an intermediate product, an indamine, is formed, thus :—

$$(CH_3)_2NC_6H_4NO + C_6H_5NH_2 + HCl \longrightarrow (CH_3)_2N=C_6H_4=N-C_6H_4NH_2$$
p-Nitrosodimethylaniline.   Aniline.   Indamine.

The indamines are too unstable to be used for dyes, but on oxidation with another molecule of an amine give azines, *e.g.* :—

$$Cl(CH_3)_2-N=C_6H_4 \underset{+}{\overset{N}{\diagup}} C_6H_4.NH_2$$
$$\underset{C_6H_5}{\overset{NH_2}{\underset{|}{}}} + 2O \longrightarrow (CH_3)_2N-C_6H_3 \underset{N}{\overset{N}{\big<}} C_6H_3NH_2$$

$$\underset{C_6H_5 \quad Cl}{}$$
Methylene Violet (a safranine).

Obviously, instead of a *p*-nitroso compound a *p*-diamine or *p*-aminoazo compound may be used.

The three components may be directly condensed and oxidised to the azine without isolation of an intermediate indamine. This was the method by which the first synthetic dye, **Mauveine**, was obtained by Perkin in 1856. Mauveine is a mixture of Safranines obtained by oxidising an impure aniline containing toluidine. It consists of—

$$NH_2C_6H_3{<}^{N}_{N}{>}C_6H_3NHC_6H_5 \quad C_6H_5 \quad Cl$$

and its homologues.

Safranine T, previously referred to (p. 61), is obtained by this method from *p*-toluylene-diamine, aniline, and *o*-toluidine, or *p*-toluidine and *o* toluidine (two molecules).

Similarly, **Phenosafranine**, mesophenyl-diaminophenazonium chloride, is obtained from *p*-phenylenediamine and two molecular proportions of aniline.

The indulines are produced by a similar method; **Induline** itself contains mesophenyl-dianilinoaminodiphenazonium chloride, and mesophenyl- tri- and -tetra-anilinophenazonium chloride :—

and is prepared by heating aminoazobenzene with aniline and aniline hydrochloride. Here arylamino groups are introduced into the molecule by means of the excess of aniline.

Nigrosine is similar in composition, and is prepared by heating aniline and its hydrochloride with nitrobenzene and a metal. These two dyes are principally used in the production of varnishes and inks (see p. 113).

4. **Another method which is a direct condensation without oxidation, viz., condensation of an *o*-diamine with an *o*-quinone,** is illustrated by the preparation of **Flavinduline** :—

Phenanthrene-quinone.　　*o*-Aminodiphenyl amine.　　Flavinduline.

A large number of other azines are known, but the above are sufficiently typical and illustrate the general methods.

Those azines which contain only amino groups are in general basic dyes, dyeing tannin-mordanted cotton or silk usually red, violet, or blue shades. When sulphonic acid groups are present, *i.e.*, when the dyes are derived from sulphonated parent materials, or are sulphonated after their production, the products are acid wool dyes; practically the only recent developments in the azine series are in the production of acid wool dyes of the Safranine type.

We may note finally that some azo dyes have been prepared by diazotising azine dyes containing amino groups and coupling with β-naphthol, etc.; **Indoïn Blue** (diazotised Safranine T + β-naphthol) is an example.

7. OXAZINE DYES

The oxazine dyes are analogous to the azines, but contain, instead of the azine ring, the oxazine ring :—

The oxazines are usually formulated as ortho-quinonoid compounds. It will be seen from the examples given below that the general methods of preparation are analogous to those employed in the production of the azines.

The most important group of oxazines is the **Gallocyanines**, which are obtained from gallic acid and its derivatives, and are employed for producing blue shades by printing on cotton or wool with chrome mordants.

Gallocyanine itself is prepared from nitrosodimethylaniline and gallic acid :—

Nitrosodimethylaniline. Gallic acid. Gallocyanine chloride.

The free base may be formulated as the anhydride :—

By using derivatives of gallic acid other gallocyanines are produced, *e.g.*, **Prune**, from nitrosodimethylaniline and methylgallate; **Gallamine Blue**, from nitrosodimethylaniline and gallamide; **Celestine Blue B**, from nitrosodiethylaniline and gallamide. In these processes the *p*-aminoazo compounds can be used instead of the *p*-nitroso bodies (*cf.* the corresponding processes for preparing azines).

Reduction converts the gallocyanines into their leuco derivatives (**1900 Blue**, **Modern Violet**, etc.), which for some purposes are preferable to the parent dyes. The action of bisulphites also give products which are probably modified leuco derivatives. Gallocyanines can be condensed with aromatic amines or phenols; for example, **Delphine Blue** is prepared by condensing gallocyanine with aniline and sulphonating the product, while **Phenocyanine VS** is obtained from diethylgallocyanine and resorcin. By heating ordinary gallocyanine in solution or suspension in an acid, neutral or alkaline medium, CO_2 splits off and a pyrogallol-gallocyanine is obtained (see English Patents, 20,802, 1906; 9,961, 1907; 1,334, 1908).

The other oxazine dyes need not be discussed at length. Examples are :—

Meldola's Blue (New Blue), from nitrosodimethylaniline and β-naphthol; **Nile Blue A**, from nitrosodiethyl -*m*-aminophenol and α-naphthylamine; **Muscarine**. from nitrosodimethylaniline and 2 : 7-dioxynaphthalene.

Meldola's blue. Nile blue A Muscarine.

8. THIAZINE, THIAZOLE, AND SULPHIDE DYES

These three groups of dyes are conveniently considered together, as they are each characterised by containing sulphur, in a ring or otherwise.

The **Thiazines** contain the six-membered ring—

which may be compared with the azine and oxazine rings.

A typical thiazine is **Methylene Blue**, tetramethyldiaminodiphenazthionium chloride, $(CH_3)_2.N.C_6H_3{<}{\stackrel{N}{\underset{S}{}}}{>}C_6H_3N(CH_3)_2$. It is prepared by oxidising dimethyl-

p-phenylenediamine together with sodium thiosulphate to give the thiosulphonic acid, $(CH_3)_2N.C_6H_3{<}{\stackrel{NH_2}{S.SO_3H}}'$, which is then oxidised with dimethylaniline to the indamine, $(CH_3)_2N{=}C_6H_3{=}N{-}C_6H_4{-}N(CH_3)_2$, which, on further oxidation, gives

first Leucomethylene Blue, $(CH_3)_2N.C_6H_3{<}{\stackrel{NH}{\underset{S}{}}}{>}C_6H_3{-}N(CH_3)_2$, and then the dye.

Methylene blue is a basic dye, dyeing tannin-mordanted cotton. It has also therapeutic properties.

New Methylene Blue N, diethyldiaminotoluphenazthionium chloride, is obtained similarly from *p*-aminoethyl-*o*-toluidine, sodium thiosulphate, and ethyl-*o*-toluidine, and has similar properties.

Brilliant Alizarin Blue, ethylbenzylaminophenodioxynaphthazthionium sulphonic acid anhydride, is obtained by oxidising *p*-aminoethylsulphobenzylaniline thiosulphonic acid and β-naphthohydroquinone :—

It dyes chromed wool, cotton, or silk.

Another method of obtaining the thiazine ring consists of the use of sulphuretted hydrogen and ferric chloride ; for example :—

Gentianine, dimethyldiaminodiphenazthionium chloride,

is obtained by oxidising by means of ferric chloride, *p*-phenylenediamine with dimethyl-*p*-phenylenediamine in presence of sulphuretted hydrogen.

5

The **Thiazoles** contain the five-membered ring :—

$$\begin{array}{c}
\text{N} \\
\text{C} \diagup \diagdown \\
\| \text{C}— \\
\text{C} \diagdown \diagup \\
\text{S}
\end{array}$$

The typical thiazole is **Primuline,** a yellow direct cotton dye ; it is obtained by heating *p*-toluidine with sulphur, whereby dehydrothiotoluidine,

$$\text{H}_2\text{N.C}_6\text{H}_4.\text{C}{=}\text{N}—\text{C}_6\text{H}_3\text{CH}_3$$
$$\diagdown \text{S} \diagup ,$$

is first formed ; this, on further heating with sulphur, condenses to the primuline base :—

$$\text{H}_2\text{N.C}_6\text{H}_4.\text{C}{=}\text{N.C}_6\text{H}_3.\text{C}{=}\text{N.C}_6\text{H}_3.\text{C}{=}\text{N.C}_6\text{H}_3\text{CH}_3 ,$$
$$\diagdown \text{S} \diagup \diagdown \text{S} \diagup \diagdown \text{S} \diagup$$

which is sulphonated to give Primuline.

As previously described, Primuline can be diazotised and combined with azo dye components, and it is used thus for producing azo dyes on the fibre (see **Developing Dyes,** p. 450).

Methylation of dehydrothiotoluidine gives **Thioflavine T,**

$$\begin{array}{c}
\text{CH}_3\ \text{Cl} \\
\diagdown \diagup \\
\text{CH}_3.\text{C}_6\text{H}_3 \diagdown \diagup \text{C.C}_6\text{H}_4\text{N(CH}_3)_2 \\
\text{S}
\end{array}$$

which dyes tannin-mordanted cotton or silk greenish yellow.

The **Sulphide Dyes** (p. 65) form a very large and important group. They are characterised in general by the property of dissolving in sodium sulphide solutions and dyeing cotton from such a bath. Some, however, are insoluble in sodium sulphide, but dissolve in alkali hydrosulphite and thus behave as vat dyes. The method of preparation is very simple, consisting in melting the parent substance with sulphur or more usually with sulphur and sodium sulphide. The parent substances used are very diverse. The first sulphide dyes were prepared from natural organic bodies, such as sawdust, bran, woodpulp, etc., and the product, **Cachou de Laval,** dyed cotton brown shades. The first sulphur dye from a synthetic organic compound was **Vidal Black** from *p*-aminophenol. A large number of sulphide dyes have been prepared from diphenylamine derivatives, *e.g.,* **Immedial Black V,** from dinitrooxydiphenylamine, **Immedial Sky Blue,** from diethyl-*p*-amino-*p'*-oxy-diphenylamine.

Cassella & Co. form indophenolic bodies by condensing *p*-nitrosophenol with carbazole or its N-alkyl, etc., derivatives ; and then sulphurise. **Hydroin Blue R** and **G** (see English Patents, 2,918, 1909 ; 9,689, 1909 ; 14,143, 1909 ; 18,822, 1909 ; 22,138, 1910) are vat dyes of this type.

The sulphur dyes derived from anthraquinone have already been referred to (see **Anthracene Dyes,** p. 458).

Although so many sulphur dyes have been prepared, their constitution is not known with certainty. Probably many of them, for example, Immedial Sky Blue, contain a thiazine ring, and also contain a thio or dithio group (R.S.H. or R.S.S.R.).

9. ACRIDINE DYES

This is a small group of basic dyes, which contain the acridine nucleus,

$$\begin{array}{c}
\text{N} \\
\diagdown \diagup \\
| \\
\text{CH}
\end{array}$$

. A typical method of preparation may be illustrated by the case of

Acridine Yellow, diaminodimethylacridine ; condensation of formaldehyde with *m*-toluylenediamine gives tetraminoditolylmethane

$$H_2N\diagdown_{H_3C}\diagup C_6H_2\diagup^{NH_2}\diagdown_{CH_2\cdot}\cdots\diagup^{H_2N}\diagdown C_6H_2\diagup^{NH_2}\diagdown_{CH_2}$$

from which, on heating with acids, ammonia splits off, giving a hydroacridine derivative:

$$HCl.H_2N\cdot\diagdown_{CH_3}\diagup C_6H_2\diagup^{NH}\diagup_{CH_3}\diagdown C_6H_2\diagup^{NH_2}\diagdown_{CH_3};$$

this on oxidation, say, with ferric chloride, gives the dye,

$$HCl.H_2N\diagdown_{CH_3}\diagup C_6H_2\diagup^{N}\diagdown_{CH}\diagup C_6H_2\diagup^{NH_2}\diagdown_{CH_3}.$$

A similar condensation, using benzaldehyde and *m*-toluylenediamine, gives **Benzoflavine**, diaminodimethyl-meso-phenylacridine,

$$HCl.H_2N\diagup_{CH_3}\diagdown C_6H_2\diagdown^{N}\diagup_{C}\diagup C_6H_2\diagup^{NH_2}\diagdown_{CH_3};$$
$$\qquad\qquad\qquad|$$
$$\qquad\qquad\qquad C_6H_5$$

dyes yellow shades.

Another yellow acridine dye, which is used for dying leather, is **Phosphine**, a diaminophenylacridine,

$$C_6H_4\diagdown^{N}_{C}\diagup C_6H_3.NH_2,$$
$$\qquad\qquad |$$
$$\qquad C_6H_4.NH_2$$

first obtained as a by-product in the manufacture of Rosaniline. Its formation may be represented thus—

$$C_6H_4\diagdown^{NH_2}_{CH_3} \quad + \quad C_6H_5\diagup^{NH_2}$$
$$\qquad +$$
$$\quad C_6H_5.NH_2$$
$$\text{\footnotesize{o-Toluidine. Aniline. Aniline.}}$$
$$\longrightarrow \quad C_6H_4\diagdown^{N}_{C}\diagup C_6H_3.NH_2$$
$$\qquad\qquad\qquad\qquad |$$
$$\qquad\qquad\qquad C_6H_4.NH_2$$

10. MINOR GROUPS OF DYES

A brief description will be given here of a number of small groups of dyes :—

(*a*) **Nitro Dyes.**—Some simple nitro compounds possess dyeing properties. Examples are: **Picric acid** (trinitrophenol), **Martius yellow** (dinitro-a-naphthol), **Naphthol yellow S** and **RS** (dinitronaphthol sulphonic acids), **Aurantia** (hexanitrodiphenylamine) ; all are acid wool dyes.

Picric acid is still used to some extent for silk and leather.

(*b*) **Nitroso-Phenol** or **Quinoneoxime Dyes.**—These are practically obsolete dyes; examples are **Fast Green O** (dinitrosoresorcin or benzoquinonedioxime), **Gambine R** and **Y** (nitrosonaphthols or naphthoquinoneoximes), **Dioxine** (nitrosodioxynaphthalene or oxynaphthoquinoneoxime) ; these are mordant dyes.

(*c*) **Quinoline Dyes.**—These are chiefly of interest because of the use of some of them in photography (see **Photographic Chemicals, p. 137**).

Cyanine, obtained by the action of amyl iodide on a mixture of quinoline and lepidine, and **Quinoline Red**, from benzotrichloride, quinoline, and isoquinoline, are examples of these.

Quinoline Yellow, quinophthalone, is obtained from quinaldine and phthalic anhydride; sulphonation of this product gives a soluble wool dye.

(*d*) **Oxyketone Dyes** (other than anthracene derivatives).—A few mordant dyes of this type may be noted. **Alizarin Yellow A**, trioxybenzophenone, from benzoic acid and pyrogallol; **Alizarin Yellow C**, trioxyacetophenone, from acetic acid and pyrogallol; **Galloflavine**, obtained by oxidising gallic acid; and **Alizarin Black S** or **Naphthazarine S**, the bisulphite compound of naphthazarine,

, obtained from dinitronaphthalene by $Zn + conc. \ H_2SO_4$, or $S + SO_3$.

(*e*) **Indamines and Indophenols.**—These are compounds of the type $NH_2C_6H_4$—$N{=}C_6H_4{=}NH$ and $NH_2C_6H_4$—$N{=}C_6H_4{=}O$, respectively. They are

<small>Indamine.   Indophenol.</small>

too unstable to be used as dyes; the production of indamines as intermediate products in the manufacture of azine and thiazine dyes has already been referred to (*q.v.*). On reduction they yield diphenylamine derivatives, and hence they are of importance as the parent materials for the manufacture of sulphur dyes.

(*f*) **Aniline Black.**—This old and still highly important dye should be more properly discussed under dyeing, since it is practically always formed on the fibre, by impregnating the material with aniline salts and oxidising by means of chlorates, etc. Many variations on the process have been suggested, chiefly with a view of obtaining a black which will not turn green. One of the most recent processes is that of Green (English Patent, 16,189, 1907), according to which a small quantity of *p*-phenylenediamine, *p*-aminophenol, or the like, is added to the aniline, and the oxidation is effected by air, the *p* phenylenediamine, etc., being supposed to act catalytically.

The constitution of aniline black has been the subject of many researches. It has the empirical formula $(C_6H_5N)_x$. According to Green and Woodhead (*Journ. Chemical Society*, 1910, p. 2388), a series of quinonoid bodies containing eight nuclei can be obtained by oxidation of aniline, viz., proto-emeraldine, emeraldine, nigraniline, and pernigraniline, the first and last of these being unstable bodies; aniline blacks prepared in substance consist of a mixture of emeraldine, nigraniline, and higher condensation products, while the blacks produced on the fibre consist largely of higher condensation products. **Emeraldine** and **nigraniline** are formulated as—

and

respectively.

In subsequent publications (*Journ. Soc. Dyers*, 1913, pp. 105 *et seq.*, 338 *et seq.*), Green develops the view that his blacks are **azonium** compounds, obtained by conjoint oxidation of products of the emeraldine series with a further amount of aniline; the "aged" and "chlorate" blacks are formulated as—

while the "bichromate" blacks are regarded as the corresponding hydroxy compounds (*cf.* English Patent, 19,124, 1912).

For **Dyeing Processes** with Aniline Black (see p. 102).

CHAPTER III

The Industry of Natural Dye-Stuffs

CHAPTER III

THE INDUSTRY OF NATURAL DYE-STUFFS

LITERATURE

H. RUPE.—"Die Chemie der naturlichen Farbstoffe." 2 vols., 1900 and 1909.
R. LOWENTHAL.—"Handbuch der Farberei." 1900.
ZERR AND RÜBENCAMP.—"Treatise on Colour Manufacture." 1908.

THE natural colouring matters of animal and vegetable origin have been used for dyeing for hundreds, and in some cases for thousands, of years. Since the manufacture of the artificial colouring matters from coal-tar their use has enormously decreased. A few, however, still possess some importance, viz., indigo and logwood. Artificial indigo, however, is now being manufactured in large quantities, and no doubt in course of time the use of the natural colouring matters will entirely die out, being replaced by superior and cheaper synthetic products.

Statistics.—The following figures show the value of the natural dye-stuffs imported into the United Kingdom :—

	1906.	1913.	Value.
	Cwt.	Cwt.	
Cochineal - - - -	2,270	1,401	£13,540
Cutch - - - - -	5,217	52,781	71,545
Natural indigo - - -	7,641	4,174	54,739
Logwood - - - -	359,820	192,580	50,701
Other dye-woods - - -	70,360	51,140	35,254

Dye wood extracts were valued in 1908 at £176,318; in 1913 at £128,437.

The United States imports were :—

	1906.	1910.	Value in 1910.
Cochineal - - - -	111,000 lbs.	151,000 lbs.	$41,000
Cutch - - - - -	...	28,000 ,,	1,278
Indigo (natural) - - -	193,000 lbs.	125,000 ,,	66,000
Annatto - - - -	...	619,372 ,,	40,000
Turmeric - - - -	...	...	28,000
Dye woods in a crude state—			
Fustic - - - -	...	5,800 tons	83,000
Logwood - - - -	37,000 tons	32,000 ,,	368,000
All other - - - -	...	923 ,,	33,000
Extracts—			
Logwood and other dyewoods	3,390,000 lbs.	3,270,000 lbs.	198,000
Persian berries - - -	...	83,000 ,,	8,000
Chlorophyll - - -	...	4,000 ,,	3,000

Black and Blue Colouring Matters

Indigo is treated under **Coal-tar Colours**, p. 46.

Logwood * (Campeachy wood, German, *Blauholz*, wood of *Hæmatoxylon campechianum* of Central America) contains a colouring matter termed **hæmo-**

---

* See also pp. 97, 98,, 112.

toxylin, $C_{16}H_{14}O_6 + 3H_2O$ (yellow prisms, p. 112), which when oxidised is converted into the real colouring matter, hæmatein, $C_{16}H_{12}O_6$. This is soluble in alkalis giving a deep blue colour, and violet precipitates with aluminium salts, blue with copper, and black with iron and chromium. For dyeing purposes the wood in the form of sawdust or chips was formerly used, but now extracts are usually employed.

1. In the **American Method of extraction** the wood is extracted five times for fifteen minutes in autoclaves at 1·5 atmospheres pressure. The largest yield is thus obtained, but it contains impurities such as resin, tannic acid, sugar, etc., which influence the dyeing unfavourably.

2. In the **French Method** the extraction is made by simply boiling the wood under ordinary pressure, yielding a good and copious extract.

3. In the **Diffusion Method** the wood is extracted similar to the extraction of beets in the sugar industry. Yield small but of best quality, and therefore dear.

The extract is settled in large tanks, filtered through cloth, and concentrated by evaporation. Up to 10° Bé. the extracts are fluid; 30°-40° Bé. yield solid extracts. Logwood is exclusively used for *black* dyeing of silk, using an iron salt and some yellow colouring matter to kill the blue tone. Also used for dyeing and printing black and grey shades on calico and wool, and for shading with a blue tone other colouring matters. Except for black silk its use is being displaced by artificial colouring matters. For **Dyeing Processes**, see pp. 97, 98.

Tests.—Logwood chips may be adulterated with syrup extracts containing tannin (*e.g.*, chestnut extract) or "foots" or with excess of moisture. (1) A microscopic examination usually reveals nature of contamination. (2) Estimate the moisture (drying weighed quantity chips at 100° C.). If it contains more than 14 per cent. (usual quantity) it is adulterated and may take up 40 per cent. moisture. (3) The only reliable test is an actual dyeing test with white wool, made with definite weights of wood, thoroughly extracted, and definite weights of mordants.

Red Colouring Matters

Madder (German, *Krapp*).—Now displaced by artificial alizarin (p. 39), which see.

Redwood, Brazil Wood (*Rotholz, Bois rouge*).—Many different varieties are known (*Family* Leguminosæ, genus Cæsalpinia, found in East Indies, Central and South America, etc.). It contains the colourless base **brasilin**, $C_{16}H_{14}O_5$, which when carefully oxidised furnishes the red colouring matter **brasilein**, $C_{16}H_{12}O_5$. The constitution of brasilin is believed to be as shown—

$$HO.C_6H_5 \begin{matrix} O—CH_2 \\ | \\ CH—C.OH \\ | \\ CH_2—C_6H_2(OH)_2 \end{matrix}$$

but the substance has not as yet been synthesised. The colour is not very fast, and its use is dyeing cotton, and printing to produce mixed shades; also for wool and oils.

Santalwood (*Sandelholz*, East Indies) contains 16 per cent. of **santalin**, $C_{15}H_{14}O_5$; the extract is used for colouring confectionery, liqueurs, tinctures, etc.

Archil (*Orseille, Oricello, Orchilla*) is obtained from the algal genera *Roccella, Variolaria*, and *Lecanora*, by extracting the plants with water and warming the liquor with ammonia, when the archil is precipitated as a paste. The actual colouring principle is **orcin**, $C_6H_3(CH_3)(OH)_2$, which in the presence of air and ammonia oxidises to the violet dye orcein, $C_{28}H_{24}N_2O_7$.

Litmus (*Lachmus, Tournesol*) is likewise obtained from certain algæ (species of *Roccella* and *Lecanora*) in the East Indies, tropical America, and Canary

Islands, Scandinavian and Mediterranean coasts. The algæ are dried, ground, mixed with ammonium carbonate, potash, and lime, allowed to stand three weeks, when the material ferments and produces a blue colour. More ammonia and chalk are added, and the mass pressed into cubes and dried. Contains several colouring matters (azolitmin, litmum, etc.), which in free state are red, but with alkali form **blue** salts (hence acids turn litmus red, alkalis blue). Used as an indicator in chemistry, also for colouring liqueurs, confectionery, preserved fruit, etc. etc.

Carotine is the yellow-red colouring matter of carrots, and is used for colouring butter and cheese.

Alkanet, $C_{15}H_{14}O_4$, is obtained by extracting the root of the *Alcanna tinctoria*, and is used for colouring oils, salves, hair-oils, etc., and other cosmetic articles, since it is soluble in such media and fast.

Carmine (Cochineal) is a colouring matter contained in the females of the insect *Coccus cacti* (Mexico and Central America). The females are collected shortly before the laying season, killed by steam, dried, and sold as colouring matter under the name **Cochineal.** The colouring matter is **carmine**, which is obtained by extracting the insects with boiling water, precipitating with alum, washing and drying; it is stated to be an **aluminium calcium protein** compound of the carmine colouring matter. The cochineal insects contain 10 per cent. carminic acid, $C_{22}H_{22}O_{13}$, which is hydrolysed by dilute sulphuric acid into sugar and **carmine red,** $C_{11}H_{12}O_7$. **Carmine** is used for making face powders, colouring sweets, puddings, etc., being non-poisonous (see also p. 98).

Lac-dye, a product similar to cochineal in origin and use, is obtained from **gum-lac,** an exudation product formed by certain tree-boring insects by extracting with sodium carbonate solution. The residue left behind forms the ordinary **shellac** (see Martin's "Industrial Chemistry," Vol. I. pp. 348, 552).

The **Purple** of the ancients was obtained from a snail inhabiting the sea-coasts of the Mediterranean.

Yellow, Brown, and Green Colouring Matters

Fustic (Brazil wood, yellow wood, *Gelbholz*), from *Morus* (Maclura) *tinctoria*, contains **Morin**, $C_{15}H_{10}O_7$, and Maclurin, $C_{13}H_{10}O_6$ (a non-colouring material). **Morin** gives a yellow lake with aluminium salts, used for colouring wool yellow. Not very fast to light (see p. 98).

Quercitron, the yellow powdered bark of the oak *Quercus tinctoria* of North America, contains quercitrin, $C_{21}H_{22}O_{12} + 2H_2O$, which, on boiling with dilute acids, hydrolyses into isodulcite, $C_6H_{14}O_6$, and the yellow dye **Quercitin** or **Flavin**, $C_{15}H_{10}O_7$. Both quercitrin and quercitin form yellow lakes with aluminium and tin salts, and are consequently used for wool dyeing and printing, and largely for shading other colours (see p. 98).

Persian Berries, Yellow Berries (*Kreuzbeeren*) contain **xanthorhamnin,** a glucoside which dilute mineral acids hydrolyse into **isodulcite** and the yellow dye **rhamnetin,** $C_{16}H_{12}O_7$; the latter substance yields, when fused with potash, proto-catechuic acid, $C_6H_3.(OH)_2.CO_2H$. Yields yellow lakes with chromium, tin, and aluminium salts, fast to soap and chlorine, but only moderately fast to light. An extract is used as painters' colour and for staining paper and leather yellow (see p. 98).

Annatto (Orleans, Anatto, *Terra orellana*), obtained from the fleshy covering of the ruccu tree (*Bixa orellana*) of Central America, contains a yellow colouring matter, **bixen,** $C_{28}H_{34}O_5$, and the extract is used for colouring butter, cheese, margarine (see Martin's "Industrial Chemistry," Vol. I. pp. 75, 87, 546), etc. When annatto has been adulterated with mineral bodies, more than 10 per cent. of ash will be found.

Turmeric (Curcuma, *Gelbwurzel*).—The powdered root of the *Curcuma longa* and *C. rotunda*, contains a yellow colouring matter, **curcumine**, which can be extracted with ether, alcohol, and alkalis. Although not fast to soap or light, the substance is a useful colouring agent for wool, silk, oil, butter, and cheese (see Martin's "Industrial Chemistry," Vol. I. pp. 75, 87, 546).

Woad (Luteolin, Wau, *Gelbkraut*), from *Reseda, R. luteola*, contains **luteolin**, $C_{16}H_{10}O_6$, and dyes silk a fast yellow (with aluminium salts as mordant).

Indian Yellow, Purree (*Purrea arabica*, Piuri) is prepared at Monghyr (Bengal) from the urine of cows, fed on leaves of the mango tree. The colouring principle is the magnesium and calcium salt of euxanthic acid, $C_{19}H_{16}O_{11}Mg + 5H_2O$. Used as a permanent water and oil colour. If adulterated with chrome yellow it gives a black coloration with H_2S. If yellow aniline lakes be present the solution remains yellow when concentrated HCl is added (if pure a colourless solution should result, depositing white flakes of euxanthic acid).

Cutch (Cachou, Catechu, Japan Earth) is the brown amorphous extract obtained by boiling with water the wood of various kinds of **Acacia** in India and the East Indies. It contains **catechin** and **catechu-tannic acid**; the latter is used for tanning purposes, and being soluble in cold water may be separated from the catechin by washing cutch with cold water; crude **catechin** remains, which, being recrystallised from hot water, is obtained as fine, white, silky needles, M.P. 217° C., and of formula $C_{21}H_{20}O_9$. Cutch is used in cotton dyeing and printing, producing brown, black, grey, and olive shades, very permanent and fast to light, soap, acids, and bleaching powder. Also used for silk and wood stains (see p 95).

Dragon's Blood is a deep or brown-red resin obtained from species of **Calamus** (India, Sumatra, Moluccas) and used for colouring spirit varnishes, toilet articles, etc., a deep red (see Martin's "Industrial Chemistry," Vol. I. p. 348).

Gamboge (*Gumigutt, Gutti*) is the resin of *Garcinia Morella* (East Indies, Ceylon); forms a yellow water colour, sometimes used for colouring spirit and other varnishes; poisonous; used in pharmacy (see Martin's "Industrial Chemistry," Vol. I. pp. 348).

Saffron, Crocus (*Safran*), from dried and powdered flowers of saffron plant, *Crocus sativus* (Orient); used for colouring confectionery (see Martin's "Industrial Chemistry," Vol. I. pp. 75, 87, 546).

A **green** colouring matter is **Chlorophyll**, found in green leaves and stalks of plants, obtained by extracting grass, etc., with alcohol (or with dilute caustic potash and precipitating by mineral acids). Is fugitive in light, but is used for colouring confectionery, liqueurs, and toilet articles.

CHAPTER IV

Dyeing and Colour Printing Industry

.CHAPTER IV

DYEING AND COLOUR PRINTING INDUSTRY

LITERATURE

KNECHT, RAWSON, LOEWENTHAL.—"Manual of Dyeing." 2 vols. London, 1910.
HERZFELD, SCHNEIDER.—"Das Färben u. Bleichen der Textilfasern." 3 vols. Berlin, 1900, 1905, 1910.
PELET, JOLIVET.—"Theorie des Färbeprozesses." Dresden, 1910.
SANSONE.—"Dyeing." 2 vols. 1888.
    ,,   "Dyeing and Calico-printing." 3 vols. 1895-1897.
HIGGINS.—"Dyeing in Germany and America." Manchester, 1907.
DREAPER.—"The Chemistry and Physics of Dyeing." London, 1906.
LAUBER.—"Praktisches Handbuch des Zeugdrucks." 4 vols. Leipzig, 1902-1905.
SCHWALBE, T.—"Farbe Theorien." Stuttgart.
ZACHARIAS.—"Färbe Theorien."
GANSWINDT.—"Einfuhrung in die Moderne Färberei." Leipzig, 1902.
    ,,   "Theorie u. Praxis der Modernen Färberei." 2 vols. Leipzig, 1903.
Journal of the Society of Dyers and Colourists.

INTRODUCTION

THE object of the dyer of textiles may be said to be to impart to them, by treatment with certain solutions, a uniform colour which should be as permanent as possible to solvents and other influences. The methods of obtaining this end are manifold, and it is not to be supposed that any one explanation will fully cover all the processes employed. Even where the operations carried out in various cases are apparently similar or identical, the theory underlying them may be entirely different.

The simplest classification of dyestuffs is that, into those which are taken out of solution directly by the fibre, and into those which are produced chemically as insoluble substances during successive operations of dyeing. The former are usually termed "**substantive**," the latter "**adjective**" dyes. Dyestuffs like indigo which are reproduced in the fibre in their original condition, during successive operations, are usually said to belong to the former class, although, according to the definition just given, they would more correctly be considered to be members of the latter. Another classification often employed is that into "direct" dyes, *i.e.*, practically the same as substantive dyes and "**mordant**" dyes, *i.e.*, such as can only be applied with the intervention of a mordant. Lastly, dyes are sometimes spoken of as "**monogenetic**" when they will yield only one colour whether applied directly or with the aid of different mordants, and as "**polygenetic**" when they will yield different colours according to the mordant employed.

Substantive or Direct Dyes.—If a piece of silk, wool, and cotton be each boiled with the solution of a basic dye, such as Victoria blue or the acidified solution of an acid dye, such as acid magenta, it will be found that the silk and the wool have been dyed, whereas the cotton will probably only have acquired a slight stain which may be easily removed by washing. If the solution of the dyestuff be fairly dilute the animal fibre will remove all of it, leaving a colourless liquid behind. Again, when wool or silk is dyed with the hydrochloride of a basic dye, such as magenta (rosaniline hydrochloride), it has been shown by Knecht and Appleyard that the whole of the hydrochloric acid is left in solution and the fibre is dyed red, in spite of the fact that the base which alone has been removed from solution is colourless. Indeed it was shown by Jacquemin as early as 1876 that when either wool or silk is boiled with a colourless solution of rosaniline base, it is dyed red. These facts all point to the conclusion that the dyeing of animal fibres with most of the basic dyes is a process of a more or less chemical nature, consisting of the combination of some substance contained in the fibre with the base of the dye. Experiments may also be adduced to show that the dyeing of animal fibres with the majority of acid dyestuffs is a similar process, a conclusion which need not surprise us, for we have every reason to believe that not only wool and silk, but also most of the substances which may be formed from them by chemical decomposition, are of the nature of amido acids, *i.e.*, they have the properties both of acids and bases, and will, therefore, readily combine with dyestuffs having basic or acid properties.

The following facts may further be adduced to confirm the conclusion that acid and basic dye-stuffs are usually held by the animal fibres in a very firm manner approaching that of chemical combination. It has been shown by Dreaper in numerous cases that, when held by the animal fibre, a dyestuff is much less readily acted upon chemically than when it is in combination with a vegetable fibre, such as cotton, or than when it is in the free state. Thus, the direct cotton dye primuline was dyed on samples of silk and cotton and then diazotised. In the former case the resulting compound was shown to be incapable of coupling with R salt, whereas in the latter combination instantly took place just as if the diazotised dye had been in the free state. Similarly, the acid dye methyl orange is not turned red so readily by acid when on silk as when in solution, which points to the conclusion that it forms an orange compound with the silk. Then again, it has been shown by Knecht that the laws which govern chemical combination are to some extent obeyed ; for when different acid colouring matters of similar composition were employed in the dyeing of wool in strong solution and under similar conditions, the quantities taken up by the fibre stood in the ratio of their molecular weights.

The action on the fibre during the process of dyeing of substances other than the dyestuff is probably of the very greatest importance. Thus it appears that two slightly soluble substances which have been named respectively lanuginic and sericinic acid are produced by the action of hot water or acid on wool or silk, and it is these substances which combine with the basic or acid colouring matters of the bath. In fact it has been shown by Knecht that if wool is first boiled with 5-10 per cent. sulphuric acid, and then thoroughly washed, it dyes fuller shades in the neutral bath of acid colours than would be obtained in the ordinary way even if acid were added. This experiment is of great interest, for it shows that what is actually dyed by chemical combination is probably not the whole of the fibre, but mainly a constituent produced from it by the action of water during the operation of dyeing. Further-more it opens up the probability that the chemical process takes place largely in solution, a chemical compound of lanuginic or sericinic acid with the dye being first produced in the liquid, and then absorbed by the fibre by one of the processes of solid solution or colloidal precipitation discussed in the sequence. The fact that many dyes may be extracted from wool and silk by alcohol is sometimes adduced as an argument against chemical combination, but what is extracted in this case may very possibly usually be the chemical compound of the dyestuff with lanuginic or sericinic acid, and not the dyestuff itself.

The dyeing of cotton is probably under all circumstances a process of a slightly different order from that usually taking place with the animal fibres. During the last twenty-five years a large number of direct cotton dyes has become known. When cotton is treated with the solution of any one of these substances, it will extract a considerable amount of dyestuff from solution, and thus become dyed ; the remaining liquid will, however, be found to be by no means colourless but to retain a very large proportion of the dyestuff. Again, if the dyed fibre be treated with pure water a considerable proportion of the dye will be extracted, and by repeating the operation almost the whole may be withdrawn. The process of dyeing in this case is thus seen to be a "reversible" one, and may fairly be compared with what takes place when the solution of a substance soluble in water such as benzoic acid is shaken with a liquid such as ether in which it is likewise soluble. The solution in ether which is thus obtained may be compared with the dyed fibres; and the latter may be termed a "solid solution" of dyestuff in the cotton.

The introduction of the idea of solid solution into the theory of dyeing is due to O. N. Witt, who, however, attempted primarily to apply it to animal fibres. A law which particularly characterises solution in contrast to chemical combination is that known as Nernst's distribution law. In its application to the dyeing of fibres this law demands that if a series of experiments is carried out in which given weights of the same fibre are dyed in a given volume of the solution of the same dyestuff, containing, however, different quantities of the latter in each experiment, then after equilibrium has been established, the expression $C_f : C_s^{\frac{1}{n}}$ should have the same value in each experiment. In this expression C_f indicates the amount of dyestuff taken up by the fibre, C_s the amount left in the solution, and n the ratio of the molecular weight of the dyestuff in solution and on the fibre respectively. It has been shown particularly by v. Georgievics that this relation does hold for the dyeing of cotton in many cases, and also in a few for the dyeing of wool and silk. It must be pointed out here, however, that a relation of similar form holds for the process of "adsorption" of colloids discussed in the sequence, and that experiments on distribution like those of v. Georgievics can, therefore, not distinguish between the phenomena of solution and adsorption.

Adjective Dyes.—In all cases where the dyestuff is produced as an insoluble substance by the interaction of two soluble ones in the interior of the fibre, the processes of chemical combination with the fibre and solid solution in it may play a part, but in addition we have the possibility of the solid being trapped by the cell walls in a purely mechanical manner, and also that it may be held by them by the phenomenon of adhesion. It must be pointed out here that there are no doubt continual gradations possible between purely mechanical processes, the physical phenomena of adhesion, adsorption, and solid solution, and finally the process of chemical combination; and very probably all these gradations occur in one or another of the manifold operations which are carried out in dyeing.

A physical phenomenon which no doubt plays an important part in many of the processes of dyeing is the formation of so-called "adsorption" compounds. This phenomenon, the importance of which in dyeing has been pointed out in particular by P. Zacharias, has recently led to a "colloid-compound" or "electrical" theory of dyeing.

A large number of substances of importance to the dyer, such as tannin, many dyestuffs, such as congo red, crystal violet (base), night blue base, etc., and the fibres themselves belong to the class of colloids. Many of these substances will dissolve in water, forming what are termed colloidal solutions, i.e., solutions in which the dissolved particles are of a much larger order of magnitude than those of ordinary solutions, so that they will not diffuse through parchment and may usually be made visible by means of the ultramicroscope. These dissolved particles have been proved to bear electric charges, those of a basic nature acquiring a positive, those of an acid or neutral nature usually taking up a negative charge. It has also recently been shown by Gee and Harrison that all the fibres become negatively charged in contact with pure water, whereas in contact with acids they usually assume a positive charge. Now, if a colloidal solution containing positively charged particles is added to one in which negatively charged particles are present, these mutually attract each other and combine, to form what are called adsorption compounds. The latter are precipitated from solution, the electrical charges being neutralised at the same time. There can be little doubt that the "triple" compounds formed between tannin, metal oxides, and dyestuffs, on which the dyeing of basic dyes on cotton mainly depends, are largely due to colloidal combination, and this same phenomenon may probably play an important part in many other processes such as the fixation of metal oxides and other substances on the fibre.

Water

Most natural waters show an alkaline reaction, and for purposes of mordanting, dyeing with basic colours, and washing after dyeing should be carefully neutralised before use by a suitable acid. Sulphuric or acetic acid may be employed. The latter, though more expensive, is preferable, since a small excess accidentally added will usually not be harmful. When employing the former it may often be advantageous to add a small amount of sodium acetate in order to neutralise the free mineral acid.

For dyeing with acid colours, it will usually be indifferent whether the water employed is originally alkaline or not, since enough acid is always added during the process of dyeing to make the bath strongly acid. For dyeing with direct cotton dyes and sulphur colours hard waters should be softened before use.

Water containing even small quantities of iron or other heavy metals is as a rule useless for dyeing and mordanting operations, since the iron will usually combine with the dye, thus acting as a mordant, and produce a dull or "saddened" colour. The iron must, therefore, be got rid of by a process of softening. For use with acid dyes a very small amount of heavy metals will as a rule not be harmful. The presence of lime in large quantity in a water must be taken into consideration, since it will act as a mordant, and may often produce undesirable results. In some cases, such as in the dyeing of turkey red, the presence of lime is desirable, since it acts as an additional mordant, and produces better shades than would be otherwise obtained.

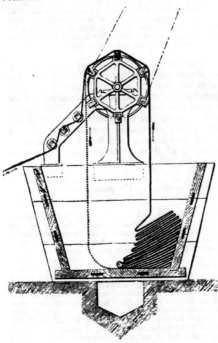

FIG. 9.—Dye Vat and Winch for Pile Fabrics.
(Mather & Platt, Manchester.)

Appliances and Machinery used in Dyeing

Preparation for Dyeing.

— The material must be freed completely from all fatty impurities by the processes described in the chapters on bleaching before it comes into the dye bath, and this refers not only to such fats and waxes as are naturally present in the fibre, but also to those which are added artificially during the operations of spinning and weaving. Bleaching is usually only necessary when delicate or bright shades are to be dyed. Wool may be carbonised either before or after dyeing in order to remove vegetable impurities such as burrs, pieces of straw, etc. In almost all cases the fibre should be thoroughly wetted out before it comes in contact with the dyeing liquid

Dissolving the Colours.

— All dyestuffs and pastes should be dissolved in condensed water and preferably filtered through cotton cloth before they are added to the dye bath. Dyewoods may be extracted in the dye vats at boiling temperature before entering the goods. For this purpose the chips are placed in bags and preferably extracted systematically, *i.e.*, the fresh chips should be employed to bring the bath completely up to strength, whereas the almost exhausted wood should be completely extracted in a bath containing fresh water. Special extractors, apart from the dye vats, are also frequently employed, and devices are also in use which may be fitted to the dye baths and in which the wood may be continuously extracted while the latter are in use.

All dyeing machinery may be said to consist of an arrangement for either moving the goods through the more or less stationary dye liquor, or for causing the dye liquor to circulate through the stationary goods. In addition, an arrangement for heating the dye vat, usually either by steam pipes or by live steam, is provided. At the present day the textile fibres are dyed in practically all stages of manufacture; the

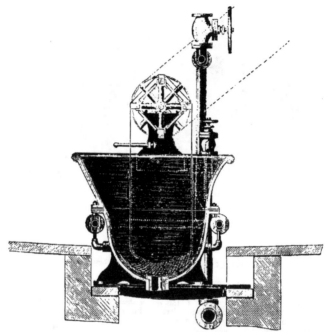

FIG. 10.—Double-Walled Copper Dye Vat.
(Mather & Platt, Manchester.)

dyeing of the finished cloth, or piece-dyeing, however, still transcends in importance that of the other partially finished forms.

Dyeing of Piece-goods.—The simplest form of machine and the one most usually employed for woollen cloth consists of the dye vat and winch.

Fig. 9 shows an arrangement of this kind in which a wooden dye vat is employed. The pieces are stitched together before dyeing and are usually run as an endless band over the winch. The

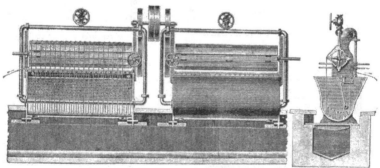

FIG. 11.—Dye Vat. (Mather & Platt, Manchester.)

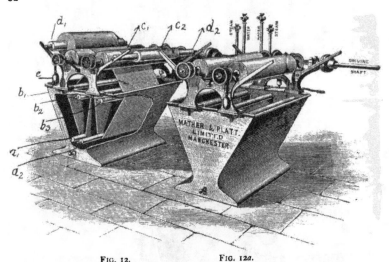

FIG. 12.   FIG. 12a.

Dyeing Jiggers. (Mather & Platt, Manchester.)

latter may be turned by machinery or by hand. The dye bath is usually heated by direct steam issuing from a perforated pipe. Fig. 10 shows a double-walled copper vat which is heated by steam introduced between the two copper walls. In this vat the steam does not mix with the dye liquor, and dilution of the latter is thus avoided during dyeing. Fig. 11 illustrates a vat in which the pieces in rope form are drawn as an endless band in a spiral over the same winch a large number of times after remaining in the liquid for a short time. Guide pegs prevent them from becoming entangled.

The machine most frequently met with in the dyeing of cotton cloth is the jigger. In this machine the cloth in full width is passed through the dye liquor several times over guide rollers.

In Fig. 12 two of these rollers, a_1, a_2, are shown submerged in the liquid, and three, b_1 b_2, b_3, are placed above. In addition, two draw rollers, c_1, c_2, and two batch rollers, d_1 and d_2, are visible above the vat. The cloth is first run from c_1 to c_2, the roller c_2 being actuated directly by the driving machinery, while the brake e is placed on c_1. The cloth is thus kept in a state of tension. When all the cloth has been run on to c_2, the motion is reversed, c_1 being made the driving roller, and the brake being put on c_2. This alternate motion is continued until the piece has been dyed the desired shade. The pipes necessary for the supply of water and steam for heating are indicated in Fig. 12a.

For **indigo dyeing**, pp. 49 and 100, vats are employed in which the cloth is run over a large series of rollers completely submerged in the liquor. It then passes through squeezing rollers, and over a series of rollers placed in the air above the vat for the purpose of oxidising the leuco compound absorbed by the fibre. Another arrangement shown in Fig. 13 for the purpose of oxidising the leuco compound, consists in piling the cloth loosely on an endless travelling band. The dye vat must be supplied with a stirring arrangement G, which can be actuated at will when the vat is being freshened up. Several vats of increasing strength are usually

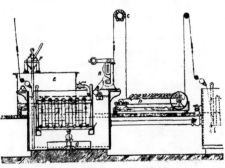

FIG. 13.—Indigo Dyeing Machine.
(Mather & Platt, Manchester.)

FIG. 14.—Jiggers for Sulphur Blue. (Zittauer Maschinenfabrik.)

employed in series. For indigo dyeing "dipping vats" are also frequently employed in which the cloth is mounted on frames that are lowered into the dye liquor, after which it is exposed to the air for oxidation.

Fig. 14 shows an arrangement of two jiggers for use in the dyeing of sulphur blue. The first is intended for dyeing, the second for washing the cloth, and an air passage for oxidising the dye is provided between the two jigs (see p. 91). These jiggers are provided with squeezing rollers.

Padding Machines, *i.e.*, machines for passing piece-goods through a concentrated solution, differ in principle from jiggers in having much smaller dye vessels or troughs. They are provided with squeezing rollers.

Machines similar in construction to the washing machine shown in Fig. 23 may also be employed in the dyeing of cloth, and like principles may also be adopted in the design of machines for the dyeing of warps.

Yarn Dyeing.—Yarn is usually dyed by hand in the hank. For this purpose a rectangular vat, Fig. 15, is employed. It is fitted with the necessary pipes for filling and emptying, and a steam coil, usually perforated, is provided for heating. A false

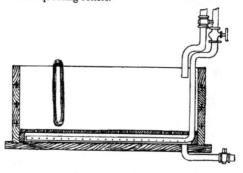

VAT FOR HANK-DYEING

FIG. 15.

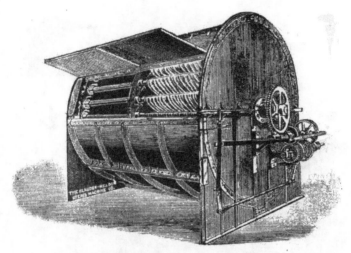

FIG. 16.—Hank Dyeing Machine for Sulphur Colours.
(Klauder-Weldon Dyeing Machine Co.)

bottom prevents the hanks from coming in contact with the latter. The hanks are suspended on square wooden rods placed across the vat, on each side of which stands a workman. One by one the rods full of yarn are taken up, and to each hank is given a quarter turn, so that the exposed part becomes submerged. This is carried out by means of a thinner rod which is inserted in the loop of the hanks immediately beneath the suspending rod. The rods are arranged in such a manner that there is always a sufficient space of about a foot available beside the rodful of hanks which is being turned.

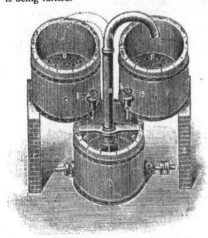

FIG. 17.—Dyeing Machine for Loose Wool, etc.
(Schirp.)

Numerous machines have been devised in which the motion given to the rods by hand is imitated mechanically. The plan most suitable for mechanical treatment seems to be the employment of a wheel on which the hanks are suspended by means of two series of rods, one series fitted near the centre, the other on the circumference of the wheel. The latter partially dips into the dye vat, and in turning slowly, alternately dips the hanks into the liquor and then lifts them out to drain ; at the same time the sticks receive a rotary motion. The whole wheel is advantageously enclosed in a case fitted with doors. Fig. 16 shows a machine of this kind constructed by the Klauder-Weldon Dyeing Machine Co. This machine may also be employed for dyeing slubbing (combed wool) in the hank.

The Dyeing of Loose Fibre, Cops, etc.—Loose fibres may be dyed in suitable boilers in which they are turned by hand by means of poles. The material, however, shows a considerable tendency to felt under these conditions, and mechanical appliances are, therefore, to be preferred.

The Klauder-Weldon Co. recommend a machine similar in appearance to the one described above for the dyeing of hanks. In it the material is placed in a perforated drum or wheel, which is divided into four sections or compartments and made to rotate inside a case in a similar manner to the wheel referred to above. In doing so, it alternately dips the fibres into the dye liquor and lifts them out to drain. The plan adopted by nearly all designers of dyeing machines for loose fibres, however, consists in placing the material in a perforated vessel or cage and forcing the dye liquor through it by means of a circulating pump, or by some other means. In many machines the direction of circulation can be reversed at will in order to ensure perfect uniformity of penetration. As a rule cotton is packed more tightly than wool, and a greater pressure of the circulating liquor is therefore necessary. Fig. 17 illustrates a simple machine for the dyeing of loose wool, etc. The material to be dyed is placed in one of the tubs *b* or *c*, of which one may be charged while dyeing is proceeding in the other. These tubs are fitted with a false bottom. The dye liquor is made up and kept continually heated in the tub *a* placed below *b* and *c*. The interior of the tub *a* is provided with a cataract pump which delivers large volumes of liquor through the pipe *n* and the movable

FIG. 18.—Dyeing Machine for Loose Fibres (Obermaier Type).
(Dehaitre.)

connecting piece *q*. The latter may be turned so as to deliver on the top of the material contained in either of the dye vats *b* or *c*. This liquid then runs back again to the tub *a* through pipes fitted to the bottom of *b* and *c*, thus producing continual circulation. The goods are covered by a sieve and a spreader for the dye liquor, and the vats *a* and *b* are kept covered during use. This same apparatus may be provided with pipes to allow circulation of the liquid to proceed alternately from above and below.

A machine very frequently employed for the dyeing of loose cotton and wool is the Obermaier apparatus. In machines of this type (Fig. 18) the material is placed in a perforated drum, with a central perforated tube. This drum is fitted inside the dye tank proper, and can be removed at will for charging. Circulation of the liquor is produced by means of a centrifugal pump in the direction shown by the arrows.

Fig. 19 shows a machine charged with cops ʊ and cross-wound bobbins v, which is also constructed in a slightly different manner for the dyeing of loose fibre. Like the Obermaier apparatus it consists, in the latter case, of a movable drum I for holding the material through which dye liquor is forced by means of the pump G. The drum is placed in the dye vat B which has a detachable front. In this apparatus the shell of the drum is not perforated, but it is divided into three compartments by perforated walls. The central compartment serves for distributing the liquor, the outer two for holding the fibre. The pump is double-acting, so that the direction of circulation can be reversed at will.

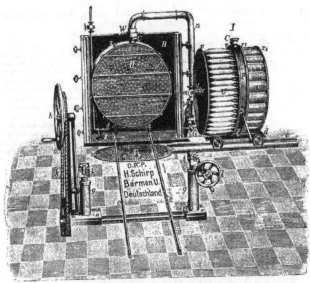

FIG. 19.—Dyeing Machines for Cops, Cheeses, etc.
(Schirp.)

Cops and cross-wound bobbins may be dyed by the "packing" system in machines similar to those used for loose cotton. In this case solid wooden skewers must be inserted to prevent them from collapsing, and all spaces must be very evenly packed by means of some packing material such as loose cotton, etc. A method that leads to satisfactory results much more easily is the hollow perforated skewer system. In this system each cop or cross-wound bobbin is placed on a perforated paper tube on a perforated spindle or skewer, and the dye liquor is forced or sucked through the

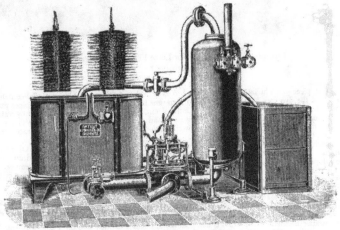

FIG. 20.—Dyeing Machine for Cops, Cross-wound Bobbins, Loose Fibres, etc.
(Pornitz.)

cop either directly by means of a pump, or else compressed air or vacuum or steam is employed for this purpose. Fig. 20 illustrates a machine of this type in which the cops or cross-wound bobbins are mounted on cylinders. In the machine already described, Fig. 19, they are inserted between two perforated metal plates, and Fig. 21 illustrates a cop-dyeing machine in which the cops are mounted on a square perforated plate.

Washing. — After dyeing, the goods must in nearly all cases be washed in water. Machines of similar or of identical construction to those used in dyeing may usually be employed. In all those cases already described in which the liquor is circulated by means of a pump, the dye liquor is usually simply withdrawn from the vat without removal of the goods and replaced by water. Most of the washing machines described in the chapter on bleaching may also be employed by

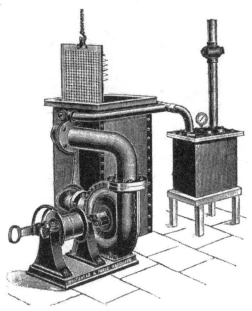

FIG. 21.—Cop-Dyeing Machine.
(Whitehead & Poole.)

the dyer. In the washing of cotton piece-goods it is often desired to cause the scouring liquor to impinge with considerable force against the cloth. For this purpose so-called beaters may be employed. These may be described as scoops which rotate rapidly on the surface of the liquor and throw it with considerable force against the cloth. Fig. 22 illustrates the action of such beaters, and Fig. 23 shows a washing machine fitted with beaters. In this figure a vertical drying machine is also shown on the right. It will be seen that the calico passes through various tanks over guide rollers alternately placed in and above the liquid. Squeezing rollers are provided.

Drying.—The process of drying may be said to consist of two operations, firstly, the removal of as much water as possible by mechanical processes, and secondly, the evaporation of the remaining moisture. The former operation may be carried out by squeezing or wringing. A more thorough method for the mechanical removal of liquid, however, consists in throwing off the drops by centrifugal force. For this purpose so-called hydro-extractors are employed. These are machines which consist essentially of a perforated metal cage for holding the goods, which can be rotated very rapidly around a vertical axis by an electric motor or otherwise

FIG. 22.—Beaters.
(Farmer.)

Fig. 23.—Washing Machine and Vertical Drying Machine. (Farmer.)

(see Fig. 24). The liquid is collected in a casing which usually forms part of the framework of the machine.

For the final drying of the fibres by evaporation, artificial heat is usually applied, although drying at ordinary temperature is sometimes carried out.

Loose fibres are usually dried in a machine consisting essentially of a chamber through which the fibres travel on an endless band, meeting a countercurrent of hot air during their passage.

Yarn is usually dried by suspending the hanks on poles or movable frames in specially constructed drying ovens through which a slow current of hot air is passed. Cops and cross-wound bobbins may be dried in a similar manner, or else the suction drying system may be employed particularly in conjunction with the machine shown in Fig. 21. The cops are left on the cylinders which are put in special machines in which hot air can be drawn through the cops.

Cloth is usually dried by passing it face upwards over steam-heated rollers (see Fig. 23). The final drying is frequently carried out in stentering machines (Fig. 25). In these the cloth which has shrunk slightly in the processes of dyeing is brought back to its original width by stretching slightly. For this purpose the moist cloth is passed between two moving endless chains which grip it at the selvedges by means of clips. These chains are not parallel but diverge slightly so that the cloth is stretched during its passage between them. At the same time it is dried by hot air drawn over steam pipes.

FIG. 24.—Hydro-Extractor.
(Dehaître.)

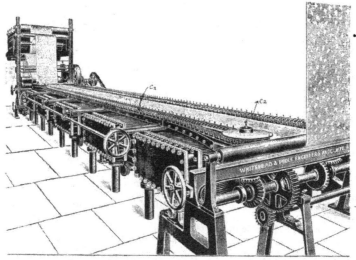

FIG. 25.—Clip Stenter with Hot-Air Drying Arrangement.
(Whitehead & Poole.)

Before leaving the subject of dyeing machinery, a brief reference must be made to the **agers** employed particularly in the development of **aniline black**, pp. 68, 102 (and also for the fixation of printed colours). These consist of chambers containing a hot atmosphere heavily charged with steam in which the cotton cloth can be hung or through which it can be passed continuously over rollers. Fig. 26 illustrates a **rapid ager** for aniline black. It is fitted with heating coils and a perforated pipe for the supply of steam. The roof and the guide rollers near the common inlet and exit of the cloth are heated by steam to prevent the formation of drops of water which would soil the goods.

Direct Dyes

The simplest dyes, from the dyer's point of view, are those which are taken up directly from their solutions by the fibre.

Direct Cotton Dyes.—During the last three decades a large number of direct cotton dyes have been put on the market. The dyes of this class appear to belong to a few well-defined groups of chemical compounds. We have firstly the congo-red group, the members of which contain the tetrazo grouping of atoms

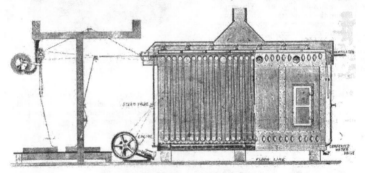

FIG. 26.—Rapid Ager. (Mather & Platt.)

$\left\{ \begin{array}{c} -N=N- \\ -N=N- \end{array} \right.$; secondly, the *primuline group*, which appear to have the radicle

$-\langle \begin{array}{c} S \\ N \end{array} \rangle C-$ in common; and thirdly, various dyes, which may be classed as *di-stilbene-azo-dyes*. Most of these dyes are also taken up by wool and silk, but a few, notably members of the last-named group, hardly dye the animal fibres at all. The direct cotton dyes are thus of particularly great importance for the dyeing of union goods, satins, etc.

The fact that these substances are not taken out of the dye-bath with the same degree of avidity as direct dyes for wool and silk, and that the process of absorption is of a more or less reversible nature, has already been referred to in the Introduction. On account of these circumstances they eminently show the desirable property of "level dyeing," but also exhibit to a marked extent an undesirable tendency towards "bleeding" or "running." It follows also that they must be dyed from as concentrated a solution as possible (weight of solution, say, ten to thirty times that of the cotton), and varying quantities of salts, such as sodium sulphate or common salt, are added to aid in the exhaustion of the dye bath. Since these colours are dyed in a neutral or alkaline bath, and most of them are precipitated by lime or magnesia, it is necessary to soften hard water before use. This is most conveniently done by boiling with a small amount of soda ash. As a rule the goods are entered at medium temperature, and dyeing is carried on at the boil, but dyeing at low temperatures is also sometimes carried out. The dye baths are not exhausted, and may be used over again after making up to strength by the addition of the necessary amount of dyestuff.

The following are two of the processes which may be employed :—

1. **Process at Boiling Temperature.**—Work the cotton at the boil for one to one and a half hours, adding 5-30 per cent. (on weight of cotton) of crystallised Glauber's salt, or 2½-10 lbs. of common salt.

The salt aids in the exhaustion of the bath but rather hinders boiling, and if difficulties are met with in this respect its quantity must be reduced, or it must be replaced by soap, turkey red oil, etc. After removal from the bath the goods are wrung and then rinsed in cold water, soda solution, or turkey red oil.

2. **Cold Bath.**—Stir the dyestuff with an equal weight of caustic soda solution of sp. gr. 1.35-1.38 (70-76° Tw.), and dissolve the whole in boiling water. Enter the cotton into the bath when cold or lukewarm and dye with the addition of a little soap and, if necessary, Glauber's salt.

The following are some of the names and prefixes employed by various firms to indicate their direct cotton colours: Benzo-, Congo-, Diamine, Union, Direct, Purpurine, Diamol, Chlorazol, Ingrain, Sultan, Titan, Primuline, Sulphine, Oxamine, Pyramine, Thiazine, Phenamine, Chrysamine, Oxyphenine, Chrysophenine, Curcuphenine, Zambesi, Chicago, Columbia, Hessian, Triazol, Toluylene, etc.

After-treatment of Direct Cotton Dyes.

—The direct cotton dyes are eminently suitable for after-treatment on the fibre, whereby not only new shades are produced but very much faster colours are obtained.

Basic dyes may be dyed upon them as on mordants (p. 95), or they may be converted into new "ingrain" colours by the processes of diazotising or coupling (pp. 30, 38, 66, 104).

Many of them are also greatly improved by after-treatment with metallic salts, such as copper sulphate, chromium salts, and the bichromates of sodium and potassium (p. 99).

Another method of after-treatment which has a marked effect on the fastness to washing and milling of certain dyes consists in working the dyed cotton for about half on hour at 60° in a bath charged with 1-3 per cent. formaldehyde (40 per cent.).

Wool and Silk are both frequently dyed with the direct cotton colours, the former in neutral or very feebly acid baths containing Glauber's salt at boiling temperature, the latter in a neutral boiled off liquor bath, the fibre being entered at lukewarm temperature and the bath being gradually taken to boiling temperature. After dyeing has proceeded for about an hour, the bath is usually made feebly acid with acetic acid to aid exhaustion.

The dyes may be subjected to after-treatment as on cotton, and the silk is finally brightened by passing through a very dilute solution of acetic or tartaric acid * and dried without washing.

Sulphur Colours

The sulphide or sulphur colours which have become of great importance in recent times for obtaining fast shades on cotton or other vegetable fibres, form a group of dyes that are obtained by fusing sodium sulphide, or a mixture of sodium sulphide and sulphur with various organic substances. They are insoluble in water and are dyed from a solution in sodium sulphide. Many of them are reduced by the bath and presented to the fibre as more or less coloured leuco compounds, being afterwards oxidised by contact with the air. They will readily dissolve in alkaline reducing agents, and may occasionally be dyed in the vat like indigo.

---

* The brightening of silk by treatment with acid is due to the fact that silk absorbs acid and retains it tenaciously, whereby its lustre is increased and it acquires the property of emitting a crackling sound called the scroop of silk when it is twisted and pressed together. The rustling of silk garments is doubtless due to this property. Tartaric acid being retained more permanently than the other acids, is the most efficient, but the most expensive of the acids employed.

They may be employed for dyeing artificial silk and also silk and wool, but the animal fibres, more especially wool, are liable to attack by the alkaline sulphide solutions unless protected by special previous treatment. The dyes are occasionally employed in the dyeing of unions. These colours are distinguished by good fastness to light, washing, cross-dyeing, etc., and they do not bleed like the direct cotton colours.

It has occasionally been observed that the cotton fibre has become tendered on storing after dyeing with the sulphur colours, and this has always been associated with the formation of sulphuric acid. When this difficulty occurs, it is best met by subjecting the cotton to an after-treatment with a feebly alkaline substance, such as soap, sodium acetate, or carbonate. A very suitable process appears to be that recently patented by Holden, in which calcium tannate is deposited on the fibre after dyeing, by steeping the material for a few minutes in tannic acid at about 40° C., squeezing, passing through limewater, and washing. The calcium tannate being insoluble has the advantage of not being liable to be removed on washing like the feebly alkaline substances mentioned above. After dyeing, the material should in all cases be wrung well and rinsed thoroughly.

In dyeing with these colours, vats made of wood or iron may be employed. Copper or any alloys containing this metal must be carefully excluded, as this metal goes into solution rapidly in the sodium sulphide solutions, and the copper compounds formed, lead to oxidation of the dyestuff and irregular dyeing. The fibre should be kept submerged, and yarn may conveniently be dyed on bent iron pipes, the ends of which have been wrapped round with cloth.

The dyestuff, to which has been added about three or four times its weight of crystallised sodium sulphide and some soda ash, is dissolved in a small amount of boiling water with stirring, and the solution obtained, is added to the bath, which usually contains an amount of water equal to about twenty to thirty times the weight of the cotton. The amount of soda ash employed is about 5 per cent. of that of the cotton, and the bath contains 10-60 per cent. (on the weight of the cotton) of common salt according as a light or dark shade is required. For dark shades the cotton may be entered at boiling temperature, turned several times, and allowed to steep for several hours. For lighter shades a lukewarm or even a cold solution may be employed and a shorter time is requisite. Turkey red oil is sometimes added to the bath to secure more even dyeing. Certain sulphur dyes, such as the kryogene blues, must be developed by oxidation in air at a high temperature in the presence of moisture, by steaming in the presence of air, or by storing in a damp warm place.

An after-treatment with oxidising metallic salts, viz., with a solution containing, say, 2 per cent. of potassium bichromate, 2 per cent. of copper sulphate, and 3 per cent. of acetic acid on the weight of the cotton at about 70° C. improves the fastness of some of these dyes.

Like the direct cotton colours they act as mordants for basic colours, and many of them may be coupled with diazo solutions (p. 104). The first dye of this description known, viz., Cachou de Laval, was discovered a considerable number of years ago. The following are some of the names employed by various firms to indicate the newer sulphide dyes: Amidazol, Crossdye, Immedial, Katigene, Kryogene, Pyrogene, Sulphur Thiogene, Thion, Thionol, Thioxine.

Natural Direct Dyes for Cotton.—Several natural dyes, such as turmeric, safflower, and annatto, are direct dyes for cotton.

ACID DYESTUFFS

This class comprises all those dyestuffs which are of an acid nature. It is obvious that some of these colours may belong to the class of direct cotton dyes, others may often be employed in conjunction with mordants, and thus the various classes of dyes merge into each other. The acid dyes are either nitro compounds or sulphonic acids, and in nearly all cases they are sold in the form of sodium or occasionally calcium salts. In many cases they have been obtained from basic dyes by introducing the sulphonic group of atoms.

Cotton.—Generally speaking the acid dyes will only stain cotton and other vegetable fibres very slightly, so that only very light and fugitive shades can be obtained by direct dyeing even when concentrated baths are employed. The results are somewhat better when the dyes are used in conjunction with gelatine or basic mordants, such as alumina or stannic oxide, but even so, the shades obtained are not fast to washing.

Wool.—The acid dyes are of the very greatest importance in the dyeing of wool. The wool is always dyed at boiling temperature, and a quantity of sulphuric acid is usually added, which is very much in excess of what is required to liberate the free colour acid from its salt. That the object of this acid is to produce lanuginic acid from the wool, which latter substance is primarily dyed, has already been mentioned in the Introduction. The mineral acid might thus be termed a "mordant" (*i.e.*, biting agent), using the word in the significance in which it was originally, though wrongly, employed by the dyers of former times.

Sodium sulphate or bisulphate is nearly always added as a levelling agent, since this substance appears to have a slight solvent action on the dye taken up by the fibre, thus removing it from those places in which it may have been deposited in excess, and generally retarding the operation of dyeing. When dyestuffs are employed which dye with exceedingly great rapidity, the sulphuric acid is replaced by acetic acid or by ammonium sulphate or acetate, substances which slowly become acid in the boiling bath owing to the expulsion of ammonia. In certain cases, particularly in the dyeing of unions, a boiling neutral bath is employed. Stannic chloride or alum is sometimes added in small quantity; tin oxide or alumina will thus be deposited on the fibre from the boiling bath, and by taking up colour from the solution increase the brilliancy of the shade. Certain acid dyestuffs, viz., the alkali blues, are not soluble in dilute acids and must be dyed from a feebly alkaline solution. The wool is afterwards treated in a hot bath containing dilute sulphuric acid. The colourless sodium salt which is originally taken up is thus converted into the blue acid.

The following may be taken as an example for the dyeing of 100 kg. of wool.

Employ a bath (5,000-10,000 l.) containing 1·4 kg. of concentrated sulphuric acid, 10-20 kg. of Glauber's salt crystals and the requisite amount of dyestuff, enter at about 70° and heat to the boil, leaving the wool in the boiling bath for about an hour.

Silk.—The acid dyes are of considerable importance in silk dyeing, although they are not fixed so well as on wool.

A bath is usually employed containing 20-30 per cent. (on volume of bath) of boiled-off liquor, which is slightly acidulated with sulphuric or acetic acid. The silk is usually entered at lukewarm temperature and dyed slightly below boiling. It is then washed with water and brightened by means of sulphuric, acetic, or tartaric acid, and dried without further washing.*

The following are a few of the more important names met with among the acid dyes : Naphthol yellow, Tartrazin, Fast yellow, Tropæolin, Brilliant orange, Brilliant scarlet, Xylidine scarlet, Biebrich scarlet, Croceïn scarlet, Fast red, Archil substitute, Orseillin, Acid magenta, Acid eosin, Acid rhodamine, Acid phloxin, Acid violet, Alkali violet, Sulphone azurin, Alkali blue, Soluble blues, Patent blue, Cyanine, Soluble induline and nigrosine, Naphthazine blue, Wool green, Naphthol green, Fast brown, Orcellin, Naphthol black, Naphthylamine black, Sulphone black, Wool black, Biebrich patent black.

BASIC DYES

This important class, which comprises some of the most brilliant and beautiful colours known, consists of coloured salts of colourless acids and organic colour bases. When the animal fibres are dyed by these subtances, only the base is taken up in a coloured form, as explained in the introduction, the acid being left behind in the bath.

Cotton.—Cotton is nearly always dyed with the intervention of an acid mordant, and the processes employed will, therefore, be considered later in conjunction with those used for mordant dyes (pp. 94-96).

---

* See note, p. 91, also Martin's "Industrial Chemistry," Vol I. p. 558.

Wool.—Although not so important as the acid dyes on account of their fugitiveness, yet the basic dyes still possess a considerable amount of importance in the dyeing of wool. They are in most cases dyed from a very feebly acid bath, but a soap bath is also sometimes employed when very soft water is available. That hard water must be feebly acidified, preferably by acetic acid, has already been mentioned under the heading of **Water**. No other addition is made.

The bath is usually started cold and gradually raised to the boil. Dyeing is continued until the bath is exhausted, which sometimes takes place before boiling. The goods are well washed after dyeing. Owing to the great tinctorial power of these dyes a very small amount is usually sufficient, ½ per cent. on the weight of the wool usually producing a medium shade. The colours should be filtered through cloth before adding to the dye bath as a precaution against the introduction of undissolved particles.

Silk.—On account of their brilliance the basic dyes play an important part in silk dyeing in spite of their fugitiveness as a class. A neutral or slightly acid bath may be employed consisting of one-third boiled-off liquor and two-thirds water. The same general precautions must be taken as in the dyeing of wool.

The silk is usually entered cold and the temperature gradually raised to a little under boiling. After dyeing, the fibre is rinsed and brightened by means of tartaric or acetic acid.*

A bath containing about 1½-2 per cent. (on the weight of the silk) of soap is frequently employed for dyeing pale shades at a temperature of 30°-40° C. (85°-105° F.).

The following are a few of the best-known basic colours: Magenta, Safranine, Magdala red, Chrysoïdine, Phosphine, Auramine, Methyl green, Malachite green, Diphenylamine blue, Victoria blue, Methylene (ethylene) blue, Meldola's blue, Nile blue, Indulines and Nigrosines, Methyl violet, Crystal violet, Mauve, Bismarck brown, Fast black.

The rhodamines, including irisamine, etc., also belong to this group, and the weakly acid eosins, including erythrosin, phloxin, rose bengal, may be dyed by similar methods.

MORDANT DYES

The mordant dyes are basic or acid substances which are not fixed on the fibre directly, but are caused to combine with a compound of an acid or basic nature termed a mordant which has usually been previously deposited on the fibre. The compound formed is termed a colour-lake.

Some dyes, such as alizarin or logwood, are only feebly coloured before combination, and yield different shades with different mordants. These are termed **polygenetic dyes.** Others have the property of dyestuffs before combination, and their lakes do not usually differ much from them in colour. These are "**monogenetic**" **dyes.**

Acid Mordants.—These mordants are of the greatest importance for the fixation of basic dyes, particularly on cotton. They are also frequently employed in order to fix basic mordants on other fibres, and in silk weighting. The most important are the tannins and the oil mordants.

The tannins† form a class of compounds which are distinguished by the fact that they are taken up readily by the animal skin, causing it to be tanned. Most of them are colloids, and their more important properties are doubtless closely connected with this circumstance. They will combine with basic dyes producing compounds insoluble in water but soluble in an excess of tannic acid. When brought together with salts of heavy metals containing a feeble acid a precipitate is formed containing the metal oxide and the tannin. This precipitate which is insoluble in tannic acid is probably what is termed a colloid compound, *i.e.*, a compound produced by the phenomenon of "adsorption" between a colloid bearing a positive and a colloid bearing a negative electric charge when in solution. These precipitates have the property of combining with basic dyes, forming the coloured so-called "triple" compounds which constitute the lakes employed in dyeing cotton with basic dyes.

---

* See p. 91. † See also p. 112.

The most important tannin is tannic acid or gallo-tannic acid, a substance obtained commercially on the large scale by the extraction of nut galls. This substance should be exclusively employed for dyeing pale shades on cotton ; for dark shades the more or less coloured extracts of the following substances containing tannin may be employed—sumach, myrobalans, divi-divi, valonia, chestnut, etc. The bath is prepared according to the amount of colour to be fixed with quantities of tannic acid, varying, say, from ½-8 per cent. on the weight of the cotton, allowing sufficient water to work the material conveniently. For pale shades the material, which must have been carefully freed from air by boiling out, is worked for a half to one hour in the bath ; for darker shades the material may be entered at boiling temperature and then allowed to steep in the cooling bath for twelve hours. It is then worked in a tartar-emetic bath containing, according to the amount of tannin to be fixed, ½-4 per cent. (on the weight of the cotton) of tartar-emetic for about a quarter of an hour. The insoluble antimony tannin compound referred to above is thus produced. The excess of antimony salt must be very carefully washed out or preferably removed by passing the dyed goods through another tannin bath. Aluminium, iron, or stannic salts are also employed for the fixation of tannic acid.

Turkey-red oil, Alizarin oil, Sulphated oil, Soluble oil,* are names applied to another class of acid mordants which are sometimes employed for fixing basic dyes on cotton. Their principal importance, however, lies in their application to the fixation of basic mordants in turkey-red dyeing. As will have been seen from the prescriptions given for dyeing with various direct dyes, turkey-red oil is also frequently employed as an assistant in the place of sodium sulphate where difficulties are met with in obtaining level shades.

Turkey-red oil is formed by the action of concentrated sulphuric acid at medium temperatures on various oils, such as olive oil, cotton-seed oil, and castor oil. The last-named is by far the most mportant. The products formed are distinguished by the fact that they are soluble in water, while they retain to a certain extent the properties of the oils from which they have been produced. Chemically, turkey-red oil is probably a mixture of various primary ethereal salts of sulphuric acid. It has the great advantage over ordinary soap that its salts with the alkaline earths are not sticky substances but fine powders which have no tendency to cause uneven dyeing.

In mordanting cotton, the material may be saturated with a solution containing 50 g. of turkey-red oil per litre, wrung, dried, and then treated for half an hour in a tepid solution of aluminium acetate of sp. gr. 1.015 in order to fix the mordant.

Dyes as Mordants.—The fact that basic dyes may be dyed on cotton on other dyes, which may thus in a certain sense be considered to be acid mordants, has already been referred to (pp. 91, 92).

Dyeing Basic Dyes on Cotton.—The basic dyes are usually dyed on mordanted cotton in the cold or at temperatures up to about 70°. A feebly acid substance, such as acetic acid or alum, is usually added to retard dyeing in order that even results may be obtained, and the dye solution is usually added during dyeing in intervals of about a quarter of an hour in about three or four portions. The operation is usually started in the cold and completed at about 60° C.

Catechu.†—In conjunction with the tannins reference must here be made to the exceedingly important natural dyes, catechu or cutch and gambier. These substances contain varying amounts of a tannin called catechutannic acid and a white crystalline substance known as catechin. In addition they contain a brown dyestuff ormed by oxidation of the preceding.

Cutch and gambier are employed largely in cotton and to a certain extent also in wool dyeing. The material is usually immersed in a boiling bath of the dye containing about 10 per cent. of copper sulphate (of the cutch employed). The latter acts as an oxidising agent and probably also as a mordant. The material is then allowed to steep for several hours and afterwards treated with a hot bath containing about 2 per cent. of dichromate. This substance effects a further oxidation. Catechu and gambier are also used in large quantity in silk weighting.

---

* See Martin's " Industrial Chemistry," Vol. I. p. 43.   † See p. 74.

Dyeing in Conjunction with Basic Mordants

Nearly all insoluble metal hydroxides may be deposited on the textile fibres as mordants, for the purpose of obtaining colour-lakes with various dyes. A brief survey of the more important methods employed for the various classes of fibres, and a short reference to the dyes used, some of which are among the most important known, is all that can be attempted here.

Wool.—Wool is capable of dissociating the salts of heavy metals at boiling temperature, taking up both the metal hydroxide or a basic salt and the acid, the former in an insoluble form, the latter in a form in which it can be washed out by water. This fact is made use of in the mordanting of wool. It is necessary to employ such salts as are not dissociated hydrolytically by the boiling water to an appreciable extent or else to hinder this dissociation by the addition of suitable substances. The deposit of metal hydroxide formed would otherwise not be held fast by the fibre. Thus in mordanting with aluminium sulphate it is necessary to make an addition of sodium bisulphate, sulphuric acid, or preferably of cream of tartar or of some other substance of an acid nature.

The following prescription for alumina may be taken as an instance of the mordanting with salts such as aluminium sulphate, chromium fluoride, ferrous sulphate, etc. Employ a bath containing about 8-10 per cent. of alum and 2½-5 per cent. of tartar (on the weight of the wool), enter at a low temperature, heat gradually to boiling and maintain at the boil for about half an hour. After cooling, the wool is thoroughly washed or preferably boiled in water to remove as much of the acid as possible. It is then dyed without allowing it to dry.

A very important mordant for wool that calls for a few special remarks is potassium (or sodium) **bichromate** (bichrome or chrome). The substance to be deposited on the fibre in this instance is chromic oxide, and reduction of the chromate originally taken up is therefore necessary. When chromate alone is employed, this reduction is probably effected to a small extent by the wool itself. The latter, however, still shows the yellow colour of chromate on leaving the mordanting bath, and the principal reduction no doubt takes place in the dye-bath later on.

It will be readily understood that care is necessary in the use of this mordant owing to its oxidising properties in order that "overchroming" of the wool may be avoided. According to Knecht, the chromate is taken up by the wool as chromic acid, and the bath consequently shows a tendency to become alkaline. If used over again it should therefore be made up to strength by the addition not only of bichromate, but also of the necessary amount of sulphuric acid.

For high-class goods bichromate is frequently employed in conjunction with reducing agents, of which cream of tartar, oxalic acid, formic acid, and lactic acid are the more important.

The following may serve as a prescription for the mordanting of wool with bichromate. Boil the wool in a bath containing 2-4 per cent. bichromate (of weight of wool). Water, fifty to a hundred times the weight of the wool. Time, one to one and a half hours; then wash with water and dye without drying.

Basic Mordants for Silk.—Silk is usually mordanted at medium temperatures at which the metal salts employed are not decomposed by the fibre. It thus becomes necessary to pass the latter through the solution of a fixing agent, such as sodium silicate, which deposits an insoluble basic precipitate on the silk. Instead of this, the fibre may in many cases simply be washed very thoroughly with water, which produces an insoluble precipitate by the process of hydrolysis. In the mordanting of silk with iron and tin salts tannin is usually employed as a fixing agent. A soap bath also has a similar effect. By passing the fibre alternately through baths containing the metal salt and the tannin extract, the fibre may be "weighted" up to about four times its weight with the metal tannate. This fact is made use of in dyeing silk with heavy logwood blacks.

Basic Mordants for Cotton.—Although cotton may absorb a certain amount of metal salts, it can in no way decompose them. Either a salt such as the acetate must be employed which can be decomposed or hydrolysed by heating yielding a basic salt; or else a fixing agent, *i.e.*, a substance which yields a precipitate of basic properties when added to a solution of the salt in question, must be employed.

In the former case the impregnated goods are subjected to the process of "age ing," which consists in exposing them to a warm moist atmosphere.

In the latter case the cotton may either be treated with tannin or some other acid mordant taken up directly by the fibre and then be passed through an alkaline bath and through the metal salt solution, or else the material is first passed through the metal salt solution and then treated with a fixing agent, such as ammonia, caustic soda, chalk, sodium carbonate, silicate, phosphate, or arsenate, which yields a precipitate of strongly basic properties by interaction with the salt in question.

When employing turkey-red oil or tannic acid, the cotton is first impregnated as described under acid mordants, it is then usually passed through clear lime water to neutralise the acid and afterwards worked in the salt solution for about an hour It is usually finally passed through a weak soap bath, thoroughly rinsed in water, and then dyed.

When one of the alkaline fixing agents indicated above is employed, the cotton is usually treated for several hours with the mordant solution, wrung out, dried at a low temperature, then worked for about half an hour in the solution of the fixing agent at medium temperature, thoroughly washed, and then dyed.

The Dyes

Although mordant dyes, both natural and artificial, are among the most important known, yet all that can be attempted here, is a brief enumeration of them, and an indication of the mordants with which they are applied.

Logwood.—This substance consists of the heart-wood of a tree known botanically as *Hæmatoxylon campechianum* which grows in various parts of America. The wood is subjected to a process of fermentation and oxidation called "ageing" or "maturing," during which a glucoside originally present in it is decomposed into a sugar and a substance called hæmatoxylin. The latter on oxidation yields a body named hæmatein which is the colouring principle of logwood. The dye is bought by the dyer either as chips, as decoctions, known as logwood liquor, or as extract, *i.e.*, a paste obtained by evaporating the decoction. In the former case it is extracted by the dyer himself by means of boiling water. Logwood is employed for dyeing both vegetable and animal fibres, and its importance lies chiefly in the production of fast blues and blacks on the latter (see also pp. 72, 112).

When employed for dyeing blacks on **cotton** it is usually applied in conjunction with an iron mordant fixed by tannin.

The following prescription may serve as an example. Work the cotton in a cold infusion of about 30-40 per cent. of sumach (of weight of fibre), allow to steep for several hours, and without washing work for about half an hour in a cold solution of "nitrate" of iron (*i.e.*, ferric sulphate), sp. gr. 1.01-1.02, treat with a cold chalk bath to remove excess of acid, and wash thoroughly. Dye in a bath containing logwood and a little fustic (say 8 per cent. solid logwood extract and 1¼ per cent. of fustic extract of sp. gr. 1.25), then treat with a bath of about 1½ per cent. copperas, or with a warm bath containing potassium bichromate (say ½ g. per litre) in order to remove the excess of logwood. Then work in a solution of soap, say 5 g. per litre, at a moderate temperature, squeeze and dry.

Chrome blacks may also be obtained on cotton; a purple is obtained by means of a tin, a blue by means of a copper mordant.

Wool is dyed black by means of either an iron or chrome mordant.

The following prescription may serve as an example. Mordant in a bath containing 3 per cent. potassium bichromate, 8 per cent. tartar, and 5 per cent. sulphuric acid (of weight of wool) at boiling

7

temperature for about an hour, wash well and dye in a boiling bath prepared from 50-80 per cent. logwood and 5-10 per cent. fustic for about an hour, having entered the wool at about 80° C. An addition of about 5 per cent. alizarin improves the fastness of the shade to light. Then fix the excess of logwood taken up in a finishing bath containing about 1 per cent. of potassium bichromate at about 80° C. Wash and dry.

In order to produce logwood blues on wool, smaller quantities of dye and mordant are employed, and the fustic is omitted in the dye bath.

Silk.—Logwood blacks play an important part in the dyeing of silk. As a rule the logwood is dyed on an iron tannin mordant, and other substances are incorporated with the dye, allowing it to weight the silk up to about 400 per cent.

The following prescription, by means of which iron tannate, tin tannate, Prussian blue, catechu, and logwood are all fixed on the fibre, allows a weighting up to about 100 per cent. and may serve to illustrate the process.

Mordant with basic ferric sulphate, then soap. Repeat these operations one to eight times, according to the amount of weighting desired ; dye Prussian blue by means of potassium ferrocyanide, treat with a catechu bath (100-150 per cent.) containing 10-15 per cent. stannous chloride at 60°-80° C. Treat with a second catechu bath containing no tin (100-200 per cent. catechu), mordant with pyrolignite of iron. Dye with logwood and soap. Brighten.

The following **natural mordant dyes** can only be referred to : Fustic (young fustic) and Quercitron bark (yellow on chromium mordant); Weld (yellow on chromium, aluminium, tin ;—olive or olive-yellow on iron and copper mordant); Persian berries (yellow or yellowish olive on tin, copper, aluminium, iron ;—brown on chromium mordant) ; Saunders wood, barwood, camwood (red to brown according to mordant); Cochineal, Kermes, and Lac dye (scarlet and crimson on tin and aluminium mordant) (see also **Natural Dyes,** p. 73).

Alizarin.—This exceedingly important dyestuff, which constitutes the principal colouring matter of madder, is at the present time obtained practically exclusively by artificial means from coal-tar (p. 39). The two substances, isopurpurin and flavopurpurin, are present in varying amounts in different brands of the commercial article and affect the shades of the dyed material to a certain extent. Alizarin is put on the market as a paste containing 20 or 40 per cent. of the dyestuff or as a powder containing from 80 per cent. upwards. Its most important application is the production of turkey red on cotton.

It would be beyond the scope of this article to give a full account of turkey-red dyeing, but it may be stated briefly that the production of this exceedingly brilliant and fast colour is based on the formation of an exceedingly complicated aluminium-calcium lake of alizarin which contains also a certain amount of tannin and oil. The latter is a decomposition product obtained by using either olive or turkey-red oil. In addition the lake often contains stannic oxide in small quantity. The following enumeration of the operations carried out in one of the simpler processes of turkey-red dyeing will give a general idea of the complicated nature of the method.

The cotton (300 kg.) is first freed very completely from fatty and resinous matter by "bowking," or boiling under a pressure of 2 atmospheres with caustic soda solution of sp. gr. 1.005 for four or five hours (p. 521). It is then treated successively three times with turkey-red oil and dried at 70°-75° C. after each treatment. The baths employed for this purpose are "standing" baths, and are freshened up as follows : The first oiling bath is freshened up with 22 kg. acid oil, 5 kg. ammonia, and 22 l. of potassium carbonate solution of sp. gr. 1.26, temperature 40°-45° C. (For a fresh bath two and a half times these quantities are needed.) Second oiling bath like the first ; the third oiling bath is freshened up with 20 kg. acid oil and 44 l. potash solutions. After drying, the cotton is now steeped for eight hours in water of 30°-35° C., hydro-extracted and again stoved at 70°-75° C. It is now ready for the alum mordanting bath, which is freshened up with 50 kg. aluminium sulphate, 4.25 soda crystals, the same amount of chalk, and 1 kg. of tannic acid. The cotton remains in this bath for fifteen to twenty hours, is well rinsed and then passed wet into the dye bath. The latter contains about 20 kg. alizarin, 300 g. tannic acid, and about 1 kg. chalk. The material is first treated in the cold bath for an hour ; the latter is then slowly heated to boiling, and afterwards boiled for about an hour. The material is then subjected to two successive processes of clearing by boiling first for three hours at 1½ atmospheres pressure with a solution containing 3-4 kg. of soda, then rinsing and finally boiling at 1½ atmospheres with 8 kg. soap, ½ kg. soda, and 400 g. of tin crystals (stannous chloride). It is then rinsed and dried in the air.

Alizarin is also dyed on cotton with chromium mordants for claret red and maroon shades, and on iron mordants for very fast violets.

Wool is dyed with alizarin on aluminium, chromium, iron, and tin mordants; red, maroon, violet, and orange shades respectively are thus produced. The mordants are applied as previously described.

In conjunction with the aluminium mordant 10 lbs. of 20 per cent. alizarin paste, 2 lbs. of calcium acetate, 1 lb. of soap, and ½ lb. of tannic acid may be employed per 100 lbs. of wool. The latter is introduced into the cold bath, which is then heated to boiling and kept so for an hour and a half. The mordant and the dye are sometimes dyed simultaneously from the same bath where only light shades are required (single bath method).

Silk may also be dyed with alizarin on aluminium, chromium, and iron mordants. About 20 per cent. of alizarin is required for a full shade.

Other Mordant Dyes.—The following are the names of some of the dyes which are dyed with mordants and are often termed alizarin dyes, although they are by no means all of them derivatives of alizarin: Alizarin bordeaux, Alizarin maroon, Alizarin orange, Resoflavin, Alizarin yellow, Galloflavin, Anthracene brown, Alizarin green, Emeraldol, Anthraquinone green, Cœruleïn, Alizarin blue, Brilliant alizarin blue, Alizarin indigo blue, Alizarin sky blue, Cyananthrol, Anthraquinone blue, Gallocyanine, Gallazine, Phenocyanine, Crumpsall fast blue, Alizarin cyanine, Alizarin cyclamin, Alizarin heliotrope, Anthraquinone violet, Anthracene violet, Alizarin black (see pp. 39-42).

In wool dyeing the order of operations is often inverted, *i.e.*, the wool is first treated ("stuffed") with the dye and then saddened with the mordant. This procedure is particularly suitable for a class of dyes of a strongly acid nature known as **acid chrome colours** which have recently been placed on the market. In this case both operations are carried out in the same vessel (single bath process). The dye is first practically exhausted from the bath, and then ½-2 per cent. of bichromate, according to the depth of shade, is added and dyeing continued at the boil for half an hour to one hour longer, after which the wool is washed and dried. Chromium fluoride may be employed instead of bichromate with those dyestuffs which will not resist the oxidising action of the latter. The following are names under which this class of dyestuff is sold by various makers: **Chrome, Acid anthracene, Acid alizarin, Diamond salicine,** etc.

After-treatment of Cotton with Metallic Salts.—Before leaving the subject of mordant dyes reference must be made to the after-treatment with metallic salts of cotton dyed with the direct and sulphur dyes (p. 91). These salts no doubt act as mordants, although in some cases an oxidising effect exerted by them may also be of importance. Copper sulphate, chromium fluoride, and potassium bichromate are the most important substances employed for this purpose. The following prescriptions will illustrate the process:—

Rinse the cotton well and treat with a cold or tepid solution of 2-4 per cent. of copper sulphate (on the weight of the cotton) for fifteen to thirty minutes; or else with a solution containing 2 per cent. $CuSO_4$, 2 per cent. bichromate, and 3 per cent. acetic acid of 30 per cent. strength under the same conditions; or else boil for half an hour in a bath containing 3-4 per cent. chromium fluoride and 2-3 per cent. acetic acid of 30 per cent. strength.

VAT DYES

Many dyestuffs are converted by reducing agents (*i.e.*, compounds capable of producing nascent hydrogen or removing oxygen) into colourless substances termed leuco compounds, which by oxidation in contact with air pass again into the original dyes. Some dyes, on the other hand, undergo so far-reaching decomposition when subjected to reduction that a simple process of oxidation cannot reproduce the original compounds. The leuco compounds are frequently soluble in alkaline liquids, and are taken up readily from these by vegetable as well as by animal fibres. On contact with the air the original dyestuff is reproduced in the fibre in an exceedingly fast form. These facts are made use of in dyeing with certain insoluble dyes known as vat dyes. The dye is brought into solution in the vat, *i.e.*, an alkaline liquid containing a reducing agent. The material to be dyed is impregnated with the leuco-compound formed, and is then exposed to the air, the dye being thus produced in it.

Indigo.—This, the most important vat dye, which may be considered to be the parent substance of most of the others in common use, is at the present day employed as natural and as artificial indigo. The former is obtained by a process of fermentation (steeping), followed by one of oxidation (beating) from the leaves of various tropical plants. A glucoside which has been named indican by its discoverer, Schunck, is thus decomposed, yielding glucose and the leuco compound indigo white, which latter is converted into indigo by oxidation. Natural indigo usually contains quantities of the pure dyestuff indigotin, varying between 30 and 70 per cent. according to the source from which it has been obtained; in addition, there may be in it quantities varying between 2 and 10 per cent. of the purple dyestuff indirubin, while the remainder is made up of more or less inert impurities. The glucoside indican is also contained in woad, a substance that is still employed as an addition to the fermentation vats used in wool dyeing.

Artificial indigo is manufactured chemically from the products of coal-tar distillation. It is met with in commerce as a powder consisting of almost pure indigotin, as a paste containing about 20 per cent. of the same substance, and in various other forms. It is also sold as "indigo vat," a substance containing about 60 per cent. of the leuco compound indigo white (see p. 46).

As already explained the indigo vat contains essentially a reducing agent and an alkaline substance which dissolves the indigo white formed. The latter is either lime, soda, or ammonia, the former may consist of a large variety of substances. Brief reference shall here be made to the hydrosulphite vats, the zinc and lime vat, the copperas vat, and the fermentation vats.

The sodium hydrosulphite employed in the first-named vats is either prepared by the dyer himself by the action of zinc dust on sodium hydrogen sulphite, or it may be obtained commercially at the present day in the form of a dry powder. Either soda, lime, or ammonia may be employed as the alkali of the vat. The vats are usually worked cold for cotton, and at a temperature of about 50° for wool. In the latter case the amount of hydrosulphite is greater, and the amount of alkali smaller, than in the former. A stock or standard vat is always prepared apart from the actual dyeing vat.

The following may be taken as an example of a hydrosulphite-soda vat for **cotton**, prepared from zinc and sodium bisulphite. Volume of dye vat, 1,000 l. A solution is prepared by mixing 15 l. of bisulphite solution (sp. gr. 1.28) in small portions with 1.5 kg. zinc dust and letting the mixture stand for a short time with occasional stirring until the sediment is pale grey in colour. A suspension of 15 kg. of 20 per cent. indigo pure paste (equivalent to about 5 kg. very finely ground natural indigo) in about 15 l. of caustic soda solution (sp. gr. 1.38) is then prepared and the first liquid added to the second. The mixture is then maintained at a temperature of about 50° C. during half an hour to an hour. When reduction is complete the stock liquor will have turned yellow. The dye vat (1,000 l.) is prepared with a mixture of 10 l. bisulphite (sp. gr. 1.28) and 1 kg. zinc dust added as above in small portions with stirring. After a short time as much stock liquor as necessary (according to the depth of shade desired) is added and the vat stirred well. It is ready for use as soon as it has become clear and yellowish green. The vat may be used continuously and fed with stock liquor and bisulphite-zinc-soda mixture to keep it up to strength.

For **wool** a corresponding hydrosulphite-lime vat may be made up by using, in the place of the quantities given above, the following: For the stock liquors 12 l. bisulphite solution, 1½ kg. zinc dust, 10 kg. indigo paste, 10 l. 20 per cent. milk of lime prepared by slaking 2 kg. quicklime in place of the soda solution; for the dye vat, ¾ l. bisulphite solution, 0.2 kg. zinc dust. As already mentioned, the wool is dyed at about 50°, and after dyeing must be passed through very dilute sulphuric acid solution (0.1 per cent.) to remove the lime and then be rinsed.

The following may be taken as an example of a vat for **cotton** in which commercial sodium hydrosulphite is employed.

The volume of the dye vat is 1,000 l. A stock liquor is prepared by stirring together well 10 kg. 20 per cent. indigo paste (equivalent to about 3½ kg. very finely ground natural indigo), 20 l. cold water, and 1¾ kg. hydrosulphite powder. To this, after ten minutes, is added 6 l. caustic soda solution (sp. gr. 1.39), and the whole is heated to 60° C. until reduction is complete. This is ascertained by dipping a piece of glass into the liquor. The glass and the drops from it should be clear yellow in colour, and the liquor should oxidise in about half a minute. The dye vat is set with 50 g. hydrosulphite to remove dissolved oxygen from the water, and after stirring, the whole or part of the stock solution is added and the vat stirred up once more.

For **wool**, the quantities for the stock solution are 10 kg. indigo paste, 10 l. cold water, 2 kg. hydrosulphite powder, and 2 l. caustic soda solution (sp. gr. 1.38). It is recommended to make the dye vat up with 50 g. hydrosulphite, about ½ l. ammonia, and 3½ l. of a 10 per cent. glue solution per 1,000 l. and then to add a portion of the above stock liquor. Dyeing takes place at about 50° C. The vat is used continuously and made up to strength from time to time.

The Zinc-Lime Vat.

—In this vat, which is extensively used for cotton, the indigo is reduced by nascent hydrogen produced by the action of zinc dust upon a lime solution. It is best to prepare a stock solution of reduced indigo.

The following prescription may serve as an example for the preparation of a vat of 1,000 l. A stock solution is prepared by mixing 10 kg. 20 per cent. indigo paste (equivalent to about 3½ natural indigo) with 1½ kg. zinc dust made into a paste with 20 l. of water of 50°-60° C. To this is added 4-5 kg. quicklime which has been previously slaked to a uniform paste. The mixture is made up with hot water to 80 l., and maintained for three to five hours at a temperature of 50°-60° C., with occasional stirring. It should then be pure yellow and ready for use. The vat is set with 250 g. zinc dust and 1 kg. lime slaked to a thin cream, stirred up and allowed to stand for some time. The stock liquor or part of it is then poured in, the vat stirred and allowed to settle. It is then ready for use. A certain amount of sediment is formed ; this may trap a small amount of indigo, producing loss, and may also lead to uneven dyeing if proper attention is not paid. These disadvantages, however, are only slight with this vat, being much less serious than in the following one.

The Copperas Vat.

—This is one of the oldest vats employed in the dyeing of cotton. The ingredients used are lime and ferrous sulphate. Ferrous hydroxide is thus produced which is converted into ferric hydroxide by the indigo contained in the vat, and thus acts as a reducing agent.

The following prescription for a vat of 1,000 l. of medium strength will illustrate the process. A stock vat of 200 l. containing 10 kg. 20 per cent. indigo paste, 12½ kg. quicklime, and 10 kg. green copperas is made up, and allowed to stand for four to six hours with occasional stirring. As soon as it has assumed a yellow colour, it is poured into the dye vat which has been about three-quarters filled with water. The latter is stirred up and dyeing commenced after it has settled completely. This vat is easy to set, but the large sediment referred to above is a grave disadvantage, and makes it unsuitable for continuous dyeing.

Fermentation Vats for Wool.

—In the fermentation vats various organic substances are allowed to ferment. Glucose is thus produced which acts as a reducing agent upon the indigo contained in the alkaline liquor. The sugar is oxidised by the latter, first to lactic and then to butyric acid. A great deal of practical experience is necessary to work a fermentation vat properly, and all that can be attempted here is to give a very rough sketch of the most important fermentation vat for wool, *i.e.*, the woad vat.

A vat containing 15,000 l. is often employed. It is filled with water and heated to 65° C., 500 kg. of woad are introduced, and after stirring left overnight. The next morning 20 kg. very finely ground indigo, 20 kg. bran, 7 kg. madder, and 12 kg. lime are added. The whole is stirred two or three times a day with the addition of 1-2 kg. of lime each time, the temperature being maintained at about 60°. After a few days the liquor should show a yellowish colour, and on gently stirring it, blue streaks should make their appearance along with a coppery scum or flurry. Before dyeing, the wool must be very thoroughly scoured and the soap removed. A trammel net is employed in the vat to preserve the wool from contact with the sediment. After dyeing, the wool is thoroughly cleansed with soap and fuller's earth in order to remove all the loosely adhering indigo, which would otherwise show the objectionable property of rubbing when in use.

Silk is not very frequently dyed with indigo. The vats must be kept less strongly alkaline than for cotton and are worked in the cold. In applying the various vats, the material is always worked in the liquor for various periods of time— for cotton yarn, three or four minutes ; for calico, ten to thirty minutes ; and for heavy woollen cloth half an hour to two hours or more. On coming out of the dye vats the goods, which show a greenish yellow colour, are squeezed or wrung and then exposed to the air. The shade quickly passes by oxidation through green to blue. The operation is then repeated either in a stronger or weaker vat until the desired shade has been attained.

Numerous machines for dyeing with indigo, some of which have been referred to in the chapter on appliances for dyeing, have been designed for use with the various forms of textile goods. They are designed to carry out the operations of steeping and oxidising the goods in a continuous manner.

Other Vat Dyes.—During the last ten years a considerable number of new vat dyes have been put on the market, most of which are distinguished by their great fastness to light and other influences, and which promise to become of the very greatest importance in the future. They are mostly employed in conjunction with the hydrosulphite vats. The following are the more important classes :—

The Thioindigo Class is of great theoretical interest. They are chemically derived from indigo by replacing NH groups by S atoms. The following are some of the more important dyes of this series : Thioindigo red, Thioindigo scarlet, Thio-indigo violet (Kalle), Vat red B (B.A.S.F.), Helindone red 3B, Helindone orange R, Helindone yellow 3G, Helindone scarlet S, Helindone fast scarlet, and Helindone brown G (M.L.B.). All these dyes may be employed for cotton and wool (see p. 51).

The Ciba Colours (S.C.I.B.) are apparently either brominated indigo derivatives or derivatives of the thioindigo class. Most of them may be applied equally well to animal and vegetable fibres. The more important ones are various indigos put on the market by M.L.B. and the B.A.S.F. Ciba blue B and 2B (S.C.I.B.), Ciba heliotrope, Ciba Bordeaux B, Ciba red G, Ciba scarlet G, Ciba grey G and B, Ciba green G, and Ciba violets (see pp. 49, 54).

The Indanthrene, Algole (B.A.S.F.) and **Leucole** (Bayer) and **Cibanone** (S.C.I.B.) colours have no chemical connection with indigo, but are mostly related to anthraquinone. They require the addition of a large amount of alkali to the hydrosulphite vat, and are therefore unsuited for use with the animal fibres. The following may be mentioned : Indanthrene yellows (flavanthrene), orange, copper, reds, Rufanthrene browns (fascanthrene), Indanthrene claret, Indanthrene blues, Indanthrene violets (violanthrene), Indanthrene grey, Indanthrene maroon (oliv-anthrene), Indanthrene brown, Indanthrene green (viridanthrene), Indanthrene blacks (melanthrene), Algole yellows, orange, scarlet, reds, grey, blues, pink, green, Bordeaux, Cibanone yellow, orange, browns, and blacks (see p. 42).

Certain of the sulphide dyes, such as kryogene black, may also be dyed in the vat, and should, therefore, be mentioned here (see pp. 46, 66).

DYESTUFFS PRODUCED BY CHEMICAL MEANS ON THE FIBRE

Aniline Black

This dyestuff, which is of the greatest importance in cotton dyeing, is always produced on the fibre as a perfectly insoluble substance by the oxidation of an aniline salt. When an acid solution of aniline is treated with suitable oxidisers, the base undergoes a very complicated series of oxidations and polymerisations, a considerable number of intermediate products is produced and ultimately a black in-soluble substance of very high molecular weight "aniline black," is formed (p. 68).

This substance appears to exist in two states of oxidation or polymerisation : the first has the property of acquiring a greenish tint under the action of sulphurous acid, the second more highly oxidised, or perhaps only more highly polymerised product does not exhibit this reaction ; and it is this form which the dyer must aim at producing, if the dyed fabric is not to turn green during use. The cotton is, therefore, usually subjected to an after-treatment in a hot chrome bath in order to convert the whole of the first into the second form of aniline black. The oxidiser employed for oxidising the aniline salt in the first instance may be sodium (or potassium) chromate; potassium ferricyanide (red prussiate of potash), or what comes to the same thing, a mixture of sodium chlorate and potassium ferrocyanide; or lastly, sodium chlorate. The last-named substance requires the intervention of a catalyst or carrier of oxygen, and as such, a salt of copper, iron, or vanadium may be employed. The same substances are sometimes also added to chromate solutions to accelerate oxidation. The oxidation takes place in the fibre, with a suitable velocity at temperatures at or about 45° C., and the following processes, producing what are termed (1) dyed blacks, (2) aged blacks, and (3) steam blacks, are in use. In the first-named process the material (say 100 kg.) is worked in a dye bath of 2,000 l. containing, say, 13 kg. aniline salt, 20 kg. hydrochloric acid (sp. gr. 1.171), 14 kg. bichromate, first in the cold for an hour. The temperature of the bath is then raised to 70°-80° C. and the cotton is worked for another half hour, during which the black is developed. It is then rinsed and soaped well, hydro-extracted, and dried. The disadvantage of this process is that the dyestuff is not held well by the fibre and rubs badly. The second or **ageing process** is the one most frequently employed. It differs from the first in making use of a much more concentrated solution, and in the fact that the oxidation is not accomplished in the liquor itself, but that the fabric is removed from it, dried, and then aged, that is, subjected to a moist warm atmosphere which develops the black. During the process of ageing large quantities of hydrochloric acid and oxides of chlorine are liberated from the aniline hydrochloride, and there is thus always a considerable risk of tendering the fabric if the temperature is not carefully regulated and the acid efficiently removed by the current of air. An addition of aluminium acetate is recommended to neutralise the mineral acid given off.

The following prescription for yarn by K. Oehler will give an idea of the process. The cotton is first thoroughly boiled out with soda, well rinsed, hydro extracted, and stretched. 25 kg. are then turned for half an hour in a padding liquor made up to 500 l., after pouring together the following solutions: 60 kg. aniline salt dissolved in 320 l., 2.75 kg. bluestone (copper sulphate) dissolved in 50 l., 18.8 kg. sodium chlorate dissolved in 37 l., 2 kg. ammonium chloride dissolved in 12 l., and 18 l. of an aluminium acetate solution (sp. gr. 1.075). The yarn is then wrung or hydro-extracted lightly until it retains about its own weight of liquor. It is then well stretched, placed on wooden laths which have been wiped over with the padding liquor, dried, and aged. The drying and ageing are conveniently carried out in the same chamber; the drying takes about four to six hours, the ageing proper is begun by carefully admitting steam until the dry bulb thermometer registers 35° C., the wet bulb 30° C. The ageing chamber is fitted with a powerful fan at the top, which draws in air through the bottom; this air is heated by means of pipes which also serve for the introduction of steam. While in the ager the yarn is turned every two hours; the ageing occupies about six to eight hours. After leaving the ager the yarn is chromed by turning quickly for ten to fifteen minutes at 75°-80° C. in a bath containing 3 kg. bichromate and 0.75 kg. sulphuric acid per 1,000 l. It is then thoroughly rinsed, soaped, rinsed again, and dried.

A process which bids fair to become of the very greatest importance in the production of aged blacks has been recently patented by A. G. Green. In it the only oxidising agent employed is atmospheric air. This is accomplished by making use of the observation that a small quantity of a diamine, e.g., paraphenylenediamine, constitutes, when associated with a copper salt, a catalytic system by means of which aniline can be readily oxidised by air alone.

In the **Steamed Blacks** the oxidising substance is essentially potassium ferricyanide. The cotton may be padded with a liquor containing 75 kg. aniline salt, 35 kg. sodium chlorate, 40 kg. yellow prussiate of potash per 1,000 litres; it is then dried at a temperature not exceeding 50° C., and the black then developed by steam in a few minutes in a suitable ager.

The advantage of this process over the ageing method lies in its rapidity and in the fact that there is little risk of tendering, as very little mineral acid is given off in the presence of the potassium ferrocyanide; its disadvantage lies in the greater expense.

Various other bases besides aniline may be oxidised on the fibre to produce aniline blacks or other dyes. Thus a black is obtained from *p*-amidodiphenylamine and a brown from *p*-phenylenediamine.

Ice Colour (see pp. 30, 38, 91).

The ice colours are employed in cotton dyeing. They belong to the class of insoluble azo dyes, and are produced on the fibre itself (p. 91) by the same chemical processes by means of which azo dyes are manufactured in the colour works.

As is well known (see p. 29), the following operations are carried out in the production of azo dyes: First an aromatic base is diazotised by dissolving it in an excess of acid, cooling the solution with ice, and adding to it a solution of sodium nitrite. As soon as the starch iodide test shows that the nitrous acid is no longer being used up in the chemical reaction, the diazotised solution is poured into an alkaline solution of a phenol, or it is allowed to act on a slightly acid, neutral, or alkaline solution of an aromatic base (see pp. 30, 38).

In the production of azo colours in the cotton fibre, the latter is always impregnated first with the alkaline solution of the phenol. β-naphthol is the substance almost exclusively employed for this purpose. The cotton is padded in small quantities at a time in a strong solution containing the naphthol and caustic soda and some turkey-red oil. The material is then hydro-extracted and dried quickly in a well-ventilated room at medium temperature. After it has been thoroughly well cooled it is ready to be developed by introducing it into the solution of the diazotised base. Various substances producing different shades, viz., diazotised paranitraniline, chloranisidine, alphanaphthylamine, and other diazo bodies are in use for this purpose, but the first-named is the easiest to work and the most frequently employed. The dye obtained is known under the name of paranitraniline red. The diazotisation is in this case carried out by pouring together the very carefully weighed out chemicals, and should take place at a low temperature (say 10° C.). The temperature should never rise higher than about 15°. Since a strongly acid solution, like the one obtained in this operation, will not couple with a phenol, it becomes necessary to make it either neutral or feebly acid by the addition of caustic soda or sodium acetate respectively. The solution must not be made alkaline since diazo solutions are unstable in this condition.

It is thus obvious that great care must be taken by the dyer in weighing out his chemicals. As a rule, his weighings alone are relied upon to give the right proportions, and are not checked by special tests. Compared with other diazo salts, those derived from *p*-nitraniline are exceptionally stable, and it is a great advantage to the dyer that these diazo-salts may be obtained commercially, ready made. They are sold mixed with indifferent substances, such as aluminium or sodium sulphate, to render them non-explosive, and are found on the market under the names of **Nitrazol C** (Cassella) and **Azophore red** (M.L.B.). Another product of a similar nature is **nitrosamine red** (B.A.S.F.) which represents *p*-nitrophenylnitrosamine sodium (antidiazo-*p*-nitrobenzene sodium). This substance is converted into *p*-nitrodiazobenzene chloride by simply adding hydrochloric acid in the cold to its solution. It is then allowed to stand for half an hour, and on the addition of sodium acetate it is ready to be employed in the process of developing.

In conjunction with the ice colours the two processes known respectively as "diazotising and developing" and as "coupling" must be considered here. Both processes are employed extensively as methods of after-treatment for the direct cotton colours. The last-named is also applied occasionally to cotton, dyed with the sulphur colours.

The majority of direct cotton colours belong to the class of amido bodies, some to the class of phenols. The former may be subjected to both methods of after-treatment under consideration, the latter only to the second. In the first-named process the dye is diazotised on the fibre, and the compound formed, coupled with the solution of a suitable developer, *i.e.*, either an amido body or a phenol. In the second process the dyed fabric is treated directly with the solution of a diazotised base, or of one of the commercial diazo bodies mentioned above.

The following prescriptions will illustrate the methods :—

Diazotising and Developing.—Wash the material well after dyeing with the direct cotton colour and then work for fifteen to thirty minutes cold in a dye bath charged with 1-3 per cent. sodium nitrite and 5-10 per cent. spirits of salt (hydrochloric acid). The cotton is lightly rinsed and passed without delay or unnecessary exposure to light and air into the cold developing bath in which it is worked for fifteen to thirty minutes. It is then washed and dried. Of the numerous developers which may be employed, the following may be mentioned: Phenol, Resorcinol, Alpha and Beta Naphthol, Para-amidodiphenylamine, etc. The first four are dissolved in caustic soda, the last named in the minimum amount of hydrochloric acid.

Prescription for "coupling" for 100 kg. cotton: Make 0.5-0.6 kg. of paranitraniline into a paste with an equal quantity of hot water, then add 1-1½ l. of cold water and 1.5 kg. hydrochloric acid (sp. gr. 1.16) and let stand until the mixture has cooled to 20° C. Then stir in 2 kg. broken ice and add all at once ¼ kg. solid sodium nitrite, taking care that the temperature does not rise above 10° C. Pour this solution into the coupling bath which has been filled with cold water, and add a solution of 1¼ kg. crystallised sodium acetate. Enter the dyed and rinsed cotton, work for about thirty minutes, rinse, and dry.

Mineral Colours

Although largely displaced by modern organic dyes, yet a few mineral colours have still retained a certain degree of importance in cotton dyeing. They are always produced in the fibre itself as insoluble pigments from substances which are not dyes.

Chrome Yellow and Orange. — These substances consist of ordinary and basic lead chromates respectively (see Martin's "Industrial Chemistry," Vol. I. p. 500). Chrome yellow may be produced by fixing lead oxide on the fibres, and then passing it through a hot dilute solution of potassium dichromate. The first-named operation is carried out by impregnating the material with a soluble lead salt, and then passing it through dilute lime water. Another method of procedure consists in impregnating the cotton first with an alkaline lead solution containing, say, $\frac{1}{10}$ per cent. lead acetate and 0.8 per cent. caustic soda (on the water), and then passing through an acidified solution of bichromate containing, say, 1 per cent. of bichromate and ½ per cent. sulphuric acid.

Chrome orange is obtained by dyeing the cotton first with chrome yellow, washing, and then working in boiling clear dilute lime water until the desired shade has been obtained.

Manganese Brown is obtained by impregnating cotton with a solution of manganous chloride, and then passing it through a hot solution of caustic soda (sp. gr. 1.01) free from carbonate. Colourless manganous hydroxide is thus precipitated, which is converted into the brown higher oxides of manganese by exposure to air and a passage through a weak solution of bleaching powder.

Mineral Khaki may be obtained by impregnating the cotton with a mixture of ferrous and chromic acetates. After drying, it is then steamed in a rapid ager which leads to the production of a mixture of basic ferric and

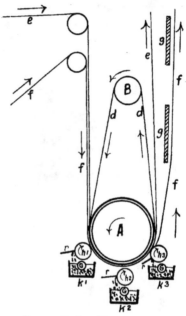

FIG. 27.—Section of Three-Colour Printing Machine.

chromic acetates on the fibre. These are further fixed by passing the goods through a boiling solution containing a mixture of sodium carbonate and sodium hydroxide.

Iron Buff consists of ferric hydroxide, and may be dyed on cotton by the same method employed for manganese brown, only substituting green vitriol for manganous chloride. It may also be obtained by successive treatment with a ferric salt and caustic soda or lime.

Prussian Blue may be obtained on cotton by first dyeing it an iron buff, and then working it in cold solution of potassium ferrocyanide containing, say, 2 per cent. ferrocyanide, 1 per cent. sulphuric acid, on volume of bath (see Martin's "Industrial Chemistry," Vol. I. p. 502). Prussian blue is frequently employed as a groundwork in the dyeing of heavy blacks on silk.

Prussian blue is also dyed on wool. It is usually obtained by the oxidation at a high temperature of hydroferro or hydroferri cyanic acid liberated respectively from potassium ferro, or potassium ferri cyanide. An addition of a stannous mordant improves the colour.

The wool may be introduced into a cold bath containing 10 per cent. red prussiate of potash and

20 per cent. sulphuric acid (on weight of wool). The temperature is gradually raised to boiling and maintained thus for about half an hour or more. About 1·2 per cent. of stannous chloride may be added towards the end of the operation.

COLOUR PRINTING OF CALICO

In colour printing the dyes are confined to certain portions of the fabric, being printed on by special rollers and prevented from spreading to neighbouring parts by the addition of thickening agents to the dye, such as starch paste, dextrine, gum arabic, gum tragacanth, albumen, casein, and similar substances. The dyes are usually applied in a water-soluble form, as in dyeing, and are fixed in the fibres by

Fig. 28.—Twelve-Colour Printing Machine. (Mather & Platt.)

suitable mordants followed by steaming in chambers. Sometimes insoluble colouring matters are fixed on with adhesives—usually blood albumen (see Martin's "Industrial Chemistry," Vol. I. p. 597); on steaming the albumen coagulates and fixes the dye in an insoluble wash-fast form on the fibre. Such colours are known as "albumen colours," and comprise insoluble mineral colouring matters, such as ultramarine, Guignet's green, chrome yellow, cinnabar, zinc white, etc.

The printing is carried out by means of hollow copper rollers, usually 1-1½ yds. long by 4-6 in. in diameter, provided with a steel core. The patterns are etched on the copper by means of acid in the usual way, the colour collecting in the hollows of the roller and being pressed on to the cloth as it passes under it. Each colour has its own roller with its own special pattern. Printing machines are now made in which one to fourteen colours are printed on the cloth in a single operation, usually on one side only of the fabric, but in duplex machines the patterns, exactly corresponding, are printed on both sides.

Fig. 27 shows the principle of a printing machine (three-colour). A is a large hollow iron roller a yard or more in diameter, covered with a thin layer of cloth; over this and over a smaller roller B runs the endless rubber cloth d; over this runs the cloth f which is to be printed, together with a supporting cloth e; h_1, h_2, h_3 are the printing rollers, which take up colours from the rotating rollers placed in the colour cisterns k_1, k_2, k_3; any excess of colour is scraped off the printing rollers by the special knife edges r, r, r pressing against them. The cloth f as it passes between each printing roll and the large iron cylinder has a coloured pattern printed on it. The cloth then passes away and is immediately dried (to prevent the colours from running) by passing over hot plates g, g or into a hot air drying chamber. The colours are then fixed by steaming in a special chamber.

FINISHING

LITERATURE

BEAN AND SCARISBRICK.—"Chemistry and Practice of Sizing." Manchester, 1906.
The EDITORS of *The Dyer and Calico Printer*.—"Cotton Finishing." London, 1911.
EDGE.—"Practical Cotton Finishing." London, 1911.
BEAUMONT.—"The Finishing of Textile Fabrics." London, 1909.
GANSWINDT.—"Technologie der Appretur." Vienna and Leipzic, 1907.
MASSOT.—"Appretur- u. Schlichte-Analyse." Berlin, 1911.
TROTMAN AND THORP.—"Bleaching and Finishing of Cotton." London, 1911.

The printed cotton cloth is always "finished" in order to weight it and give it a better appearance. The finishing materials consist of starch paste ("size"), mixed with such mineral salts as kaolin, gypsum, barium sulphate, magnesium sulphate, chalk, etc. If a highly glazed surface is required a little paraffin or soap is added. To obtain a pure white, and correct any yellowish tinge, it is usual to mix in ultramarine or other suitable colouring matter in small amount. A "soft" touch is imparted to the cloth by the presence of magnesium chloride, calcium chloride, or glycerol, which are all hygroscopic. The finishing paste is evenly spread over the cloth by means of "sizing" machines, and dried by passing the cloth over hot drums. Shrinkage is avoided by drying in a stretched condition in special frames. The goods are then "calendered" by passing between hot smooth steel rollers, whereby they acquire a fine glaze. A fine silky appearance may be given to cotton goods by stamping or subjecting to very great pressure between special rolls (satin). Woollen goods (*e.g.*, flannel) may be given a rough hairy appearance by passing over rotating cylinders provided with fine steel points.

FIG. 29.—Fourteen-Colour Printing Machine. (Mather & Platt.)

Cloth is made by mechanically working woollen goods in soap solution, whereby the fibres become more or less matted together (" milling " or " fulling "). For particulars of this and other special processes works on cloth-making must be consulted.

Acknowledgments.—The author wishes to express his thanks to the following firms who supplied him with many samples of dyed material and with much information regarding the newest processes of dyeing : Read Holliday & Sons, Ltd., Cassella & Co., The Badische Aniline u. Soda Fabrik, Meister Lucius & Brüning, Kalle & Co., Farbenfabrik F. Bayer & Co.

CHAPTER V

Inks

CHAPTER V

INKS

LITERATURE

C. AINSWORTH MITCHELL AND T. C. HEPWORTH.—"Inks, their Composition and Manu-
facture." 1904. (Gives English Patents to 1904.)
SIGMUND LEHNER.—"Ink Manufacture." 1902.
SCHLUTTIG AND NEUMANN.—"Untersuchungen Eisengallustinten." 1909.
A. BUCHWALD.—"Bleistifte, Farbstifte." 1904.

Black Writing Inks

Gallotannic Inks.—The ordinary writing inks consist, principally, of the iron salts of gallotannic and gallic acid substances contained in vegetable tannins. Gallotannic acid occurs in gall tannin and has the formula : *—

$$C_6H_2(OH)_3—CO—O—C_6H_2(OH)_2.COOH.$$

When hydrolysed by hot acids, or by fermentation, it breaks down into **gallic acid,** $C_6H_2(OH)_3.COOH$. Gallotannic acid yields blue or black compounds with iron salts. Gallic acid, however, produces no coloration with ferrous salts, but the solution on standing gradually oxidises to the ferric state, becomes black, and deposits an insoluble black precipitate. In consequence of this property the ordinary writing inks of commerce are ferrous (unoxidised) inks with gallic or gallotannic acid, and being usually of a very pale colour, have added to them a provisional colouring matter, such as indigo sulphonic acid, soluble blue, etc. The ink on penetrating into the fibres of the paper oxidises after some days into the black ferric compound, and so is not easily removed by washing. The presence of indigo increases the permanency of the ink, and makes it more resistant to the action of bleaching agents.

A good ink of this nature consists of an extract of 42 parts Aleppo galls in 120 parts of water, mixed with 1-2 parts of indigo solution (indigo sulphonic acid), or some other blue aniline dye, such as aniline blue, fast blue, etc. To this are added 5.5 parts of ferrous sulphate and 2 parts of metallic iron dissolved in crude acetic acid (pyroligneous liquor). A certain amount of anti-septic—say 2 lbs. phenol to 1,000 gals. of ink—is usually added to prevent the ink from becoming mouldy.

State of Massachusetts official ink contains : Dry gallotannic acid, 23.4 ; gallic acid crystals, 7.7 ; ferrous sulphate, 30 ; gum arabic, 25 ; dilute hydrochloric acid, 25 ; phenol, 1 ; all dissolved in 1,000 parts of water.

Dieterich recommends the following ink : 60 g. tannin are dissolved in 540 c.c. of water ; 40 g. of ferric chloride solution, containing 4 g. of iron, are mixed with 1 g. of sulphuric acid and 400 c.c. of water. The solutions are mixed, boiled ten to fifteen minutes, and then 30 g. of sugar and 10 g. of aniline water blue 1B are added. The ink flows easily from the pen with a deep blue colour, and dries blue-black ; copies taken are blue at first but become black.

Gallic Acid Inks.—When gallotannic acid is hydrolysed by acid or allowed to ferment it breaks up into gallic acid, $C_{14}H_{10}O_9 + H_2O = 2C_7H_6O_5$. After the conversion of gallotannic acid into gallic acid twice as much ink is produced from a given amount of ferrous sulphate—a fact which has given rise to Gallic Acid Inks, which we will briefly describe :—

Ink from Fermented Gall Extract.—200 parts of powdered Chinese galls are kept moist (but not wet) at 20°-25° C. until mouldy (eight to ten days), when most of the gallotannic acid has fermented into gallic acid. The galls are thoroughly extracted with hot water, talc is added, the

---

* Recent research has shown that the tannins consist of several complex substances.

solution filtered, and made up to 1,000 parts by weight; then 100 parts of ferric chloride solution containing 10 per cent. of iron are added, and the ink left for two weeks in closed flasks, decanted, and a provisional colour added, which, for a **blue-black** ink, consists of 3 parts of phenol blue in 400 parts water + 1 part phenol; this is added to 600 parts of the ink solution, the whole kept for a week in a loosely-covered flask, and then decanted. A **black ink** is given by 10.5 parts aniline green + 9 parts ponceau red R + 1 part phenol blue 3F dissolved in water and added to the ink solution.

Ink from Hydrolysed Tannin Solution.—100 parts of tannin, 100 of water, 200 of ferric chloride solution (10 per cent. iron), and 10 parts of crude hydrochloric acid (sp. gr. 1.16), are heated for ten hours at 80°-90° C. (in order to hydrolyse the gallotannic acid into gallic acid), then diluted with 700 parts of hot water, heated to 80° C. for one hour, cooled, kept in a closed bottle for two weeks, filtered, and diluted to 1,000 parts. A provisional colour must be added, since the writing at first is barely susceptible, although it ultimately oxidises to deep black. The provisional colour may be the same as that in the preceding ink.

Chemical Nature of Tannin Inks.

—Schluttig and Neumann showed that benzene derivatives containing three or more hydroxyl derivatives in juxtaposition yield permanent inks with iron compounds. For instance, hydroquinone, $C_6H_4(OH)_2$, does not yield an ink with iron salts, whilst gallic acid, gallotannic acid, and hæmotoxyline (the colouring principle of logwood), each of which contain three adjacent hydroxyls, all yield permanent inks with iron salts:—

$$C_6H_2 \begin{cases} OH\ (1) \\ OH\ (2) \\ OH\ (3) \\ COOH \end{cases}$$

Gallic acid.

$$CO \begin{cases} C_6H_2(OH)_3\ (1:2:3) \\ O-C_6H_2(OH)_2\text{·}COOH \end{cases}$$

Gallotannic acid.

$$\begin{array}{c} C_6H_2(OH)_3\ (1:2:3) \\ | \\ C_6H_4 \\ | \\ C_6H_2(OH)_3\ (1:2:3) \end{array}$$

Hæmatoxyline.

The precise nature of the iron compounds which occur in tannin inks is unknown; no doubt several individual bodies exist and contribute to the effect. The experiments of Pelouze, Wittstein, and Schiff point to the existence of the basic tannate $(C_{14}H_9O_9)_3Fe-Fe(C_{14}H_9O_9)_3$. Chemically, however, the whole subject is very obscure.

Tannin Materials for Inks.

—Tannins of various kinds occur widely distributed in the vegetable kingdom, and consequently there exist a large number of vegetable products from which inks can be made. Among these may be mentioned: **Galls,** vegetable excrescences formed upon the branches, shoots, and leaves of trees by the puncture of the young tissues by the females of certain insects for the purpose of depositing eggs. Many varieties of galls occur, such as **Oak Apple Galls, Aleppo Galls** (Turkey or Levant Galls), **Chinese Galls, Japanese Galls, Acorn Galls,** etc. These contain from 40-70 per cent. of tannin, estimated as gallotannic acid.

Other ink-making materials are: **Chestnut Extract** (from the wood or bark of chestnut tree), **Sumach, Divi-Divi, Myrobalans, Valonia, Oak Bark,** etc., all of which materials are rich enough in tannins to yield good inks. (See also under **Leather Manufacture** (Martin's "Industrial Chemistry," Vol. I. p. 573).)

Tannins may be divided into "**iron-blueing**" and "**iron-greening**" according to the colour of the precipitate they form with iron salts. Only the **iron-blueing** tannins are suitable for the manufacture of black ink. Oak-bark tannin, although an iron-greening tannin, contains a substance giving a blue precipitate with iron salts and consequently can be used for ink manufacture. Tannins suitable for leather (see **Leather Manufacture**), are often unsuitable for inks.

Statistics.—The amount of galls imported into Britain was 18,500 cwt. (value, £62,000) in 1906, and 15,600 cwt. (value, £37,000) in 1910. The amount of the other vegetable tannins is given under Leather.

Logwood Inks.

—Logwood extract (see **Logwood, Natural Colouring Matters**) is often added to iron gall inks, improving its colour without injuring its permanency. A common recipe is 3 parts of galls, 1 of ferrous sulphate, 1 of logwood, in 50 parts of water, with gum arabic in proportion of 1 part to 40 of ink.

A **copper** logwood ink consists of logwood extract, 20 kilos. in 200 kilo. water, mixed with 10 kilos. of ammonium alum previously dissolved in 20 kilos. of boiling water, 0.2 kilo. sulphuric acid, 1.5 kilos. copper sulphate in 20 l. of water. A provisional colouring matter (indigo sulphonic acid, phenol blue, etc.) must be added. The copper destroys steel pens.

Dieterich's School Ink is a bichromate logwood ink, consisting of 200 parts of a 20 per cent. logwood extract solution diluted to 500 c.c. and heated to 96° C. Then a solution of 2 parts of potassium bichromate, 50 of chrome alum, and 10 of oxalic acid dissolved in 150 of water are added drop by drop, the mixture maintained at 90° for thirty minutes, and then diluted to 1,000 parts, 1 part of phenol added, and the whole allowed to stand two to three days, decanted, and is then ready for use.

Black Aniline Inks.—A black ink stylographic pen consists of a solution in water (1 part dye to 80 parts water) of the various brands of water-soluble nigrosines (the sodium salts of the sulphonated nigrosines, see **Dyes**, p. 63). Such solutions have no action on metallic pens, and dry well, but lack the permanency of a good iron gall ink. Induline blue (B) (p. 63) forms a similarly constituted **blue** ink.

Coloured Writing Inks

These are usually made from water-soluble aniline dyes such as the following, the proportions being 1 part dye to 50-80 parts of water.

For Red Inks.—Eosin, erythrosin, ponceau scarlet, or cotton scarlet.

For Green Inks.—Neptune green S.G., diamond green G.

For Blue Inks.—Indigo carmine, or soluble blue T.

A good blue ink (fast) is made by triturating 10 parts freshly precipitated Prussian blue, 1 part of oxalic acid, and adding water gradually.

Violet.—Acid violet 4B.L.

Yellow.—Fast yellow or tartrazin in water.

Gold Ink.—Gold leaf, mixed with honey, is ground fine, washed, dried, and suspended in gum-arabic (1) + 1 of soluble potash glass dissolved in 4 of water. Substitutes for gold are Dutch leaf or bronze powder. **Silver ink** = powdered silver (or Aluminium foil) rubbed up with gum or the preceding medium.

Essentials of a Good Writing Ink.—(1) The writing should be permanent. (2) The ink should flow readily from the pen. (3) It must penetrate deeply into the fibres of the paper without passing right through. (4) It must not become mouldy or thick in the ink pots. (5) It must not extensively corrode metallic pens. (6) The writing must rapidly dry and should not be sticky—unless it is a copying ink.

Copying and Hectographic Inks

I. Writing Inks.—Ordinary iron-gall and logwood writing inks are rendered capable of giving one or two good copies in a press, or less readily in a rapid-roller copying machine, by the addition of glycerol, gum, sugar, glucose, etc., to a previously concentrated ink.

Better results are obtained by using concentrated solutions of the water-soluble aniline dyes with the addition of a small proportion of glycerol.

Many of the copying inks on the market contain an excess of acids and gums or other thickening substances which are not only unnecessary but actually deleterious.

Any of the basic dyes are suitable for the manufacture of copying inks, the proportion to be used varying with the strength of the dye and the number of copies required.

Hectograph inks are merely concentrated copying inks. Occasionally it is desirable to add a small proportion of alcohol and a very slight excess of a weak acid to prevent thickening due to deposition of the dye.

Typewriter Ribbon Inks.—The manufacture of typewriter ribbons has increased enormously in recent years. There are quite a number of firms who have placed on the market machines for cutting, inking and winding typewriter ribbons ; whilst the manufacture and cutting into the required widths of the fabric is a separate branch of the industry.

The firms selling inking machines also provide suitable grinding mills and formulæ for manufacturing the inks.

Typewriter ribbons may be divided into two classes :—

(a) **Record or Non-Copying.**—The only really permanent ribbons are those inked with a composition having lamp or a similar carbon black as a basis.

For use on a modern inking machine the lampblack, or in the case of coloured ribbons an aniline lake, is ground in a suitable mill with a non-drying oil, thickened if necessary with petroleum jelly. Occasionally a little volatile solvent such as petrol, carbon tetrachloride, etc., is used to facilitate absorption.

Oil-soluble aniline colours may also be employed for the manufacture of one-colour record ribbons.

(*b*) **Copying Ribbons.**—Copying ribbons are made in several varieties.

Slow-copying, two-sided ribbons, for use with the old-fashioned screw press using damp rags; and one or two sided-rapid copying ribbons for use on machines such as the Roneo Copier using rolls of prepared paper.

The slow-copying ribbons contain a lake or colour and a small proportion of a water-soluble dye, whilst the rapid roller ribbons consist of a strong water-soluble dye ground in a non-drying oil. It is not necessary to add glycerol or indeed any other substance beyond the oil and dye.

Testing Typewriter Ribbons.—A well-made typewriter ribbon should give fine sharp impressions, exhibit no tendency to fill the type and be cleanly in use and last a reasonable time without losing its writing or copying properties or wearing into holes.

The general character of a ribbon can best be judged by an extended and careful test carried out on the machine for which the ribbon is intended.

For purposes of comparison short definite lengths of the ribbons to be tested should be worked backwards and forwards through the typewriter a stated number of times and the results compared.

If the letter "e" is alone used for this test the type-filling property can also be judged.

To test the life of a ribbon a special testing machine similar to that described in the United States Bureau of Chemistry Bulletin No. 109 revised, p. 51, is necessary.

Some idea of the life of a ribbon can be obtained, however, from the results obtained in the character and filling tests described above.

In order to obtain concordant and comparable results, it is absolutely necessary that the tests should be carried out under exactly similar conditions.

A good copying ribbon should give eight to twelve readable copies from one original. The copying test should preferably be carried out on a "Copier" in order to obtain comparative results.

As a rule one-sided ribbons give neater work and are cleaner to handle than two-sided ribbons and are absolutely non-filling, but the life is somewhat shorter than that of a two-sided ribbon. One-colour record ribbons are always two-sided.

Record ribbons may be tested for resistance to sunlight and chemical reagents if necessary.

As mentioned previously only black record ribbons are absolutely permanent, but for ordinary commercial use a good copying ribbon is generally preferred owing to the convenience of being able to obtain actual copies of the correspondence without using carbon paper.

Unless actually exposed to sunlight or to the action of chemicals both the original and copies are sufficiently permanent for commercial office use.—FRANK B. GATEHOUSE, F.C.S.

Copying Ink Pencils are made by making a paste of powdered graphite and kaolin clay with a very concentrated solution of methyl violet, pressing into **sticks** and drying.

Manifold Copying Apparatus.—The block of *Rosefeld's* apparatus (English Patent No. 2,256, 1879) consists of gelatine, glycerol, molasses or sugar, acetic acid, iron oxide, and sodium bisulphite. The ink is aqueous methyl violet.

The drawback of gelatine beds is that they become ultimately saturated with ink. *Smith's* apparatus (English Patent No. 7,149, 1888) obviates this, as **ink** is sponged or scraped off when used. The slab consists of china clay, starch, glycerol, and water. The ink is an aniline dye in water, alcohol, and hydrochloric acid. Similar pads consist of water (10), dextrine ($1\frac{1}{2}$), sugar (2), gelatine (15), glycerol (15), zinc oxide (2). Barium sulphate is sometimes used instead of zinc oxide, while the addition of soap makes the surface smooth and easily washable.

Marking Inks

(*a*) **Natural Vegetable Inks.**—A number of plants give black marking inks. Among these we may mention the **juice** of *Coriaria thymifolia*, a plant occurring in New Granada and New Zealand ("ink plant").

The fruit of the Indian tree, *Anacardium orientale* or *Semecarpus anacardium*— the "marking nut"—yields a juice which when mixed with lime water or alkali marks linen an almost indelible black. Similar inks are prepared from the **Cashew Nut** (fruit of Anacardiaceæ, *A. occidentale*, found in India, West Indies, tropical South America), the *Rhus toxicodendron* (North America), *Rhus venenata* (North America), and *Rhus radicans*.

(*b*) **Chemical Marking Inks—Silver Inks.**—These inks contain a silver salt—usually silver nitrate—the reduction of which within the fibres of the material leaves an insoluble black deposit.

Thus *Dieterich's* marking ink consists of 25 parts **silver nitrate** and 15 gum arabic in 60 parts ammonia solution, to which are added 2 parts of lampblack or indigo. The ink must be used with a **quill pen**, and fixed by passing a hot iron over it. With 25 parts of gum it may be used with a rubber stamp.

Aniline Black Marking Ink is obtained by mixing 2 parts aniline black, 40 parts 95 per cent. alcohol, and 2 parts hydrochloric acid; add this to 3 parts shellac in 150 parts of the concentrated alcohol. Not very resistant to alkalis.

Often a solution of india-rubber (in benzene or similar solvent) + aniline or other colours is used; *e.g.*, for black, india-rubber + lampblack + solvent.

Foertsch's Pencil for Glass is made by stirring Prussian blue into a melted mixture of 8 parts white wax and 2 parts tallow, and when nearly cold rolling into a pencil on a slab and covering with a paper case.

Printing Inks

These really are rapidly drying **paints,** consisting of pigments of various colours, thoroughly incorporated with varnish made of boiled linseed oil, rosin oil, or other "vehicles" for paints.

Black Printing Inks are made by mixing lampblack with **varnish.** The proportion and quality of the lampblack varies widely according to the purpose for which the ink is employed, ranging from 20-40 per cent., as shown by annexed table (*Andes,* "Oel und Buchdruckfarben," 1889, p. 239), while occasionally a little blue pigment is added.

	Rotary Machine Ink.	Newspaper Ink.	Book Ink.	Illustration Ink.	
	Per Cent.	Per Cent.	Per Cent.	Per Cent.	Per Cent.
Oil varnish	70-72	76-78	77-79	78	78
Lampblack	30-28	24-22	23-21	20	19
Paris blue	...	...	...	2	2
Indigo	...	...	...	...	1

As regards **Newspaper ink** formerly (and still to some extent) rosin varnish was the vehicle used, made by the destructive distillation of rosin, separated from its water and spirit and from the residual pitch products. Recently heavy mineral oils have largely displaced the resin. Soap is also often added, the presence of soap causing the ink to "lift" well. These vehicles or varnishes are carefully ground with lamp-black, the varnish being made of varying consistencies according as whether the ink is required for slow or fast printing, cold or hot climates. In the inks used now there is a tendency to add blue or blue-black pigments to the lamp-black in order to obtain an intensification of colour and to overcome the brownish tendency which often develops owing to lightness of impression. The exact composition of these inks are carefully guarded trade secrets, but some recipes have been published some of which are given below. In **letterpress inks** the black pigments used are of a more varied character, careful blending of several kinds being resorted to in order to allow the ink to flow at the proper rate for allowing the presses printing machines to run at their proper rate. In **ink for illustrations** the exclusive use of black pigments has now been departed from, delicate shades in ink being now used which greatly heightens the effects of the pictures shown.

The following are some published recipes for printing inks:—

1. To each gallon of **Linseed oil varnish** (prepared by heating the oil to 380°-400° F. in boilers provided with a closely-fitting lid) add 4 lbs. rosin and 1 lb. brown soap in slices. Mix in the proper weight of lampblack (about 30 per cent. of weight of vehicle) or other pigment,

grind and mix in special grinding machinery, between polished granite or steel rollers, then seal up in suitable receptacles, when the ink is ready for use.

2. **Brackenbusch's mineral oil inks** consist of 25 parts paraffin oil, 45 parts of rosin (colophony) and 15 parts of lampblack. For soft inks for high-speed work reduce the percentage of rosin.

3. **Fireman's ink** (U.S. Patent., 802,928) consists of manganese dioxide or oxides of iron pigments ground into varnish. The paper can be bleached and re-made into white paper, which cannot be done with lampblack inks.

The following are some published "*vehicles*" for inks :—

Mineral Oil Vehicles.—Rosin, 1 part, dissolved in 1 part of mineral oil of sp. gr. 0.880 to 0.920, previously heated to expel volatile components.

Rosin Oil Vehicle.—Rosin, 50 ; rosin soap, 5, dissolved in rosin oil, 50 ; boiled linseed oil, 50 ; partly boiled linseed oil, 6.

Linseed Oil Vehicle.—Boiled linseed oil, 100 ; partly boiled linseed oil, 6 ; rosin soap, 10 ; rosin, 50.

Composition Vehicle.—(1) Olein (added hot), 4 ; soft soap, 10 ; thick turpentine, 10. (2) White wax, 1 part mixed at 100° C. with castor oil, 15, and Venice turpentine, 5.

Coloured printing inks are obtained by adding pigments to the oil while it is being heated.

Red—Vermilion, madder, Indian red, Venetian red, orange mineral, orange lead, burnt sienna, rose pink, rose red, red lead, are the colours most used. A bright red is got from pale vermilion + carmine. Also orange red and vermilion (very permanent). For **Pink** use carmine or crimson lake. **Blue**—Ultramarine, Prussian blue, Antwerp blue, Chinese blue, indigo. Indigo makes a good dark blue, but is difficult to lighten. Prussian blue dries quickly and hence requires the roller to be often cleaned. Chinese, Antwerp, and Prussian blues are difficult to grind and print greenish with thin varnish. **Purple** = red + blue pigments. **Lilac** = carmine + cobalt blue. **Green**—Mixtures of yellow and blue pigments, also chrome green, cobalt green, emerald green. **Emerald Green** = pale chrome + Chinese blue. Antwerp blue + yellowish varnish gives greenish tints. **White**—Heavy spar (barium sulphate) ; zinc white, lithophone, white lead. The latter darkens in air. **Yellow**—Chrome yellow, yellow ochre, gamboge. For bright tints use chrome yellow (lead chromates). For dull tints use yellow ochre. **Brown**—Burnt umber + scarlet lake ; burnt sienna alone or with scarlet lake. Avoid heavy colours. See **Pigments**, p. 497 *et seq.*

For **Copperplate printing** and **lithographing** thicker ink is used, which is mixed with a denser black than that used in ordinary printing. The varnishes, made with utmost care from linseed oil thickened by extremely high temperatures.

Modern recipes not published. Old recipes are :—(1) wax, 18 ; shellac, 14 ; rosin, 7 ; tallow, 10 ; soap, 18. Fuse and incorporate 6 of lampblack and 2 of rubber dissolved in 5 of oil of turpentine. (2) Shellac, 12 ; mastic, 8 ; turpentine, 1. Melt, and add 16 wax and 6 tallow, mix wel and incorporate 4 of lampblack. For an **autographic ink**, melt white wax, 8 ; white soap, 2.5 ; incorporate 1 of lampblack, heat strongly and mix in 2 of shellac. Heat again.

The author desires to thank Mr J. W. Barker, A.R.C.S., B.Sc. (H.M. Patent Office), for looking through the MS. of inks and giving me many suggestions. Also Mr Frank B. Gatehouse, of Messrs Roneo, Ltd., for supplying some details of hectographic and copying inks.

Statistics.—The United States imported *Ink* and *Ink powders* to the value of $75,000 in 1906, and $44,000 in 1910. The figures for 1910 are :—

Printers' ink	$4,787.
Writing and copying ink	19,416.
All other, including ink powders	20,162.

The United States exported (principally to England, Canada, and Mexico) :—

	1906.	1910.
Printers' ink	$275,000.	$326,000.
All other	174,000.	192,862.

The British import of printers' ink in 1913 was £23,000. In 1907 Great Britain made £536,000 of printers' ink and £69,000 of other inks (writing, endorsing, marking, etc.).

CHAPTER VI

SACCHARINE AND OTHER ARTIFICIAL SWEETENING CHEMICALS

Within the last few decades chemicals of enormous sweetening power have been placed on the market. The most important of these is the **Saccharine** of Fahlberg, o-anhydrosulphamine-benzoic acid or benzoic sulphimide, $C_6H_4\diagdown^{CO}_{SO_2}\diagup NH$; discovered in 1879 by Ira Remsen and C. Fahlberg, and now manufactured by Fahlberg, List, & Co., in Salbke-Westerhüsen near Magdeburg. **Toluene** is converted into o- and p-toluene-sulphonic acid, $C_6H_4(CH_3)(SO_3H)$, by treating with concentrated H_2SO_4 at 100° C. The acid is converted first into the calcium salt (by $CaCO_3$) and then into the sodium salt (by Na_2CO_3), which is dried, treated with PCl_5 and Cl gas, whereby toluene sulpho-chloride, $C_6H_4(CH_3).SO_2Cl$, is produced. This, by treating with NH_3 gas or with Am_2CO_3, yields o-toluol-sulphamide, $C_6H_4(CH_3).SO_2NH_2$, which is oxidised by an alkaline solution of $KMnO_4$ to $C_6H_4.(COOH).SO_2NH_2$, which when treated with HCl is immediately converted into free o-sulphaminebenzoic acid, $C_6H_4(COOH)SO_2NH_2$, which then spontaneously splits off water, forming the anhydride, $C_6H_4\diagdown^{CO}_{SO_2}\diagup NH$, which separates out.

Saccharine is a white crystalline powder with difficulty soluble in water, melts at 223.5° C. and is *five hundred times* sweeter than cane sugar. **Easily soluble saccharine** consists of the sodium salt, $C_6H_4\diagdown^{CO}_{NH}\diagup N.Na$, prepared by treating saccharine with alkali carbonates.

Dulcin or **Sucrol** is another sweet chemical, about two hundred times sweeter than cane sugar. It is mono-p-phenetol-carbamide, $NH_2.CO.NHC_6H_4.OC_2H_5$, prepared by evaporating a solution of p-amidophenetol cyanate thus :—

$$C_2H_5O.C_6H_4.NH_2-(HO-C \vdots N) \longrightarrow C_2H_5O.C_6H_4.NH-CO-NH_2.$$

It may also be obtained by heating urea with phenetidine hydrochloride,

$$C_6H_4\diagdown^{OC_2H_5}_{NH_2.HCl} + CO\diagdown^{NH_2}_{NH_2} = CO\diagdown^{NH_2}_{NH.C_6H_4.OC_2H_5} + NH_4Cl.$$

White needles, M.P. 173° C. ; soluble in 800 parts of cold or 55 parts of boiling water, also in 25 parts of alcohol.

Other very sweet chemicals are **Glucine** (amidotri-azinesulphonic acid or its Na salt), **Sandoce** or **Methyl Saccharine**, $C_6H_3(CH_3).\diagdown^{CO}_{SO_2}\diagup NH$, etc.

Saccharine and similar sweetening chemicals possess no food value at all, while sugar, on the other hand, is a valuable food. The use of saccharine has on this account been made illegal in many countries as a sweetening agent for cakes, liquors, etc., intended for human consumption (except in the case of certain medicines). Saccharine must be made under Government supervision, and it is sold by apothecaries to diabetic patients as a substitute for sugar. It has considerable antiseptic or preserving qualities.

Statistics.—Saccharine is subjected to a duty of 7d. the oz. in Great Britain, the duty raised from this source being £36,000 in 1913 on 1,234,000 oz. The quantity imported in 1913 was 1,242,000 oz., of value £14,435. The quantity exported was 21,278 oz., of value £4,402. No saccharine was manufactured in the United Kingdom prior to 1903.

The United States imported 2,977 lbs. (value, $3,395) in 1908, and 1,405 lbs. (value, $1,901) in 1909 ; the United States export reached 2,513 lbs. (value, $2,225) in 1910 ; the United States duty is $1.50 per lb. and 10 per cent.

CHAPTER VII

The Industry of Modern Synthetic Drugs

CHAPTER VII

THE INDUSTRY OF MODERN SYNTHETIC DRUGS

LITERATURE

FRANCIS AND FORTESCUE-BRICKDALE.—"The Chemical Basis of Pharmacology." Bristol, 1909.

FORTESCUE-BRICKDALE.—"Guide to the Newer Remedies." Bristol, 1910.

FRÄNKEL.—"Arzneimittelsynthese." 3rd Edition. Berlin, 1912.

NELSON.—"Analysis of Drugs and Medicines." New York, 1910.

MERCK'S INDEX.—1902.

MERCK'S ANNUAL REPORTS.

WAUGH, ABBOTT, AND EPPSTEIN.—"Alkaloidal Therapeutics." Chicago, 1907.

KEANE.—*Journ. Soc. Chem. Ind.*, 15th April 1910, 388.

MARTINDALE AND WESTCOTT.—"Salvarsan (606)." London, 1911.

EHRLICH AND HATA.—"Die experimentelle Chemotherapie der Spirillosen." Berlin, 1911.

MAY.—"The Chemistry of Synthetic Drugs." London, 1911.

JOWETT AND PYMAN.—"Relation between Chemical Constitution and Physiological Action." *Proc. Internat. Congress of Applied Chemistry,* 1909, Sect. IV. A, I.

The following works deal with natural alkaloids :—

WINTERSTEIN U. TRIER.—"Die Alkaloide." Berlin, 1910.

PICTET.—"Die Pflanzenalkaloide und Ihre Chemische Konstitution." Berlin, 1900.

BRÜHL, HJELT, U. ASCHAN.—"Die Pflanzenalkaloide." Braunschweig, 1900.

J. SCHMIDT.—"Pflanzenalkaloide (Konstitution u. Synthese)." Stuttgart, 1900.

    „   "Die Alkaloidchemie in den Jahren 1900-1911." 3 vols.

For the Patent Literature up to 1905 see WINTHER'S "Patente der Organischen Chemie." 1877-1905. 3 vols. For **Trade Names** of the newer drugs, see MARTIN'S "Industrial Chemistry," Vol. I., list on p. 667 (Appendix II.).

INTRODUCTION

IT is impossible in the space at our disposal to give a complete account of the enormous number of new drugs now on the market. The reader is referred to the above-mentioned literature for further information. All that is attempted is a brief account of some of the more important of the drugs—especially the newer synthetic ones—which within the last few years have been placed on the market, and which will in the future play an important part in therapeutics.

The larger modern chemical firms—such as Burroughs Wellcome & Co. ; Merck ; Meister, Lucius, & Brüning—employ a staff of university-trained scientists to synthesise and test new drugs, and some of the recent discoveries made by these firms are certainly epoch making. The whole chemistry of Ergot, for example, has been revolutionised by recent work carried out in the laboratories of Messrs Burroughs Wellcome & Co. by Barger and others, while equally important work has been done by Meister, Lucius, & Brüning of Höchst on Adrenaline and on the new organic arsenic compounds used in treating sleeping sickness and syphilis.

Statistics.—The following figures show the magnitude of t]e import and export of drugs into the United Kingdom :—

IMPORT.

	1905.	1913.	Value, 1913.
Opium - - - - - - -	825,836 lbs.	566,834 lbs.	£507,261
Quinine and quinine salts - - -	1,973,039 oz.	2,422,944 oz.	102,101
Peruvian bark - - - - - -	24,602 cwt.	26,122 cwt.	58,000
Chloral hydrate - - - - -	19,978 lbs.	23,501 lbs.	2,080
Chloroform - - - - - -	972 ,,	1,366 ,,	347
Other drugs and medical preparations -	...	...	1,302,800
Total - - -	...	...	£1,972,589

The amount of imported tea for the manufacture of **caffeine** was 1,500,000 lbs. (value £10,300) in 1913.

EXPORT.

	1906.	1913.	Value, 1913.
Cocaine - - - - - - -	...	3,300 oz.	£1,000
Morphia - - - - - - -	...	400,000 ,,	193,000
Opium - - - - - - -	...	12,100 lbs.	12,400
Quinine and quinine salts - - -	1,059,948 oz.	1,374,000 oz.	72,600
Other medicines and drugs - - -	...	...	2,072,000

The United States imports (entered for consumption) in 1910 were :—

	Quantity.	Value.
Caffeine - - - - - -	60,500 lbs.	$100,500
Chloroform - - - - - -	960 ,,	1,500
Cinchona bark - - - - - -	3,300,000 ,,	242,000
Quinine sulphate, quinine, and other alkaloids from cinchona bark - -	3,000,000 oz.	398,000
Cocaine - - - - - -	29,600 ,,.	38,000
Cocaine salts, ecgonine - - -	24,900 ,,	42,000
Ergot - - - - - -	181,600 lbs.	53,000
Ichthyol - - - - - -	14,400 ,,	21,500
Iodoform - - - - - -	31 ,,	97
Opium - - - • - -	439,000 ,,	1,575,000
Morphia and salts - - - -	13,000 oz.	60,000
Other opium alkaloids - - -	23,020 ,,	66,000
Santonin and salts - - - -	7,300 lbs.	53,000
Strychnine and salts - - -	2,000 oz.	1,000

ANÆSTHETICS

Anæsthetics may be divided into (*a*) General Anæsthetics, (*b*) Local Anæsthetics.

(*a*) General Anæsthetics

Produce total insensibility to pain. Usually administered by inhalation. The most important are :—

Chloroform, $CHCl_3$.—For manufacture and properties see Martin's "Industrial Chemistry," Vol. I. p. 377. For anæsthetic purposes it should contain 1 per cent. absolute alcohol, or it undergoes decomposition. Used for operations where a considerable interval of anæsthesia is required.

Ether, $C_2H_5.O.C_2H_5.$—For preparation and properties see Martin's " Industrial Chemistry," Vol. I. p. 381. Anæsthesia endures for a shorter time than that produced by chloroform.

Ethyl Chloride, $C_2H_5Cl.$—Obtained by passing dry HCl gas into ethyl alcohol in the presence of $ZnCl_2$ (see p. 377). B.P. 12.5° C., hence is gaseous at ordinary temperatures. Miscible with alcohol. Sparingly soluble in H_2O. Produces anæsthesia in 30 to 120 seconds, which endures for fifteen to twenty minutes. Only one nineteenth the paralysing action on the heart of that possessed by chloroform.

Ethyl Bromide, $C_2H_5Br.$—Now produced very pure by Merck. Colourless liquid of B.P. 38.4° C.; sp. gr. (13° C.) 1.47. Produces extremely rapid anæsthesia, but has a somewhat irritating action on the lungs.

Narcotil is a mixture of methyl and ethyl chlorides.

Somnoform consists of the same ingredients with the addition of **ethyl bromide**.

(b) Local Anæsthetics

There is a large and increasing number of organic compounds which, under suitable conditions, can render certain definite portions of the body insensible to pain ("local anæsthesia"). Certain alkaloids, for example, when dropped upon the eye in the form of solution, render possible operations which would otherwise have to be performed under the influence of chloroform or one of the other general anæsthetics. Similarly, when such a substance is injected at the base of the spine, the whole of the region of the loins is rendered completely insensible to pain.

The discovery of the action of these drugs is one of the very greatest importance to the medical man, and during the last ten years they have almost superseded chloroform for the performance of several of the less serious operations. Moreover, in cases where, for several reasons, it is not yet considered advisable to dispense with the use of a general anæsthetic, the quantity of the latter which is required has been considerably reduced by administering a local anæsthetic as well. This is of special importance in cases where, owing to certain diseased conditions of the organism, the use of chloroform is attended with more than the usual amount of danger.

Most of these drugs are administered by injection into the region which it is desired to anæsthetise. For operations upon the eye, the solution is usually applied in the form of drops.

The chief local anæsthetics employed are :—

Cocaine, $C_{17}H_{21}NO_4$, a white crystalline alkaloid occurring in the leaves of *Erythroxylon coca* of Bolivia and Peru. The leaves contain 1 per cent. ether soluble alkaloids, about half of which is cocaine, the other alkaloids including tropacocaine, truxilline, cinnamylcocaine, and hygrine. The leaves are exhausted with water at 60°-80° C., protein matter precipitated with lead acetate, excess of lead removed by Na_2SO_4, the filtered solution concentrated, made alkaline with ammonia, and the alkaloid extracted with ether.

Cocaine is methylbenzoylecgonine, ecgonine being a carboxyl derivative of tropine. Its relationship to atropine, the alkaloid of *Atropa belladonna* or the Deadly Nightshade, will be seen from the constitutional formulæ :—

Tropine.   Atropine.

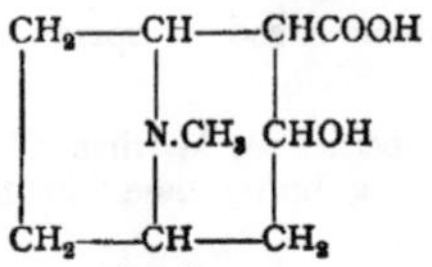

$$CH_2—CH—CHCOOH$$
$$N.CH_3 \quad CHOH$$
$$CH_2—CH—CH_2$$
Ecgonine.

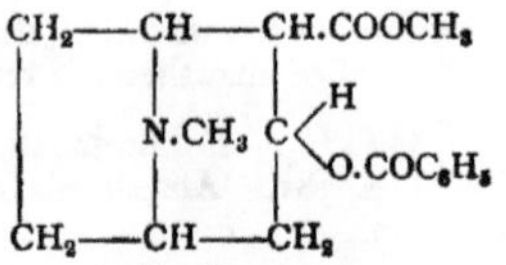

$$CH_2—CH—CH.COOCH_3$$
$$N.CH_3 \quad C \overset{H}{\underset{O.COC_6H_5}{<}}$$
$$CH_2—CH—CH_2$$
Cocaine.

Other alkaloids, with very undesirable action, which occur in the coca leaves, may be converted into ecgonine by heating with HCl. Pure cocaine can then be prepared synthetically from ecgonine.

Properties.—Large colourless crystals, M.P. 98° C.; bitter taste; very sparingly soluble in water; soluble in alcohol, ether, benzene, chloroform, etc. Forms monovalent salts with acids.

In small doses the drug sustains muscular energy, raises the body temperature and blood pressure. Dilates the eye pupil. Excess causes death by convulsions. Its chief value is its power of paralysing nerve-ends, and so causing local anæsthesia for minor surgical operations. Maximum daily dose, 0.15 g.; maximum single dose, 0.05 g. For injections a 5-10 per cent. solution is used.

Tropacocaine = benzoyl-ψ-tropine, $C_{15}N_{19}NO_2$. Accompanies cocaine in the leaves of *Erythroxylon coca*; sixty-three times less toxic than cocaine, and its action commences more quickly. No dilation of the pupil. It is an excellent local anæsthetic, and is coming more and more into use.

Synthetic substitutes for **cocaine** are :—

Anæsthesine, $NH_2.\langle\quad\rangle.COOC_2H_5.$—Obtained by reducing p-nitrobenzoic

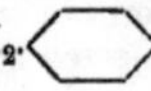

ethyl ester with Sn + HCl. Excellent anæsthetic of low toxicity and non-irritant power. Used for anæsthising wounds and checking vomiting.

Novocaine, $NH_2.\langle\quad\rangle CO_2.CH_2.CH_2.N(C_2H_5)_2, HCl.$ — Excellent local

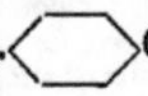

anæsthetic, used in dentistry, and for the production of spinal anæsthesia. Often used with adrenaline.

Stovaine forms white, lustrous scales, M.P. 175°, readily soluble in water; prepared by the interaction of magnesium ethyl bromide and dimethylaminoacetone, and subsequent benzoylation of the product thus formed. It has the constitution :—

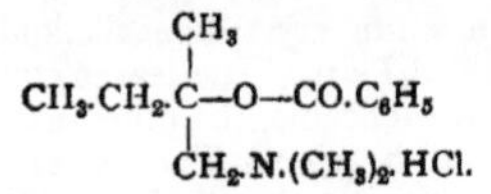

$$CH_3$$
$$CH_3.CH_2.C—O—CO.C_6H_5$$
$$CH_2.N.(CH_3)_2.HCl.$$

As little as 0.3 c.c. of a 10 per cent. solution are sufficient to produce anæsthesia in the legs below the knees.

Much used as a local anæsthetic in dental, ophthalmic, and minor surgical operations. Much less toxic than cocaine.

Alypine has the constitution

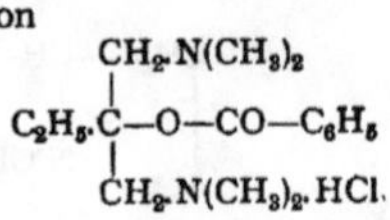

$$CH_2.N(CH_3)_2$$
$$C_2H_5.C—O—CO—C_6H_5$$
$$CH_2.N(CH_3)_2.HCl.$$

Readily soluble in H_2O and probably superior to stovaine as a local anæsthetic. Used as a substitute for cocaine in 1-5 per cent. solution.

When administered along with heroine (diacetylmorphine) the demulcent and sedative effects of the latter drug are enhanced, and the combination has proved very successful in allaying the nocturnal cough of pulmonary tuberculosis.*

The Eucaines.—The important results which usually follow the determination of the chemical constitution of any important physiologically active substance are well instanced by the existence of α- and β-eucaine.

The preparation of these two compounds was a direct outcome of the various attempts which were made to prepare substances chemically related to cocaine.

Preparation of the Eucaines.—By the condensation of 2 molecules of acetone with 1 of ammonia, diacetoneamine is formed (I.). If this be allowed to react with a third molecule of acetone, the symmetrical triacetoneamine is obtained (II.). If instead of allowing the diacetoneamine to react with acetone, acetaldehyde be used, the product is a substance known as vinyldiacetoneamine (III.). Thus :—

$$(CH_3)_2C \mid O$$
$$H_2N \mid H \qquad H \mid CH_2COCH_3$$

Vinyldiacetoneamine (III.) ← Acetaldehyde $CH_3C \diagdown^O_H$ + Diacetoneamine (I.) + $(CH_3)_2CO$ Acetone → Triacetoneamine (II.)

Triacetoneamine is a crystalline solid, M.P. 39°-40°. It has a strong alkaline reaction and its odour is ammoniacal, and also similar to that of camphor. When converted into its cyanhydrin, and then hydrolysed, methylation and benzoylation of the resulting hydroxy acid yield α-eucaine.

Triacetoneamine → (hydroxy acid, COOH/OH) → α-Eucaine.

Vinyldiacetoneamine is a volatile base, M.P. 27°, B.P. 200°, which forms salts with acids. When the carbonyl group in this substance is reduced, benzoylation yields a derivative, the hydrochloride of which is β-eucaine.

Vinyldiacetoneamine → (OH/H) → β-Eucaine.

α- and β-eucaine are colourless crystals, the former soluble in 10 parts and the latter in 30 of water. α-Eucaine has been abandoned in practice owing to its irritant action on the tissues.

The anæsthetic action of β-eucaine is somewhat feebler than that of cocaine, and in consequence of its vasodilatory properties it gives rise to hæmorrhage and causes pain when injected. It has also a tendency, when used in ophthalmic surgery, to cause hardening. This difficulty seems to have

---

* Laufer, "Merck's Reports," 1907, 21 ; *Reichs-Medisinal-Anzeiger*, 1907, 17.

been largely overcome by Langgaard * by combining β-eucaine with lactic acid, when a product is obtained which is non-irritant and causes neither local anæmia, hyperæmia, nor shrinkage. Injections of β-eucaine have been employed by Opitz † with very great success in the treatment of sciatica and neuralgia, the drug having a decided curative as well as analgesic effect.

In spite of the similarity in chemical constitution between the eucaines and cocaine, they are hardly such satisfactory substitutes for the latter drug as tropacocaine.

SYNTHETIC ANTIPYRETICS

Acetanilide, or Antifebrin, $C_6H_5.NH.COCH_3$, prepared by heating in earthenware vessels for one to two days equal parts of aniline and glacial acetic acid :
$C_6H_5.NH_2 + CH_3.COOH = H_2O + C_6H_5.NH.CO.CH_3$.

Used as a febrifuge in cases of typhoid fever, small-pox, phthisis, rheumatism, and erysipelas. Prolonged use is dangerous.

Acetylsalicylic Acid (Aspirin), $C_6H_4(CO_2.CH_3).CO_2H$, prepared by heating salicylic acid with acetic anhydride or acetyl chloride, and recrystallising from chloroform. See also American Patent 749,980 and English Patent 15,517/02. White needles, M.P. 135°. Moderately soluble in water, easily in alcohol and ether. Dose, 0.5 g. ; 4 g. may be given daily for rheumatism and neuralgia.

Phenacetine is acetyl *p*-phenetidine, $C_6H_4\diagup\diagdown^{O.C_2H_5}_{NH.CO.CH_3}$.   *Preparation.—*

Phenol, C_6H_5OH, is nitrated, aud the *p*-nitro-phenol, $C_6H_4.(NO_2).OH$, is separated from the *o*-compound, and ethylated with ethyl sulphate, whereby $C_6H_4(NO_2).OC_2H_5$ is produced. This is reduced with Sn + HCl, thereby producing **Phenetidine,** $C_6H_4(NH_2).OC_2H_5$, which is then acetylated by boiling with acetic acid, thus producing phenacetine, $C_6H_4.(OC_2H_5).NHCOCH_3$. White crystals; tasteless; valuable antipyretic and antineuralgic. Dose, 0.5-0.75 g. Very largely used, England importing about 8½ tons yearly. Owing to its sparingly soluble nature its action takes place slowly. This defect is partially overcome by introducing an NH_2 group into its acetyl group, thus producing **Phenocoll.**

Triphenine is propionyl-*p*-phenetidine, $C_6H_4(OC_2H_5)NH(CO.CH_2.CH_3)$, prepared similarly to phenacetine by heating *p*-phenetidine with propionic acid. Very sparingly soluble in H_2O. M.P. 120° C. Antipyretic and antineuralgic.

Phenocoll, $C_6H_4(OC_2H_5).NH.CO.CH_2.NH_2$.—It is prepared by acting on phenetidine with chloracetyl chloride, and treating the resulting compound with ammonia ; its salts are soluble in water. It is a rapidly acting antipyretic and antineuralgic, but is transitory in its effects.

Neraltein, a new drug, is the sodium salt of *p*-ethoxyphenylaminomethane-sulphonic acid ; white crystals, soluble in 10 parts of cold water.

$$C_2H_5O\diagup\hexagon\diagdown NH.CH_2.SO_2ONa + H_2O.$$

Only slightly toxic, and in small doses produces no irritation of the kidneys ; possesses good analgesic properties, and has been used in slight cases of rheumatism.

Antipyrine is the most important member of the " pyrazolone drugs."

Manufacture.—Phenylhydrazine (II.) (216 parts) is dissolved in dilute sulphuric acid (300 g. of acid in 2 l. of water). Ethyl acetoacetate (I.) (260 parts) is then allowed to flow into the solution at a temperature of about 40°, the mixture being stirred constantly. Atter the reaction is at an end, excess of caustic soda solution is added and the mixture extracted with ether. From the ethereal extract, after washing with caustic soda solution and drying over calcium chloride, methyl-phenyl-pyrazolone (III.) is obtained as an oil which can be distilled *in vacuo*.

When 200 parts of this are heated with 140 parts of methyl iodide and 200 parts of methyl alcohol at 100°-110° for twelve hours, methylation takes place. After removing the alcohol by evaporation

---

* " Merck's Reports," 1904, 63 ; *Therapeutische Monatshefte*, 1904, No. 8, 416.
† *Ibid.* 1907, 97 ; *Klinisch-therapeutische-Wochenschrift*, 1907, No. 14.

the residue is decolourised with a little dilute solution of sulphurous acid. Caustic soda is then added and the precipitated oil extracted with benzene from which solvent the drug can be crystallised.

$$CH_3CO \quad H_2N \quad CH_3.C—CH_2 \quad CH_2C=CH$$

CH_2		$N \quad CO$ $\longrightarrow$	$CH_3.N \quad CO$
$OC.OC_2H_5$	$HN.C_6H_5$	$N.C_6H_5$	$N.C_6H_5$
(I.)	(II.)	(III.)	(IV.)
Ethyl acetoacetate.	Phenylhydrazine.	Methyl-pnenylpyrazolone.	Antipyrine.

$$CH—CH_2$$
$$N \quad CO$$
$$NH$$
Pyrazolone.

Antipyrine (IV.) forms colourless, inodorous, scaly crystals possessing a bitter taste; readily soluble in water, chloroform, or alcohol. M.P. $112°$-$113°$. Acts as a base forming salts directly with acids. Much valued for the treatment of fever, neuralgia, and rheumatism. Dose, 0.25-2 g. daily.

Tussol—prescribed for whooping cough—is the antipyrine salt of Mandelic acid.

Migräneine is a mixture of caffeine citrate and antipyrine, used for headaches, etc., as an antipyretic and antineuralgic.

Salipyrine is antipyrine salicylate.

Pyramidone, 4-dimethylamino-antipyrine, is prepared from antipyrine hydrochloride by the action of nitrous acid whereby a nitroso-antipyrine is produced (I.). On reduction this is converted into aminoantipyrine (II.) which is isolated in the form of its benzylidene derivative. On treatment with methyl iodide it yields pyramidone (III.). This forms small colourless crystals of slightly bitter taste which are readily soluble in water. M.P. 108°.

$CH_3C=CH$	$CH_3C=C.NO$	$CH_3C=C.NH_2$	$CH_3C=C.N.(CH_3)_2$
$CH_3.N \quad CO$ $\longrightarrow$	$CH_3.N \quad CO$ $\longrightarrow$	$CH_3.N \quad CO$ $\longrightarrow$	$CH_3N \quad CO$
$N.C_6H_5$	$N.C_6H_5$	$N.C_6H_5$	$N.C_6H_5$
Antipyrine.	(I.)	(II.)	(III.)
			Pyramidone.

Pyramidone possesses advantage over antipyrine in that it may be prescribed in cases where there is cardiac weakness. The effective dose is only one-third that of antipyrine while it has no irritant effect on the stomach or kidneys.

It has been largely used to allay the high temperatures of typhoid fever and of phthisis, and also in neuralgia and rheumatism.

Trigemine is dimethylaminoantipyrine + butyl chloral hydrate, $C_{17}H_{24}O_8N_8Cl_3$, or :—

$$
\begin{array}{cc}
CH_3 & CH_3 \\
C & CHCl \\
CH_3—N \quad C—N{<}^{CH_3}_{CH_3} & + \quad CCl_2 \\
C_6H_5—N—CO & CH \\
& HO \quad OH
\end{array}
$$

It is prepared by mixing dimethylaminoantipyrine with butyl chloral hydrate. M.P. 85°. Soluble in H_2O, alcohol, and benzene; less so in ether and ligroin. Has an analgesic effect, and is prescribed for headaches, neuralgia, etc. Mild antipyretic. Dose, 0.5-1.2 g.

HYPNOTICS

An ideal hypnotic will produce a normal sleep as differentiated from a **narcotic** which produces unconsciousness by intoxication.

The first hypnotic used was **Chloral Hydrate**, $CCl_3.CH(OH)_2$ (1869), the manufacture and properties of which are treated on p. 379. Chloral hydrate, while producing sleep, exerts a depressing action on the heart, sometimes acts as a toxic agent, and often sets up the "chloral habit." Consequently a large number of substitutes have been sought.

Dormiole is amylene chloral, $CCl_3.CH(OH).O.C_5H_{11}$, produced by mixing 6 parts amylene hydrate + 10 of chloral. Colourless oily liquid, insoluble in water, soluble in alcohol, ether, acetone, etc. Useful and harmless soporific in **heart disease** and **nervous troubles**, etc.

Isopral is **trichlorisopropyl alcohol**, $CCl_3.CH(OH).CH_3$, prepared by treating chloral with methyl magnesium iodide and decomposing with dilute acid—

$$CCl_3.CHO + CH_3.Mg.I = CCl_3.CH.(OMgI).CH_3 + H_2O = CCl_3.CH(OH).CH_3 + Mg(OH)I.$$

Colourless crystals, M.P. 49° C., soluble in alcohol, ether; sparingly soluble in H_2O. Twice as powerful hypnotic as chloral hydrate. Dose, 0.5 to 1 g. In insanity, 2-3 g.

Acetone Chloroform, Chloretone, $(CH_3)_2.C.(OH).CCl_3$, is used as a soporific, inhalation anæsthetic, and a remedy for sea-sickness.

Sulphonal, diethylsulphonedimethylmethane (III.), is prepared by condensing acetone with ethyl mercaptan (I.) and oxidising the resulting compound (II.) with potassium permanganate.

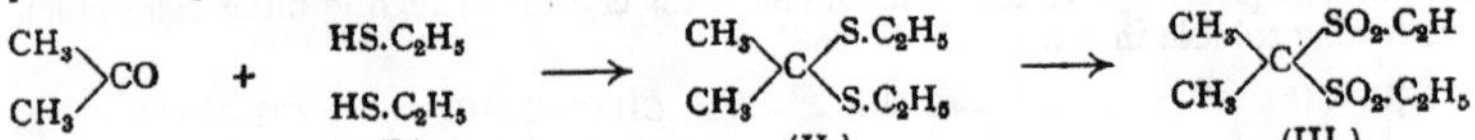

Acetone.   Ethyl mercaptan.   (I.)   (II.)   (III.) Sulphonal.

Heavy, colourless prismatic crystals, M.P. 125.5°, soluble in 500 parts of water, 133 parts of ether, and 65 parts of alcohol at 15° C., and in 15 parts of boiling water. It should be free from odour. Used as a sleep producer (dose, 10-20 gr. = 0.65-1.3 g.), also prescribed in epilepsy and in diminishing the sweats of phthisis.

Single, occasional doses do not affect the health, but the continued administration of the drug has been known to lead to serious consequences, such as mental confusion, difficulty of speech and breathing, paralysis of the legs, and finally death.

Trional and **Tetronal** are two drugs closely allied to sulphonal. Their constitution is shown below :—

(I.) Trional.   (II.) Tetronal.

The methods employed in their manufacture are analogous to those employed for sulphonal.

Trional forms colourless crystals, M.P. 76°, readily soluble in alcohol and ether, slightly so in water. The dose for insomnia is from 1-2 g., as an anhydrotic from 0.25-0.5 g. It is contra-indicated in certain affections of the heart.

Tetronal forms lustrous leaflets melting at 85° and possessing the solubilities and general action of the last two drugs. Dose, the same as for trional.

The physiological action of these drugs depends on the presence of the ethyl groups, since dimethylsulphonedimethylmethane (I.) is practically without hypnotic effect. Moreover, the intensity of the physiological action increases as we pass from sulphonal to tetronal, *i.e.*, as the number of ethyl groups increases. In this connection it is interesting to note that if one of the methyl groups in sulphonal be replaced by a phenyl group, the resulting substance (II.) is devoid of soporific effect, but if both methyl groups are so replaced an intensely poisonous compound (III.) is obtained.

$$
\begin{array}{ccc}
\underset{CH_3}{\overset{CH_3}{>}}C\underset{SO_2.CH_3}{\overset{SO_2.CH_3}{<}} & \underset{C_6H_5}{\overset{CH_3}{>}}C\underset{SO_2.C_2H_5}{\overset{SO_2.C_2H_5}{<}} & \underset{C_6H_5}{\overset{C_6H_5}{>}}C\underset{SO_2.C_2H_5}{\overset{SO_2.C_2H_5}{<}} \\
(I.) & (II.) & (III.)
\end{array}
$$

Keane,[*] in a lecture delivered before the Liverpool Section of the Society of Chemical Industry, draws attention to the fact that the ethyl groups of the sulphone hypnotics are the agents whereby the grouping $>C<\substack{SO_2- \\ SO_2-}$, which is really the carrier of the soporific action, can be brought into combination with the protoplasm of the living organism.

Hedonal, methylpropylcarbinolurethane, $NH_2.CO.O.CH(CH_3)(C_3H_7)$, is prepared by acting on secondary amyl alcohol, $(CH_3)(C_3H_7).CHOH$, with ethyl chlorocarbonate, and then treating with NH_3. Crystals; M.P. 76°; sparingly soluble in cold, easily in hot H_2O. Hypnotic in cases of hysteria or neurasthenia. Dose, 1.5-2 g. in alcohol.

Veronal,[†] diethylmalonylurea, or diethylbarbituric acid, $C_8H_{12}O_3N_2$, introduced into therapeutics in 1903 by Emil Fischer and von Mering, is prepared by the condensation of diethylmalonyl chloride (I.) or ethyl diethylmalonate (II.) and urea :—

Small transparent crystals; M.P. 191°; soluble in 145 parts H_2O at 20° C., 12 parts H_2O at 100° C. The monosodium derivative is more soluble, and so is frequently employed. An excellent soporific (dose, 0.5-1 g.), superior to most synthetic soporifics in that it is free from unpleasant bye-effects. No injurious effects on the heart. Used in sea-sickness, vomiting, etc.

---

[*] *Journ. Soc. Chem. Ind.,* 15th April 1910.
[†] See Merck's "Annual Reports," 1903-1910, and a pamphlet entitled "Veronal" also published by the same firm.

It is very much to be preferred to other drugs in cases where the patient may have to receive a hypnotic for a protracted period, since there seems to be no evidence to show that it produces a habit, although in time the effective dose of the drug may have to be raised slightly. In such cases the treatment may advantageously be varied by the prescription of proponal (see below). It has been successfully used as a partial substitute for morphine in the early stages of treatment of patients striving to break off a habit for that drug.

Proponal* is dipropylmalonylurea or dipropylbarbituric acid :—

$$
\begin{array}{c}
NH—CO \\
\ \ \ \ \ \ \ \ \ \ \ C_3H_7 \\
CO\ \ \ C \\
\ \ \ \ \ \ \ \ \ \ \ C_3H_7 \\
NH—CO
\end{array}
$$

The preparation is analogous to that of veronal. It is less soluble than the latter drug, dissolving in 70 parts boiling and 1,640 parts cold water. Dose in simple insomnia $= 0.15$-0.2 g.

It not infrequently produces a remarkably prolonged effect, a feeling of drowsiness persisting for some hours after awakening. This drug seems to be quite equal to veronal in its freedom from unpleasant effects.

It is probably the presence of the urea residue which is responsible for the soporific effect in veronal and proponal. This is evident from the fact that while the amide of diethylmalonic acid (I.) has no hypnotic effect, diethylacetyl urea (II.)—in which a urea residue has been introduced—is as strong a hypnotic as sulphonal. The action of the urea radical is greatest when it is present in the form of a cyclic ureide, as in the veronal group of hypnotics (III.).

$$
\begin{array}{ccc}
CO.NH_2 & CO.NH.CONH_2 & \\
\ \ |\ \ C_2H_5 & \ \ |\ \ C_2H_5 & CO—NH \\
C & C & C\ \ \ \ \ CO \\
\ \ |\ \ C_2H_5 & \ \ |\ \ C_2H_5 & CO—NH \\
CO.NH_2 & H & \\
(I.) & (II.) & (III.)
\end{array}
$$

Amide of diethylmalonic acid. Diethylacetyl urea.   Hypnotic group in veronal and proponal.
No hypnotic properties.   Hypnotic properties. Strong hypnotic properties.

Overton† has shown for a large number of hypnotics that the intensity of the narcotic action of a given drug is proportional to the ratio between its solubilities in oil and in water (*i.e.*, distribution coefficient).

The discovery is important because the material of nerve cells is largely composed of oily or fatty substances (lipoids).

The narcotic drug, after introduction into the system, rapidly finds its way into the blood, in which condition it is practically in aqueous solution ; the extent of its narcotic action, or, in other words, the extent to which it permeates the nerve cells, depends, therefore, on the ratio between its solubility in the serum and in the cell lipoids. This applies, of course, to drugs such as chloroform and ether as well as to sulphonal, trional, etc.

ADRENALINE

Adrenaline (epinephrine, suprarenine, hemisine), the active principle of the suprarenal capsules, has the constitution—

$$
\begin{array}{c}
OH \\
\ \ \ OH \\
\bigcirc \\
CH(OH).CH_2NH.CH_3
\end{array}
$$

Adrenaline forms white, light crystals, M.P. $210°$-$212°$, very sparingly soluble in water, alcohol, and ether; soluble in dilute acids. The aqueous solution has a

---

* Merck's "Reports," 1905-1909.
† "Studien über Narcose," Dissertation, Jena, 1901 ; see also Pfluger's *Archives*, 92, 115-280.

bitter taste and is faintly alkaline. In alkaline and neutral solution it is a strong reducing agent, absorbing oxygen from the air and turning brown, the change being accompanied by a diminution in physiological activity.

Adrenaline is known in all three possible forms, viz., laevo-rotatory (l), dextro-rotatory (d), and racemic (dl).

In the suprarenal capsules only the laevo-rotatory base occurs, and this is by far the most physiologically active, being (as regards rise of blood pressure) twelve to fifteen times stronger than the d-modification, and *twice* as strong as the dl or racemic variety.

(a) Extraction of l-Adrenaline from the Suprarenal Glands.—Takamine extracted at 95° C. the disintegrated suprarenal glands of sheep or oxen with water acidulated with HCl or acetic acid, concentrated the extract, added alcohol until no further precipitate was thrown down, filtered, evaporated *in vacuo*, and rendered alkaline with ammonia. In a few hours adrenaline crystallised out and was purified by solution in acid and reprecipitation with ammonia. 112 kg. of fresh tissue yield 125 g. adrenaline. $[a]_D = -51.4°$ in HCl.

(b) Synthetic Preparation of Adrenaline (Stolz).—Chloroacetylchloride (I.) or a mixture of monochloroacetic acid and phosphorus oxychloride is made to react with catechol whereby chloroacetylcatechol * (II.) is produced. This is then mixed with alcohol, and an aqueous solution of methylamine run into the cooled mixture.

The methylamine salt of the chloroacetylcatechol is first produced, but on standing changes to methylaminoacetylcatechol (III.) which crystallises out. This ketone is known as adrenalone; its salts with acids differ from those of adrenaline in that sodium acetate precipitates from them the free base.

By reduction of a solution of adrenalone sulphate by means of aluminium turnings † in presence of mercuric sulphate, adrenaline (IV.) is obtained.

Dakin ‡ has also reduced adrenalone electrolytically.

CH₂Cl.COCl			
(I.)	(II.)	(III.)	(IV.)
Chloracetyl chloride.	Chloracetyl catechol.	Adrenalone.	Adrenaline.

This preparation of synthetic adrenaline was carried out by *Stolz* whilst working in the laboratories of Messrs Meister, Lucius, & Brüning.

The product is known as **synthetic** or **racemic** adrenaline, and is about half as physiologically active as the natural l-rotatory adrenaline. The resolution of this racemic adrenaline into l-adrenaline —identical in all respects with the natural product—and d-adrenaline, has been achieved by Flächer (also of Meister, Lucius, & Brüning's staff) as follows :—

Resolution of Synthetic Racemic Adrenaline. §—Synthetic adrenaline is dissolved in a hot methyl alcohol solution of the molecular equivalent of d-tartaric acid, the alcohol removed *in vacuo* at 35°-40°, and the residue crystallised by seeding with the acid d-tartrate of l-adrenalin. The crystals of the acid d-tartrate of dl-adrenaline are then stirred with methyl alcohol, when the acid d-tartrate of the l-base remains undissolved while the isomeric salt passes into solution. The crystals are filtered off, washed, and recrystallised from alcohol until a product is obtained melting at 149°. The **laevo-adrenaline** recovered from this showed a rotation of $[a]_D - 51.4°$ in dilute hydrochloric acid solution, melted at 211°-212° (the melting point of dl-adrenaline), and was identical in all respects with the natural l-adrenaline from the suprarenal glands.

The **dextro-adrenaline** is obtained by regenerating the base from the methyl alcohol mother liquors, and submitting it to a similar treatment with l-tartaric acid, M.P. 211°-212°; $[a]_D = +51.9°$ in dil. HCl. Very little physiological action.

---

* *Bull. Soc. Chim.* [3], **12**, 1911 (1894).
† *Cent. Blatt.*, 1905 (I.), 315.
‡ *Ibid.* (II.), 57.
§ Flächer, Hoppe-Seyler's *Zeitschrift*, Vol. 58, part 3, p. 189.

Clinical Uses of *l*-Adrenaline.—When injected subcutaneously it intensely contracts the arteries and increases the blood pressure.

So enormously powerful physiologically is adrenaline that the injection of one-millionth of a gram for every 2 lbs. weight of an animal causes the blood pressure to suspend a column of water 7 in. higher than it would otherwise do. A dose of one-twentieth of a milligram intravenously injected in rabbits doubles the general arterial blood pressure, and less than one-millionth of a gram gives a distinct action.

The contractile effect on the arteries is so great that it drives blood away from the injected tissues and thus allows "bloodless" surgery, adrenaline being to-day the most valued styptic known.

It has been' used in ophthalmic surgery in conjunction with cocaine or similar drugs (see Section I., p. 603) for the production of local anæsthesia along with anæmia of the conjunctiva. If administered along with an anæsthetic such as chloroform or ether, adrenaline tends to prevent the fatal collapse which sometimes occurs under these conditions, while for minor operations, as in dentistry, when employed along with cocaine, it prevents severe bleeding.

It is employed in the earlier stages of Addison's disease, which arises from a diseased condition of the suprarenal glands. It is also used in cases of catarrh. Strength of solution used for injection is 0.1-0.01 per cent., maximum dose for injection = 0.0005 g.

The introduction of adrenaline into Surgery is largely due to the scientific work of the firm Meister, Lucius, & Brüning.

A number of important recent researches have been made on the connection between the physiological action of adrenaline and its chemical constitution, with the object of ultimately synthesising other drugs with similar or more powerful characteristics. See Dakin, *Proc. Roy. Soc. Lond.*, **76**, Series B, 498-503; also *Cent. Bl.*, 1905, ii. 1458, and *Journ. Physiol.*, 1905, **32**, p. 35; Loewi and Hans Meyer, *Cent. Blatt.*, 1905, 1111; Barger and Dale, *Journ. Physiol.*, 1910, **41**, 19.

3 : 4-Dihydroxyphenylethylmethylamine, $HO\langle\ \rangle CH_2.CH_2.NH.CH_3$

HO

is closely allied to adrenaline both in formula and physiological action. It is prepared by the degradation of papaverine (compare Pyman, *Trans. Chem. Soc.*, 1910, **97**, 264), and is placed on the market by Burroughs Wellcome & Co. under the name "**Epinine.**"

ERGOT, ETC.

Ergot (*Claviceps purpurea*, *Sclerotium clavus*, and *Spermaldia clavus*), a dark-coloured fungus which attacks damp rye and other grasses, and when contained in flour causes the disease known as **Ergotism**, is much used in midwifery for causing powerful contractile action of the pregnant uterus. When injected, it produces a rise in blood pressure, and is sometimes used to check hæmorrhage from the lungs and other internal organs.

Formerly no method of testing the efficiency of the various ergot preparations was known, but now the strength is ascertained by noting the quantity required to blacken (cause gangrene) a cock's comb.

Ergot is detected in flour by extracting with boiling alcohol, acidifying with H_2SO_4, and examining the alcoholic extract spectroscopically. If ergot is present the solution is reddish and shows characteristic absorption bands.

Chemical Constituents of Ergot.—Ergot is a complex mixture of alkaloids. The chief physiologically active ones isolated are :—

* Ergotoxine, $C_{35}H_{41}O_6N_5$, white amorphous powder, is the physiologically active principle of ergot, since it produces a strong rise in blood pressure, causes gangrene of the cock's comb, and powerfully contracts the pregnant uterus, although having little effect on the isolated non-pregnant uterus.

p-**Hydroxyphenylethylamine,** $HO.\langle\ \rangle CH_2.CH_2.NH_2$, is present in the aqueous extract of ergot, from which it was extracted and later on synthesised by

---

* Barger and Carr, *Trans.*, 1907, **91**, 347 ; Barger and Ewins, *ibid.*, 1910, **97**, 284.

Barger (*Proc. Physiol. Soc.*, 1909, **37**, 77; *Biochem. Journ.*, 1907, ii. 240; *Trans. Chem. Soc.*, 1909, **95**, 1123, 1720). M.P. 161°. Is now placed on the market by Messrs Burroughs Wellcome & Co. under the name **Tyramine**. In addition to raising the blood pressure and producing strong contraction of the pregnant uterus, it greatly increases the vigour of the heart's action, and may be administered in case of shock or collapse.

Iso-amylamine, $(CH_3)_2CH.CH_2.CH_2.NH_2$, isolated by Barger (*loc. cit.*) from aqueous extract of ergot by steam distillation. Increases the blood pressure and contracts pregnant uterus.

Both p-hydroxyphenylethylamine and isoamylamine are present in putrid meat.

4 (or 5)-β-Aminoethylglyoxaline, also known as β-iminazolylethylamine, is also contained in ergot. (Barger and Dale, *Trans.*, 1910, **97**, 2592; Ewins and Pyman, *Trans.*, 1911, **99**, 339; Ackermann, *Zeitsch. Physiol. Chem.*, **65**, 1910, 504). It

has the constitution

$$NH_2.CH_2.CH_2.C \begin{array}{c} CH-NH \\ \| \qquad \diagdown \\ \diagdown \qquad CH \\ \diagup \\ ---N \end{array}, \text{ and is prepared synthetically}$$

(Windaus and Vogt, *Ber.*, **40**, 1907, 3691; Pyman, *Trans.*, 1911, **99**, 668). It is now placed on the market by Burroughs Welcome & Co. under the name "**Ergamine**." It decreases the blood pressure and powerfully contracts the isolated uterus even in a non-pregnant condition.

Hordenine, $HO.C_6H_4.CH_2.CH_2.N(CH_3)_2$, was isolated by Leger [*] from barley-malt germs, in which it is present to 0.2-0.5 per cent., by extracting with alcohol in the presence of tartaric acid, filtering, neutralising, extracting with ether, and crystallising the product from alcohol. It is a strong base, sparingly soluble in water, soluble in alcohol, ether, $CHCl_3$, etc., and forms crystalline salts with acids. Hordenine retards coagulation of the blood and when injected raises the blood pressure, although not to the same extent as adrenaline or the ergot bases. Not very toxic. Used in dysentery and as a heart tonic. Preparations are placed on the market by Merck and by Burroughs Wellcome & Co. It has been synthesised by Barger (*Trans. Chem. Soc.*, 1909, **95**, 2193).

SYNTHETIC DRUGS USED IN PARASITIC DISEASES, SUCH AS SLEEPING SICKNESS, SYPHILIS, Etc.

Atoxyl, Arsamin, or Soamin, the mono-sodium salt of p-aminophenyl-arsonic acid, $NH_2.C_6H_4.As \begin{array}{c} O \\ \diagup \\ \diagdown OH \\ ONa \end{array}$, is prepared by heating arsenic acid with aniline at 190°-200° C., converting into the sodium salt by agitating with Na_2CO_3, and recrystallising from water.

A white powder, tasteless and odourless, easily soluble in H_2O. Decomposes in stomach and so is given subcutaneously. Used in the treatment of sleeping sickness and syphilis. Dose, about 0.5 g. Incautious treatment may lead to blindness and symptoms of poisoning, (headache, colic). Also used in tuberculosis.

Acetylatoxyl or Arsacetin, $CH_3CO.NH.C_6H_4.As \begin{array}{c} O \\ \diagup \\ \diagdown OH \\ ONa \end{array}$, is soluble in water (1 part in 10). More chemically stable and less toxic than atoxyl. It has been successfully employed in sleeping sickness, skin diseases, and syphilis. Dose, 0.6 g. injected in 10-15 per cent. solution.

---

[*] *Compt. rend.*, 1906, **142**, 108, **143**, 234, 916 *et seq.*

Salvarsan, "606," is dihydroxydiaminoarsenobenzene dihydrochloride, and is believed to have the constitution :—

$$HO.\langle\ \rangle-As{=}As-\langle\ \rangle-OH$$
$$\quad NH_2.HCl \qquad\qquad NH_2.HCl$$

It is prepared, according to the English Patent 13,485, 1910, by nitrating the Na-salt of p-hydroxyphenylarsonic acid, $HO.\langle\ \rangle.As{\lesseqgtr}^{O}_{OH}$, whereby the nitro-body

$HO.\langle\ \rangle.As{\lesseqgtr}^{O}_{OH}$ is produced; this on reducing with Na-amalgam or Na_2S,
$\quad\ NO_2$

condenses, with the ultimate production of the dihydroxydiamino-compound, whose hydrochloride is known as **Salvarsan.** Salvarsan is a bright yellow powder supplied in glass tubes filled with an inert gas to prevent oxidation.

The introduction of **Salvarsan** by Ehrlich and Hata in 1910-1911 caused a sensation in the medical world. It is stated to be a specific cure for syphilis, a single injection into the buttocks having effected a complete cure in many cases. It is placed on the market by Meister, Lucius, & Brüning. See "Salvarsan," by Martendale and Westcott (London, 1911); also Ehrlich and Hata's treatise, "Die Experimentelle Chemotherapie," Berlin, 1911.

Arsenophenylglycine ("418"), a predecessor of salvarsan, has the formula

$COOH.CH_2.NH\langle\ \rangle As{=}As\langle\ \rangle NH.CH_2.COOH.$ Also a powerful curative

agent for syphilis, but not so popular as salvarsan.

Ichthyol is a volatile oil containing sulphur obtained by heating "stink-stone" or "oil-stone"—a bituminous schist found in the Tyrol (Seefeld). The salts of ichthyol sulphonic acid (obtained by treating ichthyol with concentrated H_2SO_4) are used therapeutically, the ammonium salt, **ammonium "sulphoichthyolicum,'** being obtained by neutralising the sulphonic acid with ammonia and evaporating to a syrup. It is sometimes called "ichthyol." It forms a reddish brown syrup, soluble in water, with a smoky taste and smell. Much used externally in cases of skin diseases and internally in cases of tuberculosis, catarrh of the lungs, chronic diseases of the stomach and intestines. The Na-, Li-, and Zn salts are also used.

Ichthyol-Albumen (= Ichthalbine) is obtained by precipitating albumen solution with a solution of ichthyol sulphonic acid. Grey-brown powder, soluble in water, insoluble in the stomach. It decomposes in the intestine into ichthyol and albumen, and is used for intestinal catarrh.

Ichthoform is a compound of ichthyol sulphonic acid and formaldehyde. Dark powder, insoluble, almost odourless and tasteless. Used externally as an **iodoform substitute** for wounds, and internally as an intestinal antiseptic.

Santonine, $C_{15}H_{18}O_3$, the lactone of santoninic acid, $C_{15}H_{20}O_4$, is separated from the blossoms of wormseed and used for destroying intestinal worms. Dose, 0.025-0.05 g. twice daily for children. Maximum dose, 0.1-0.3 g. per diem. Colourless, odourless crystals, M.P. 170°. Sparingly soluble in cold water, more soluble in hot, readily soluble in alcohol, ether, chloroform. Turns yellow in light.

For Trade Names to other new Drugs, see Martin's "Industrial Chemistry," Vol. I., Appendix II., p. 667.

VEGETABLE ALKALOIDS

Alkaloids of Opium.—Opium is a very complex mixture containing along with protein matter and various acids, carbohydrates, gums, waxes, etc., numerous alkaloids of which the most important are: Morphine, about 9 per cent., Narcotine 5 per cent., Papaverine, 0.8 per cent., Thebaine, 0.4 per cent., Codeine, 0.3 per cent., Narceine, 0.2 per cent.

Morphine, $C_{17}H_{19}NO_3$, the most important, is extracted as follows: The aqueous extract of opium is concentrated, and alkaloids precipitated with sodium carbonate. The precipitate is extracted first with water, and then with cold alcohol when most of the morphine remains behind. This is dried, dissolved in dilute acetic acid (any narcotine is insoluble), filtered through animal charcoal and precipitated with ammonia. Purified through its salts or by crystallising from boiling alcohol. Dose of morphine hydrochloride, $\frac{1}{8}$-$\frac{1}{2}$ **grain**.

Atropine, $C_{17}H_{23}NO_3$, occurs in the deadly nightshade (*Atropa belladonna*) and in *Datura stramonium*. It forms heavy needles of M.P. 115°, and is intensely poisonous, and strongly dilates the pupil of the eye, for which purpose a 0.5 per cent. solution is used in ophthalmology. Maximum dose = .001 g.; maximum per day, 0.003 g.

It is also used as a narcotic, and in the night sweats of phthisis. Its constitution is given under **Cocaine** (section on **Local Anæsthetics**).

Strychnine, $C_{21}H_{22}N_2O_2$, occurs along with brucine, $C_{23}H_{26}N_2O_4$, in the seeds of *Strychnos nux vomica*.

Extraction.—The crushed, water-sodden nuts are ground to a pulp, and extracted with hot alcohol, the latter evaporated, the extract treated with lead acetate, and excess of lead removed by H_2S or H_2SO_4. The strychnine is then precipitated with caustic soda, the more soluble brucine remaining almost completely behind.

Colourless crystals, intensely poisonous, a typical spinal poison. Dose, $\frac{1}{30}$-$\frac{1}{12}$ of a grain. It is a valuable tonic, and is employed in paralysis, and in cases of lead poisoning.

Quinine, $C_{20}H_{24}N_2O_2$, is obtained from various kinds of cinchona bark, in which it occurs along with other alkaloids such as quinidine, cinchonine cinchonidine, etc.

Extraction.—The powdered bark is mixed with lime and extracted with high boiling petroleum, the solution being then shaken with dilute sulphuric acid and neutralised *while hot* with Na_2CO_3. The most of the quinine then separates as sulphate, which is further purified by precipitating as insoluble tartrate with Rochelle salt solution.

A white crystalline powder almost insoluble in water, sparingly soluble in cold alcohol, the aqueous solution of its sulphate fluoresces blue. Perhaps the most important drug known, its annual production amounting to 485,900 kg.

Pilocarpine, $C_{11}H_{16}N_2O_2$, occurring in Jaborandi leaves, is the physiologica antithesis of atropine. It is a thick liquid and is used as a sudorific and to check salivation.

For the chemistry of pilocarpine see papers by Jowett, *Trans.*, 1901-1905.

Hydrastine, $C_{21}H_{21}NO_6$, found in the root of a North American plant *Hydrastis canadensis*, is employed similarly to ergot.

Veratrine.—The commercial product, obtained from the seeds of *Veratrum sabadilla*, is a mixture of various alkaloids. It is a white powder causing violent sneezing and general irritation of the mucous membrane when inhaled.

Yohimbine is an alkaloid obtained from the Yumbehoa tree (Africa). It is employed internally in cases of impotence.

Purine Alkaloids.—Three important drugs belonging to the purine compounds are Caffeine, $C_8H_{10}O_2N_4 + H_2O$, Theobromine, $C_7H_8O_2N_4$, and Theophylline or Theocine, $C_7H_8O_2N_4$.

Caffeine.
1:3:7-Trimethylxanthine.

Theobromine.
3-7-Dimethylxanthine.

Theophylline.
1:3-Dimethylxanthine.

Caffeine occurs in tea and coffee, about 1.4 per cent. in tea. From the waste dust of tea it is extracted by boiling with water, precipitating tannin with lead acetate, removing excess of the latter with H_2S, filtering, and concentrating, when caffeine crystallises out. It is also obtained as a bye-product in the manufacture of caffein-free coffee. Unroasted coffee beans are treated with superheated steam and extracted with benzene, whereby much of their caffein is removed. It is now prepared on the large scale from guano by Böhringen & Sons, of Mannheim.

Caffeine forms white silky needles which lose water at 100°, sublime at 180°, and melt at 230.5°. It is soluble in 80 parts of water at 15° and in 2 parts of boiling water, but is sparingly soluble in many organic solvents such as cold alcohol. Chloroform readily dissolves it.

Used in headache and neuralgia alone or combined with phenacetin, and as a heart tonic. Dose, 0.5 g.; maximum daily dose, 1.5 g. It is employed internally and subcutaneously.

Theobromine, a colourless, odourless, crystalline powder, sublimes at 290°, neither melting nor decomposing. It occurs in cocoa. Combined with a molecular proportion of sodium salicylate, its sodium salt is employed under the name of Diuretin. This is a white powder, soluble in water, and employed in dropsy and in diseases of the kidneys and heart. Theobromine has been synthesised by Traube (*Berichte d. deutschen Chemischen Gesellschaft*, **33,** 1371 and 3035) starting from cyanoacetic acid and methylurea.

Theophylline or Theocine is a stronger diuretic than theobromine. It occurs to a small extent in tea leaves. Sodium theophylline acetate is a valuable diuretic.

Synthetic Preparation.—See D.R. Pat., 151,133, 144,761, 148,208, 138,444 Theophylline itself forms colourless crystals, M.P. 208°. It is difficultly soluble in water, hence the use of soluble double compounds.

The writer desires to thank the following firms for much information regarding the newer synthetic drugs:—Messrs Burroughs Wellcome & Co., London; Messrs Meister, Lucius, & Brüning, Höchst; Messrs Merck, Darmstadt; Messrs Evans, Sons, Lescher, & Webb, Liverpool.

CHAPTER VIII

The Industry of Photographic Chemicals

CHAPTER VIII

THE INDUSTRY OF PHOTO-GRAPHIC CHEMICALS

LITERATURE

VOGEL-KÖNIG.—"Photochemie." 5th Ed. Berlin, 1906.

E. VALENTA.—"Photographische Chemie." Halle, 1899.

" "Chemikalien u. Präparate für Photographie." Article in Vol. I. of Dammer's "Chemische Technologie der Neuzeit." Stuttgart, 1910.

L. MATHET.—"Traité de Chimie Photographique." 2 vols. Paris, 1901.

CHAPMAN JONES.—"Science of Photography." 4th Ed. London, 1904.

SHEPPARD AND MEES.—"Investigations on the Theory of the Photographic Process." London, 1907.

R. MELDOLA.—"Chemistry of Photography." London, 1889.

C. E. KENNETH MEES.—"The Photographic Industry." *Journ. Soc. Chem. Ind.*, 1912, 31, 307.

THE manufacture of photographic chemicals is a modern industry of great and rapidly growing importance.

We can only give in this place an account of the more important substances especially manufactured for photographic purposes. Chemicals which are widely employed in other industries—such as sodium thiosulphate, salts of gold, silver, platinum, etc.—cannot be discussed here, since an account of these technically important salts will be given in the second volume of this work.

Statistics.—The United States imported in 1910—Moving picture films, 12,830,000 lin. ft., of value $771,000. Photographic plates and other films, value $416,000. Photographic paper, value $762,000.

The American export of **photographic goods** is shown by the following figures :—

1906	1907	1908	1909	1910
$256,000	$1,090,000	$2,840,000	$4,185,000	$4,765,000

The United Kingdom in 1913 *exported* £1,065,700 of photographic materials. The *import* in 1913 was £2,372,000. The value of the photographic materials (plates, paper, and films), produced in Great Britain in 1907 was £909,000.

Although exact statistics are at present unobtainable, the magnitude of the industry of photographic chemicals may be gauged by the fact that one factory in England alone orders its potassium bromide in 30-ton lots, and that one company is the largest user of silver except a Government mint ! The production of the biggest English photographic paper factories runs to *miles*, and of plates to *acres* per day. Many thousands of workers are employed in the industry.

CHEMICALS EMPLOYED IN THE MANUFACTURE OF PHOTOGRAPHIC PLATES AND FILMS

Dry Plates.—The ordinary dry plate is a specially selected best quality thin glass sheet, covered with an extremely light-sensitive layer of silver bromide particles suspended in gelatine. The glass, cleaned by automatic machinery by brushing and spraying with soda and water, is coated with a substratum consisting of a weak solution of gelatine containing chrome alum, which causes the emulsion to adhere to the glass and prevents "frilling," then dried by hot air and coated with the sensitive emulsion by a special machine, dried in a special room, cut to the proper size by machinery, examined for defects by red light, and packed.

The **Emulsion** is made by adding a concentrated solution of silver nitrate to a potassium bromide solution containing gelatine. Negative emulsions usually have a small percentage of KI added to the gelatine, while diapositive and "gaslight" paper emulsions consist chiefly of silver chloride with a very little bromide. After mixing, the emulsion is "ripened" by keeping at a high temperature for some time, or by digesting at a lower temperature with ammonia, then it is cooled by ice until it sets to a jelly, forced by hydraulic pressure through small holes in a metal plate, and the threads thus produced washed free from the KNO_3 (formed thus: $AgNO_3 + KBr = KNO_3 + AgBr$). The "fastness" of the plate depends upon the size of the grains of AgBr—the larger the grain the faster the plate.

The British Patent, No. 1,689 of 1908, describes a plate containing derivatives of hydrazine, which, it is stated, cannot be over-exposed.

Collodion Wool is simply nitrated cotton, the manufacture of which is described in Martin's "Industrial Chemistry," Vol. I., on pp. **207, 624.**

Collodion is its solution in a mixture of alcohol and ether, usually containing 5 per cent. of wool.

The solvent rapidly evaporates in the air, leaving a skin. It is used for making light sensitive surfaces in the wet plate process, in the manufacture of silver bromide collodion emulsions, and for making light filters.

Celluloid is used for the manufacture of films, cinematographic pictures, etc., also as a protective covering for pictures, being for the latter purpose coated with an adhesive. For the manufacture of celluloid see Martin's "Industrial Chemistry," Vol. I. p. 208.

Cellite, or **Cellulose Acetate,** is used for the same purposes as celluloid ; although dearer it has the great advantage over celluloid that it is practically non-inflammable. For its manufacture see Martin's "Industrial Chemistry," Vol. I. pp. 210, 216.

Gelatine is largely used for the manufacture of dry plates, and for making light-sensitive emulsions of silver halides. For the manufacture and properties of gelatine see Martin's "Industrial Chemistry," Vol. I. p. 595.

The ordinary dry plate is covered with an extremely light-sensitive layer of silver bromide particles suspended in gelatine. The gelatine on the plate may be hardened after development by soaking in a solution of formalin or of alum.

Albumen and **Casein** used in the manufacture of photographic papers. For manufacture and properties of albumen see Martin's "Industrial Chemistry," Vol. I. p. 597, and for casein, p. 79.

DYES USED IN THE PREPARATION OF PHOTOGRAPHIC PLATES AND FILMS

Silver halides are most sensitive to blue and violet light rays, and least sensitive to red rays. Various dyes are used to render silver halides treated with them more sensitive to red, yellow, and green rays, so that the true colours are better reproduced in the resulting picture than would otherwise be possible.

The dye may be added to the sensitive emulsion either before pouring it on to the plate, or it is applied to the dry plate after manufacture by immersing it in a dilute solution of the dye and then allowing the plate to dry. For example, in the case of cyanin dyes a solution containing 1 part dye : 1,000 water is used, and 2·4 c.c. of this solution is added to 100 c.c. of a mixture of 40 c.c. alcohol + 60 c.c. water. The plates are bathed in the solution for two to three minutes and then dried at 18°-24° for ten minutes—the whole operation being carried out in the dark. Plates which have been thus rendered almost equally sensitive to all the rays of the spectrum are termed "**panchromatic,**" while those which are especially sensitised for green and yellow—very important for landscape pictures—are the so-called "**orthochromatic**" plates.

When ortho plates are bathed in pinacyanol, the plate is hypersensitised, and exposure necessary reduced to one-fourth its original amount. The plate is immersed for ten minutes in the bath, which consists of 1 milligram of pinacyanol in 1 c.c. alcohol + 1,000 c.c. H_2O + 2 drops NH_3.

Lumière's **autochrome** plates give very beautiful results. The plates are prepared with a sensitive gelatine film and a multicolour light filter composed of blue, green, and red starch grains (see German Patents, 172,851 and 182,099), only one copy being at present attainable.

The screen of the **Paget colour plate** is prepared by giving it a preliminary coating all over with a collodion film dyed red. This is then coated with a resist in such a way that two-thirds of the total area is unprotected, and this is bleached out and dyed green. So that at this stage the plate is covered with a series of red and green lines, the latter being twice the width of the former. A resist is again applied, but with its lines at right angles to those of the first, and the unprotected portions are bleached and dyed blue. The result is a very transparent and uniform screen firmly attached to the glass. **Omnicolore** and **Dufay** plates are well-known colour plates.

The following are the most important dyes used as sensitisers :—

The Phthaleins.—Of these **erythrosin** and **eosin** are widely used for rendering silver bromide sensitive to yellow and green rays, and consequently for the manufacture of " **Ortho-chromatic** " plates.

Monobromfluorescein is used as a green sensitiser for silver bromide.

Among the **Rosaniline dyes** we may mention that **Ethyl violet** and **Formyl violet** are used as red sensitisers of silver bromide collodion emulsions. **Akridin dyes** are used to some extent as sensitisers for green and blue.

Among the **Azo dyes** used as sensitisers we may mention : **Benzonitrol brown** (By), **Dianil black R** (M., L., & Br.), **Glycin red** (By), **Pluto black** (By), **Wool black 4B** (Agfa). The dyes known as **Alizarin blue bisulphite** and **Nigrosin D** are used to some extent as red sensitisers.

Quinoline Dyes

Are now very important sensitisers (see p. 67). Among them we must mention :—

a. Cyanines

Cyanin (Lepidinquinolineamylcyaniniodide), a blue dye, quite useless for textile purposes on account of its fugitiveness, but used as a sensitiser for silver bromide plates where a panchromatic effect is desired. It renders silver bromide sensitive to red, orange, and yellow rays, with a minimum of sensitiveness between E and F. Its defects are a tendency to fog and speck the plate, accompanied with a diminution in its light-sensitiveness. As a red sensitiser it has been displaced by isocyanines, but it is still used for wet plates and for special kinds of work. Vogel uses a mixture of this dye with quinoline red under the name " Azalin " for sensitising dry plates for green and yellow.

Ethylcyanin (Lepidinquinolinethylcyaninbromide), being more soluble than cyanin, has been proposed as a substitute.

Dicyanin (prepared by action of KOH+atmospheric O on a-γ-Dimethylquinolinium salts) sensitises silver bromide gelatine plates up to the red line *a*, with a strong minimal effect between E and F. Used as a red sensitiser for scientific work, but the prepared plates are not very sensitive.

b. Isocyanines

Of these dyes the most important are :—

Ethyl red, or quinaldinquinolinethylcyanin iodide, which forms green crystals soluble in water and alcohol, with a violet-red colour. In dilute solution (1 : 50,000) it sensitises silver bromide gelatine plates almost uniformly from the red (C) to the violet, with only a small minimum in the green. It does not sensitise far into the red.

Preparations of isocyanines and similar dyes, which are sensitive further in the red, have been put on the market by Meister, Lucius, & Brüning in Höchst-a.-M., under the names **Orthochrom T** (which is *p*-Toluquinaldin-*p*-Toluquinolinethylcyaninbromide), **Pinachrom** (which is *p*-Ethoxyquinaldin-*p*-methoxyquinolineethylcyaninebromide), and **Pinacyanol** (which is obtained by treating quinaldinium salts with formaldehyde, followed by alkali), the latter sensitising in the red up to the B line. **Pinaverdol**, produced by the same firm, is a green sensitiser for silver bromide collodion emulsions, and consists of *p*-Toluquinaldinquinoliniummethyl-cyaninbromide.

Fr. Bayer in Elberfeld also places several sensitisers on the market. Among these we may mention :—

" **Perikol**," prepared by treating with alcoholic KOH the addition product obtained from Toluquinaldin and the ethyl ester of Toluene sulphonic acid, sensitises plates to a maximum between $\lambda = 590$ and $\lambda = 560 \ \mu\mu$. "**Isokol**" is a similar preparation. "**Homokol**" is a mixture of quinoline red with an isocyanine dye.

Some of Fr. Bayer's more interesting patents are German Patents, 158,078, 170,048, and 170,049, where the process of manufacture of a number of sensitising dyes are described by acting with alkalis on the addition products of dialkylsulphates with quinaldin and its homologues. The new colouring matters are stated not to fog or fleck plates.

Dyes used for Colour Filters and Similar Purposes

Coloured screens or filters are an absolute necessity in many photographic processes, and a very large number of coal-tar colours are used for the manufacture of these colour filters, which may consist of collodion, gelatine, or aqueous fluids coloured with special dyes which only allow special wave lengths to pass, or which greatly diminish the intensity of the actinic rays.

The screens most widely used consist of glass plates covered with gelatine coloured with a suitable dye.

For developing ordinary dry plates in the dark room the filters used consist of red dyes, and for bromide, yellow dyes. For very fast plates both yellow and red filters are used. For panchromatic and colour-screen plates a faint green light is used.

Auramine O is very suitable, as it absorbs blue and violet, allowing red, green, and yellow rays to pass.

Tartrazin and **Fast Red D** (M., L., & Br.) are good red filters, so also is **Chrysosulphite** (Lumière), which is a mixture of magnesium picrate and sodium sulphite.

Coxin is also a very suitable red filter.

The dyes used for colouring gelatine must be water soluble and free from other adjuncts such as dextrin, Glauber's salt, etc. etc., otherwise the gelatine will not dry clear. The following dyes (among others) are used for colouring the gelatine :—

Auramine, Brilliant green, Crystal violet, Fuchsin, Methylene blue, Phenosafranin, Rhodamin (these also can be used for colouring collodion), also **Acid green, Congo red, Naphthol green, Naphthalene green, Filter yellow, Rapid Filter red, Rapid Filter yellow** (Meister, Lucius, & Brüning), **Patent blue, Tartrazin**.

LIGHT FILTERS

The following light filters are recommended by *Meister, Lucius, & Brüning*, the filters produced being toned for orthochromatic and panchromatic plates :—

Light Filters for the Three-Colour Process

Red Filter.—2.5 g. filter red I. are dissolved in 100 c.c. warm water. 100 c.c. of 8 per cent. gelatine solution are mixed with 4 c.c. of the colour solution and the whole filtered, and 7 c.c. of the gelatine used for every 100 c.c.

Blue Filter.—4 g. crystal violet are dissolved in 100 c.c. warm water and 5-6 drops of acetic acid are added ; then 6 c.c. of coloured solution are added to 100 c.c. of 8 per cent. gelatine solution, and the whole is filtered.

Green Filter.—2.5 g. tartrazine + 6 g. patent blue + 4 g. naphthol green dissolved in 400 c.c. water ; 5 c.c. of colour solution are then added to 100 c.c. of 8 per cent. gelatine solution and the whole filtered.

Time of exposure with orthochromatic plates is blue : green : red :: 1 : 3 : 6.

Light Filters for the Additive Three-Colour Prints

Red Filter.—4 g. tartrazine + 7.5 g. filter red II. in 150 c.c. water.   Add 7-8 c.c. of this solution to 100 c.c. of 8 per cent. gelatine solution and filter.

Blue Filter.—3 g. crystal violet + 1 g. methylene blue (free from $ZnCl_2$) + 100 c.c. warm water + 6 drops acetic acid.   Add 7-8 c.c. of this coloured solution to 100 c.c. 8 per cent. gelatine solution and filter.

Green Filter.—6 g. tartrazine + 1 g. patent blue + 2 g. naphthol green + 180 c.c. water. 8-9 c.c. of coloured solution is used for 100 c.c. of **8** per cent. gelatine solution.

Times of exposure for orthochromatic plates are blue : green : red = 1 : 5 : 8 ; for panchromatic plates 1 : 4 : 3.

To make the dry filters 7 c.c. of the coloured gelatines made as above described are poured over every 100 sq. cm. of plate surface and allowed to set; then two coloured plates are taken together and fixed with Canada balsam.

In the three-colour photographic process such dyes as **Aurophenin** or **Naphthol yellow S, Erythrosin, Diamine pure blue** or **Fast bluish green** are used to colour the partial pictures.

FLASHLIGHTS

Powdered magnesium was introduced as a flashlight in 1887.   Since then many other flashlights have been introduced—usually by mixing the magnesium with an oxygen-rich substance.   Many of these preparations are very explosive, and must not be blown into a flame.   We may notice the following recipes :—

1. 2 parts Mg powder + 3 parts powdered potassium permanganate.

2. 15 parts Mg powder + 30 parts $KClO_3$ + 5 parts antimony sulphide, finely powdered and mixed dry.   Explosive, so must not use a mortar.

3. Smokeless flashlight mixtures giving an intense light consist of magnesium or aluminium powder + nitrates of rare earths (thorium, zirconium).   See German Patent, 158,215 ; see also English Patent, 27,267 (1904), where rare earths are added to Mg or Al flashlights.   Fr. Bayer & Co. (German Patent, 136,313) place a number of excellent flashlights on the market ; they appear to consist of Mg + manganese peroxide, to which are added bodies like $Sr(NO_3)_2$, which yield a coloured flame.   See also English Patent, 27,466, 1904.   Such mixtures are termed ortho- or panchromatic flashlights, since they give out orange rays in addition to the blue or violet rays emitted by the ordinary mixture.   Other proposed mixtures are : of Mg powder + silica + boric acid (German Patent, 101,528) ; Al powder + $KClO_3$ (German Patent, 101,735) ;   Mg powder + red phosphorus + peroxides.   Very powerful photo effects are obtained by adding cadmium nitrate in quantity equal to magnesium powder.   Zinc nitrate also is used.

Time Lights do not flash, but burn slowly, an effect attained by adding to magnesium (sometimes mixed with aluminium) powder bodies such as carbonates, silicates, or oxides of the alkaline earths—*e.g.*, $SrCO_3$.   Bayer (German Patent, 165,259) proposes Mg or Al powder + Na_2WO_4, or WO_3, as a smokeless time light.   Novak proposes Mg powder + cerium nitrate + $SrCO_3$ as a smokeless time light.

Kreb's panchromatic time lights give out coloured rays, thus enabling the taking of photographs of objects by colour sensitive plates without the use of a yellow light filter.   Electric metallic filament lamps are also used now.

DEVELOPERS

We can give here only a brief mention of some of the more important reducing substances used in the manufacture of developers.

Iron Oxalate is one of the oldest developers, and is still used to some extent—usually in the form of two solutions, I. and II., I. consisting of 300 g. neutralised potassium oxalate in 1,000 c.c. of water, and II. of ferrous sulphate solution (100 g. $FeSO_4$ + 300 c.c. water + 5 drops concentrated H_2SO_4).   For use, 3-4 parts of I. are used with 1 of II.

Developers derived from Monohydric Phenols

Paramidophenol, $C_6H_4\diagdown^{OH}_{NH_2}$ ($1:4$), produced by reducing p-nitrophenol with tin + HCl.   Colourless crystals, M.P. 184°; forms a crystalline hydrochloride, $OH.C_6H_4.NH_2.HCl.$

" Rodinal" contains p-amidophenolhydrochloride.   "Unal" is rodinal in a solid form.

Monomethylparamidophenol, $C_6H_4(OH)(NHCH_3)$, $1:4$, is prepared by methylating p-amidocresol.

It is an excellent developer, giving results free from stain. It is known as "scalol." Two solutions are used : (A) "Scalol," 1.5 g. + hydro-quinone, 3 g. + sod. sulphite (crystals), 28 g. + KBr, 0.25 g. + H₂O, 284 c.c.; (B) Na₂CO₃ (crystals), 30 g. + H₂O, 300 c.c. Use equal parts of A and B.
"Metol" is the sulphate of this body. The developer "Satrapol" also contains it. Metol works exceedingly rapidly. Stock solution : 15 g. metol + 150 g. cryst. sod. sulphite + 75 g. K₂CO₃ + 2 g. KBr + 1,000 c.c. H₂O.
"Metolhydroquinone" developer, now widely used, consists of the two solutions : (A) 2 g. metol + 3.5 g. hydroquinone + 4 g. Na₂HPO₄ + 400 c.c. H₂O + 2 c.c. sodium sulphite solution (1 : 100). (B) 40 g. K₂CO₃ + 400 c.c. H₂O.   For use mix equal parts of A and B.

Diamidophenol, $C_6H_3(OH)(NH_2)(NH_2)$, $1:2:4$, is prepared by reducing with Sn + HCl $1:2:4$-dinitrophenol; forms salts with HCl and H_2SO_4.

"Amidol" consists of 20 g. diamidophenol sulphate or chloride + 200 g. cryst. sod. sulphite + 1,000 c.c. H₂O. Solution will not keep. Best developer for bromides and gaslight papers. Valenta proposes acetonesulphite + diamidophenol hydrochloride as a powerful developer.

p-Amido-saligenin, $C_6H_3(CH_2OH)(OH)(NH_2)$, $1:2:3$, in the form of its hydrochloride, occurs as an easily soluble white powder, similar in properties to amidol, but having the advantage of allowing very concentrated solutions being formed.

"Edinol" (made by Fr. Bayer, Elberfeld) consists of 5 g. p-amido-saligenin + 7.5 g. acetone sulphite + 30 g. KOH + 0.5 g. KBr + 100 c.c. H₂O. Edinol-hydroquinone developer consists of 2 g. p-amido-saligenin + 1 g. hydroquinone + 5 g. acetone sulphite + 30 g. cryst. sod. sulphite + 30 g. K₂CO₃ + 150 c.c. H₂O.

Diamido-oxydiphenyl, in the form of its sodium salt, is used in a manner $C_6H_3\diagdown^{ONa\ (1)}_{NH_2\ (4)}$ similar to "Rodinal." Placed on the market under the name "Diphenal" by Cassella & Co.

$|$
$C_6H_4.NH_2$

p-Oxyphenylglycocoll, $C_6H_4(OH)(NH.CH_2.CO_2H)$, $1:4$, is manufactured by heating p-amidophenol, $C_6H_4(OH)(NH_2)$, with monochloracetic acid, $CH_2Cl.COOH$, in aqueous solution.

Used as a developer, it gives pure black tones and keeps well. It is placed on the market as "Glycin." Stock solutions are : 5 g. glycin + 25 g. cryst. sod. sulphite + 100 c.c. H₂O + 25 g. K₂CO₃ Another good keeping solution is 2 g. glycine + 800 c.c. H₂O (recently boiled) + 2 g. cryst. sod. sulphite + 15 g. K₂CO₃. It is used chiefly for stand development because it does not produce chemical fog by long action.

Methylorthoamidophenol, $C_6H_4(OH)(NHCH_3)$, 1 : 2, 2 molecules of which, combined with 1 molecule of hydroquinone, forms the basis of the excellent developer " Ortol."

Two naphthalene compounds are used as developers :—

Sodium a_1-amido-β_1-naphthol-β_2-sulphonate, $C_{10}H_5(OH)(NH_2)(SO_3Na)$, a good developer if used at 20° C. or a little below. It forms the basis of Eikonogen. One of the best developers for plates which have received very short exposure.

Hydroquinone-eikonogen developer consists of two solutions, A and B : (A) 100 g. cryst. sod. sulphite + 16 g. eikonogen + 4 g. hydroquinone + 900 c.c. boiling water ; (B) 40 g. K_2CO_3 + 200 c.c. H_2O. For use, 40 c.c. of A are added to 180 c.c. B, together with 3 drops 10 per cent. KBr solution.

Sodium amidonaphtholdisulphonate, $C_{10}H_4(NH_2)(OH)(SO_3Na)_2$, which forms the basis of the developer " Diogen."

Developers derived from Dihydric Phenols

Hydroquinone, $C_6H_4(OH)_2$, 1 : 4, is a developer much used by amateurs, giving strong hard negatives of a bluish black tone.

The best preparation occurs as yellowish crystals, and is obtained by recrystallising the commercial product in the presence of SO_2. The stock solution consists of 5 g. hydroquinone + 40 g. cryst. sod. sulphite + 6.5 g. KOH + 150 c.c. H_2O. It is frequently combined with other developers. See Edinol, Eikonogen, Metol.

Monochlor and Monobromhydroquinones, $C_6H_3Cl(OH)_2$ and $C_6H_3Br(OH)_2$, are now used as developers under the name " **Adurol** " (see German Patent, 111,798).

Monochlorhydroquinone is obtained by leading Cl gas through hydroquinone dissolved in benzol, while the bromo derivative is obtained by adding a solution of Br in benzol to a hydroquinone benzol solution, evaporating the benzol and crystallising from ligroin.

" Adurol " developer consists of the stock solutions : (A) 10 g. adurol + 80 g. cryst. sod. sulphite + 500 c.c. H_2O ; (B) 60 g. K_2CO_3 + 500 c.c. H_2O. One part A, one part B, and one part H_2O are taken to develop. Adurol comes between hydroquinone and the "rapid developers" (metol, rodinal, etc.) in properties. It does not turn brown by oxidisation in air, and so may be repeatedly used.

Pyrocatechol, $C_6H_4(OH)_2$, 1 : 2, has been proposed as a developer, and under the name "Kachin" has been placed on the market.

Resorcin, $C_6H_4(OH)_2$, 1 : 3, is of no use as a developer. Two amido derivatives of it, however, are used for this purpose, namely, **Diamidoresorcin,**
$\overset{(4:6)\ (1:3)}{C_6H_2 \cdot (NH_2)_2(OH)_2}$, and **Triamidoresorcin,** $C_6H(NH_2)_3(OH)_2$ (" Reducin ").

Developers derived from Trihydric Phenols

Pyrogallol, $C_6H_3(OH)_3$ (1 : 2 : 3), is the basis of most of these. Pyrogallol developers work rapidly, but have the drawback that they stain the fingers, are poisonous, and do not keep well.

Pyrosoda Developer.—Stock solutions : (A) 10 g. pot. metabisulphite + 83 g. pyrogallol + 13 g. KBr + water up to 1,000 c.c. ; (B) 100 g. Na_2SO_3 + 100 g. Na_2CO_3 + H_2O up to 1,000 c.c. For use mix 1 part A with 1 part B and 1 part H_2O.

Pyropotash Developer.—Stock solutions : (A) 25 g. cryst. $Na_2SO_3 + 100$ c.c. $H_2O + 10$ g. pyrogallol $+ 3.4$ drops H_2SO_4 ; (B) 45 g. $K_2CO_3 + 12.5$ g. Na_2SO_3 in 100 H_2O. Use 3 c.c. A and 3 c.c. B with 100 c.c. H_2O.

Pyrometol.—Stock solutions : (A) 5 g. metol $+ 14$ g. pot. metabisulphite $+ 6$ g. pyrogallol $+ 2$ g. $KBr + H_2O$ up to 1,000 c.c. ; (B) 200 g. $Na_2CO_3 + 1,000$ c.c. H_2O. Use equal quantities of A and B. Gives a good printing yellow negative.

"**Pinakol P**" is an excellent developer made by replacing in the pyropotash developer the alkali by half the equivalent amount of **sodium amidoacetate**, $CH_2NH_2.COONa$. Developing with "Pinakol P" gives stronger, clearer, and more rapid results than the old pyro developers ; moreover, it does not stain the fingers.

Pinakol Salt N is a 20 per cent. solution sodium amidoacetate, $CH_2NH_2.COONa$. It is used for replacing alkali in organic developers since it does not affect the skin of the operator and the gelatine film in the unpleasant way that alkali does ; moreover the results attained are superior to those of soda and potash.

Acetone bisulphite, acetone-sulphite "Bayer," is now largely used as a substitute for sodium or potassium bisulphite in developers. It is antiseptic, a restrainer for rapid developers, a clearing agent for fixing baths and developing papers, and is used also for darkening the negative after the use of mercury intensifiers.

FIXING, TONING, AND COMBINED BATHS

Sodium Thiosulphate, $Na_2S_2O_3 + 5H_2O$, is now practically the only fixing salt used. The fixing occurs according to the equation :—

$$2AgBr + Na_2S_2O_3 = Ag_2S_2O_3 + 2NaBr ;$$

the $Ag_2S_2O_3$ then combines with the excess of $Na_2S_2O_3$ to form the soluble double salt $Ag_2S_2O_3.2Na_2S_2O_3$.

The thiosulphate may be used in neutral solution (1 : 4 H_2O) but is best used in acid bisulphite fixing solution, and sometimes alum is added (to harden the gelatine). The following are well-known gold **toning** baths :—

Ordinary Toning Bath.—(A) 4 g. borax in 1,000 c.c. H_2O ; (B) 4.5 g. anhydrous sodium acetate in 1,000 c.c. H_2O ; (C) 1 g. gold chloride in 50 c.c. H_2O. Use 8-10 c.c. of C + 100 c.c. A + 100 c.c. B.

Neutral Toning and Fixing Bath.—250 g. sodium thiosulphate $+ 20$ g. lead acetate $+ 10$ g. calcium chloride $+ 0.4$ g. gold chloride $+ 1,000$ c.c. H_2O.

Acid Toning and Fixing Bath.—250 g. sodium thiosulphate $+ 25$ g. ammonium sulphocyanide $+ 10$ g. lead acetate $+ 5$ g. citric acid $+ 0.4$ g. gold chloride $+ 1,000$ c.c. H_2O.

Platinum toning baths are also used, the basis being $PtCl_4$ or $PtCl_2$, which reacts with Ag salts thus : $4Ag + PtCl_4 = 4AgCl + Pt$.

Palladium Chloride, used as a toning bath for silver pictures, gives beautiful brown tones.

Sodium Thiosulphate Destroyers.—A lengthy washing is required to remove the last traces of sodium thiosulphate, and the durability of the print largely depends on its complete removal. Consequently attempts have been made to find substances which rapidly destroy the last traces of thiosulphate. The best known substances are **Anthion** = potassium persulphate, **Thioxydant Lumière** = ammonium persulphate. More recently **percarbonates, perborates,** and **permanganates** have been suggested.

Bayer's "Hypo-destroyer" = persulphate + percarbonate. "Antihypo" is potassium percarbonate. 10 g. are dissolved in 1,000 c.c. H_2O and the plates and paper, after rinsing, are immersed for a few minutes after which only a short rinsing is necessary. A great time-saving is thus effected.

REDUCERS AND INTENSIFIERS

Reducers are chemicals which act by dissolving the fine silver particles. A large number of such substances are known, being oxygen-rich substances such as chromic acid, mercuric nitrate, ferric-, manganic-, ceric-, and titanic-salts, persulphates, etc.

Farmer's reducer = 100 c.c. sodium thiosulphate solution 1 : 4 + 8 c.c. of a 10 per cent. potassium ferricyanide solution. This destroys the fine middle tones, and so increases the contrasts. **Ammonium persulphate reducers** diminish the contrasts by acting on the darker parts of the plate. **Cerium sulphate** makes a very uniform reducer.

Intensifiers are used to increase the density of thin negatives, and bring out the contrasts better. The **mercury intensifying process** consists in treating the negative with a solution containing 2 per cent. mercuric chloride + 2 per cent. KBr. When the negative is grey it is removed, rinsed, and immersed in a 12 per cent. solution of sodium sulphite, when the negative becomes black again : $2Ag + 2HgCl_2 = 2HgAgCl_2$, then

$$4AgHgCl_2 + 7Na_2SO_3 + xNa_2SO_3 = Ag_2 + Hg + Ag_2SO_3.xNa_2SO_3 + 3HgNa_2(SO_3)_2 + 8NaCl.$$

The **uranium** intensifying process requires two solutions : (A) 1 g. uranium nitrate + 100 c.c. H_2O ; (B) 1 g. potassium ferricyanide + 100 c.c. H_2O. For use, 50 c.c. A + 11 c.c. acetic acid + 50 c.c. of B are mixed. Other intensifying solutions used are : $CuSO_4$ + pot. ferricyanide + pot. citrate, and $HgI_2 + Na_2SO_3$. Intensifiers containing **bichromate** are also used.

PHOTOGRAPHIC PAPERS

An enormous number of these exist : we may class them into—

1. **Printing-out Papers.** — The p.o.p. papers are still made (although developing papers are said to be rapidly supplanting them) and usually employ silver chloride as the sensitive substance. Four well-defined groups of papers are manufactured : (a) **Albumen papers** in which the ground is albumen and the sensitive substance silver chloride. (b) **Silver chloride gelatine paper ;** here the ground is gelatine and the sensitive substance silver chloride. (c) **Silver chloride collodion papers.** (d) **Silver chloride casein papers** give good results and resist high temperatures. Direct printing platinum papers are also on the market.

On exposure to light the chloride is converted to a "photo-chloride," Ag_2Cl, of a purple or reddish colour, and stated to be an adsorption compound of silver chloride and silver, of variable composition. After the paper has been printed the colour of the deposit is modified by immersion in a bath containing a gold or platinum salt, associated with a weak reducer, so that metallic gold or platinum is precipitated ("Toning"). The unused silver chloride, AgCl, is then dissolved out by thiosulphate ("Fixing"), which only slightly attacks the photo-chloride.

2. **Developing Papers.**—These may also be grouped into five classes, namely : (a) **Silver bromide papers** consisting of an emulsion of silver bromide + gelatine ; used for printing and enlargements ; very sensitive and must be worked in a dark room. (b) **Silver chlorobromide papers** can be used for printing in ordinary shaded daylight or by gaslight. (c) **Silver phosphate papers** may be printed in weak daylight or by gaslight. When developed they give p.o.p. effects. (d) **Platinum** developing papers give excellent results. (e) **Pigment papers** are covered with chromgelatine, which under the influence of light becomes insoluble in hot water. As any pigment can be mixed with the gelatine very beautiful

coloured results are obtainable.   In the bromoil process the bleached bromide print is worked up with special inks.

The chief difference between emulsions for development papers and those for plates is that paper emulsions are of a much lower sensitiveness (finer grain), and contain a larger proportion of silver to gelatine, the coating being thin so as to keep the image on the surface of the paper.   The colour of the image obtained depends upon the size of the grain, and developers can be used by which the silver is deposited in a very finely divided state, almost approaching to colloidal solution. By the admixture of such fine grain silver with larger grains, various tones can be obtained upon development.   The papers, which are sometimes faced with $BaSO_4$, are manufactured by passing through a trough containing the emulsion, then over a cold roller to set the gelatine, then hung up in loops in a long drying chamber, through which it slowly travels, emerging dry after about two and a half hours.   It is then rolled direct and cut.   Surface-coated papers without gelatine, such as platinum papers, are dried almost instantly on a short machine by hot air, and do not require the elaborate hanging and slow drying arrangements used for gelatine-coated papers.

Acknowledgment.—My best thanks are due to Mr S. Allen for expert advice and many suggestions.   He kindly revised the proof sheets of the above article.

INDEX

A

Printed at THE DARIEN PRESS, *Edinburgh.*

CPSIA information can be obtained
at www.ICGtesting.com
Printed in the USA
BVHW080250091121
621094BV00011B/122

9 780343 392437